SECOND EDITION

GRADED READER of BIBLICAL HEBREW

Other Resources by Miles V. Van Pelt and Gary D. Pratico

Basics of Biblical Hebrew Grammar

Basics of Biblical Hebrew Workbook

Charts of Biblical Hebrew

Old Testament Hebrew Vocabulary Cards

The Vocabulary Guide to Biblical Hebrew and Aramaic

Biblical Hebrew Laminated Sheet

Biblical Hebrew Vocabulary in Context

Other Resources by Miles V. Van Pelt

English Grammar to Ace Biblical Hebrew

Biblical Hebrew: A Compact Guide

Basics of Biblical Hebrew Video Lectures

Basics of Biblical Hebrew Vocabulary Audio

Basics of Biblical Aramaic: Complete Grammar, Lexicon, and Annotated Text

Basics of Biblical Aramaic Video Lectures

SECOND EDITION

GRADED READER *of* BIBLICAL HEBREW

A GUIDE TO READING THE HEBREW BIBLE

MILES V. VAN PELT
GARY D. PRATICO

ZONDERVAN ACADEMIC

ZONDERVAN ACADEMIC

Graded Reader of Biblical Hebrew

ISBN 978-0-310-09335-0 (softcover)

Requests for information should be addressed to:
Zondervan, *3900 Sparks Dr. SE, Grand Rapids, Michigan 49546*

Cover Design: LUCAS Art & Design
Typesetting: Miles V. Van Pelt

Printed in the United States of America

HB 10.15.2024

to

Benjamin Trent
Katharine Claire
Madeline Grace
Max Kenneth
and now
Elizabeth Gray
and
Brooks Jameson

and to

Madeline Pearl
Our gift and treasure from the Lord.
May you come to love God's Word
as do your grandparents.

דָּבְקָה לֶעָפָר נַפְשִׁי חַיֵּנִי כִּדְבָרֶךָ

Psalm 119:25

Table of Contents

Writings

Preface to the First Edition

Almost every instructor of biblical Hebrew would agree that the best way to reinforce the first year of language instruction is immersion in the Hebrew text. The purpose of this reader, therefore, is to provide students with a structured introduction to the reading of biblical Hebrew. The book's primary goals are: (1) to review and reinforce basic Hebrew grammar; (2) to introduce students to issues of intermediate grammar; (3) to familiarize students with normative Hebrew syntax through significant exposure to narrative and poetic texts; and (4) to provide students with a measure of encouragement as they build their confidence in the handling of the Hebrew Bible. This volume may be used at the end of a first year language course, as part of an intermediate language or exegesis course, or as part of an independent (directed) study course. This reader can also be used by students to maintain or revive Hebrew language skills that have diminished due to a lack of use.

With the publication of this volume, the team of Pratico and Van Pelt bring to a conclusion their efforts to provide students with a number of helpful and integrated resources for beginning studies in biblical Hebrew. During these past eight years, we have worked with Zondervan to produce a grammar, workbook, vocabulary guide, vocabulary cards, a laminated study guide, and now this reader. In addition to these printed resources, we have also participated in the development of an electronic flashcard program, and have produced over four hundred supplementary color charts and overheads, as well as video lectures. These efforts stem from our conviction that facility with the biblical languages is vital for the study of God's Word, especially for those preparing for pastoral ministry. In the early part of the twentieth century, B. B. Warfield (1851-1921) exquisitely expressed this conviction:

> No second hand knowledge of the revelation of God for the salvation of a ruined world can suffice the needs of a ministry whose function it is to convey this revelation to men [and women], commend it to their acceptance and apply it in detail to their needs – to all their needs, from the moment they are called into participation in the grace of God, until the moment when they stand perfect in God's sight, built up by his Spirit into new men. For such a ministry as this the most complete knowledge of the wisdom of the world supplies no equipment; the most fervid enthusiasm of service leaves without furnishing. Nothing will suffice for it but to know; to know the book; to know it at first hand; and to know it through and through. And what is required first of all for training men for such a ministry is that the book should be given them in its very words [Hebrew, Aramaic, and Greek] as it has come from God's hand and in the fullness of its meaning, as that meaning has been ascertained by the labors of

> generations of men of God who have brought to bear upon it all the resources of sanctified scholarship and consecrated thought.

We recognize that not every person or institution will share this level of commitment to and enthusiasm for the biblical languages. In fact, the study of the biblical languages by those training for ministry appears to be in steady decline, despite the increasing abundance of resources. This is not, however, a new situation. Martin Luther (1483-1546) made this same observation almost five hundred years ago when he wrote:

> For the devil smelled a rat, and perceived that if the [biblical] languages were revived a hole would be knocked in his kingdom which he could not easily stop up again. Since he found he could not prevent their revival, he now aims to keep them on such slender rations that they will of themselves decline and pass away. They are not a welcome guest in his house, so he plans to offer them such meager entertainment that they will not prolong their stay. Very few of us, my dear sirs, see through this evil design of the devil.

We trust that these resources will provide both the opportunity and the inducement for the study of biblical Hebrew. It is not an easy path, but it is the right one and well worth the journey.

> The main point is, with all and above all, study the Greek
> and Hebrew Bible, and the love of Christ.
> – John Wesley, 1703-1791

We are indebted to a number of individuals and institutions. We would like to thank Zondervan for their support in the preparation of this volume – especially Verlyn Verbrugge and Jack Kragt. We also recognize Lee Fields for his editorial work. Special thanks are due to James Forsyth for his reading of the manuscript, to Brad and Aleta Irick for their support in data entry and to Jamie Viands. We wish to express a word of special gratitude to Jonathan Kline for his significant contribution to the production of this volume. We are indebted to Reformed Theological Seminary and to Gordon-Conwell Theological Seminary for their support of our teaching and scholarship. Finally, we are indebted to our families, and especially to our wives, whose encouragement, support, and love have sustained us in our work.

Miles V. Van Pelt
Gary D. Pratico
January 31, 2006

Preface to the Revised Edition

Just over thirteen years ago, we made this statement in the preface of the first edition of this resource:

> With the publication of this volume, the team of Pratico and Van Pelt bring to a conclusion their efforts to provide students with a number of helpful and integrated resources for beginning studies in biblical Hebrew.

While reflecting on this statement we were reminded of Proverbs 16:9, "The heart of man plans his way, but Yahweh establishes his steps." Now, with over two decades of collaboration and many more resources, we give thanks to the Lord for his kindness to us by allowing us to continue to serve together in the production of resources for the study of the Old Testament in Hebrew.

This revised edition does, in fact, bring to a conclusion the process of revising and updating all of the Zondervan Hebrew language resources produced by the team of Pratico and Van Pelt over the past twenty years. We have updated the fonts, rendered the divine name as "Yahweh," and revised many of the textual notes appearing in the grammatical commentary. All of the references to *Basics of Biblical Hebrew* now correspond to the 3rd edition of the grammar (Zondervan, 2019). We have also included a lexicon in the appendix following the parsing answer key.

We are thankful for our friends at Zondervan and their commitment to producing the best original language resources in the service of the church and the academy. Nancy Erickson is a wonderful scholar, editor, and friend. We also recognize with gratitude Alaina di Staulo Garcia for all of her excellent assistance during the process of revision.

Introduction

This reader contains 30 Hebrew texts, 202 verses, and 4,585 words for translation. There are 622 verbs to parse and an answer key to check your work. These texts have been selected as appropriate readings for the beginning student who has completed a basic introduction to biblical Hebrew. For the most part, the grammatical composition and syntax of these readings is appropriate to a beginner's capability with the language. Some texts are more difficult than others. As a general observation, the texts in section one (Law) are easier than those in the Prophets or Writings. It should also be noted that we have intentionally selected a number of shorter texts rather than fewer texts of greater length. The rationale for this decision is: (1) to cover a larger cross section of the Hebrew Bible (both in terms of genre and canonical exposure); (2) to provide more discrete units of text for the time management of the beginning student; and (3) to attract a greater audience with diversified interests. It is important to understand that the limits of each reading were determined on the basis of grammatical and syntactical simplicity. These texts, therefore, are not necessarily intended to represent "pericopes," that is, discrete units of thought. Despite these self imposed restrictions, this selection nevertheless represents some of the most important biblical texts in the Old Testament from the perspective of biblical history, theology, and exegesis.

This volume focuses primarily on morphology, with an emphasis on the morphology of verbs. Sentence syntax and the syntax of forms are also emphasized, but not to the degree of considering how verbal and non-verbal forms are spelled and translated. By design, this volume in not an introduction to exegesis or to exegetical method and, in fact, we have fastidiously refrained from making exegetical and interpretive observations. Our commentary on the Hebrew text focuses, in significant measure, on the identification of forms with a view to observing the features of spelling that promote and enhance the student's ability to read, understand, and translate accurately. Some readers may consider our primary emphasis on morphology to be too narrow a focus and so a word of explanation is perhaps necessary.

Most teachers of biblical Hebrew would likely agree that students who have completed their first year of basic language study have only a tenuous grasp of grammar, especially in the categories of morphology and syntax. The basic elements of grammar are in hand, to be sure, but important paradigms and the nuances of sentence syntax will soon be lost apart from continued study. At this critical point, students need to solidify the basics and advance their skills in the identification of grammatical forms. They will not have access to the subtleties of syntax apart from competence in the ability to fully and accurately identify words. An understanding of sentence syntax and the syntax of form is essential for working with the text. Dynamic exegetical insight is more likely to be the result of understanding syntax than morphology. Nevertheless, understanding morphology is the prerequisite to understanding syntax.

On the assumption that we have correctly identified the greatest need for students who have completed their first year of Hebrew language study (or for those whose skills have languished), this book focuses on teaching and, hopefully, reminding a student how to recognize and understand the spelling of words. While we have engaged syntax in some measure, this area of language study is not our intended focus. The language of biblical exegesis, like the exegetical process itself, must be learned systematically, progressively, and incrementally. The study of morphology is one of the essential increments. Some readers will want more and perhaps others will want even less, but the content of this volume represents our best determination of what students at this stage of study both want and need.

The order of the texts follows the order of the Hebrew Bible as presented in *Biblia Hebraica Stuttgartensia* (*BHS*). The student will quickly discover that the order of the Hebrew Bible differs from the order of the English Old Testament. In general, the books of the English Old Testament are arranged by genre (law, historical books, poetical books, and prophetical books) and chronology (historical sequence). The Hebrew Old Testament, on the other hand, is organized into the three groups known as the Law, Prophets, and Writings (Luke 24:44) – beginning with Genesis and concluding with Chronicles (Matt 23:35; Luke 11:51). Given the substantial differences in arrangement, students will want to familiarize themselves with the ordering of the books in the Hebrew Bible. After this introduction (p. xv), we have provided both the English and Hebrew arrangements in parallel columns for comparison.

Each of the 30 translation exercises in this reader has three basic parts. The first part consists of the Hebrew text following *BHS*. Hebrew words that appear fewer than 50 times in the Hebrew Bible are glossed in footnotes. These definitions have been taken (and modified) from our vocabulary guide (*VGBH*). When necessary, we have also consulted *HALOT*, *NIDOTTE*, BDB, and Holladay.

With regard to the layout and presentation of the Hebrew text, there are two important notes. First, for the sake of simplicity and for other pedagogical reasons, we have decided not to include the system of Masoretic accents that appear with the Hebrew text in *BHS*. Some may express a measure of disapproval with this decision, but given the purpose of this reader and its intended audience, we were convinced that the benefits outweigh the liabilities. The only circumstances that consistently present any potential difficulty are instances of pausal spelling (see *BBH* 36.3). We have identified the majority of these forms and provided appropriate explanations and references.

Secondly, with regard to the presentation of Qere and Kethiv readings (see *BBH* 36.5), we have followed the convention of Accordance by placing the Qere reading in brackets following the Kethiv reading. In the selection of texts that appears in this reader, there are only three such instances. For the sake of convenience and clarity, these readings are listed below.

	Qere	Kethib
Joshua 24:15	[מֵעֵבֶר]	בְּעֵבֶר
1 Kings 8:26	[דְּבָרְךָ]	דְּבָרֶיךָ
Psalm 100:3	[וְלוֹ]	וְלֹא

Following the presentation of the Hebrew text with footnotes containing lexical information, we have laid out selected verbs from each passage for the student to parse. The answer key for each of the parsing exercises appears in Appendix 1 of this volume. Note that while certain verbal forms may have more than one possible identification, we have selected the parsing that best suits the context.

Following the parsing exercises, we have provided in the third section extensive grammatical commentary on selected words, phrases and clauses from the text under study. The grammatical commentary at the end of each translation exercise covers: (1) basic elements for review; (2) issues of intermediate Hebrew grammar; (3) grammatical or syntactical constructions that signal significant exegetical observations; (4) the nuances of idiomatic expressions; (5) selected lexical issues; and (6) occasional notes on miscellaneous issues regarding the Masoretic Text. These notes also include additional bibliographic references and are intended to provide students with an inductive introduction to some of the standard Hebrew grammar reference works.

As stated above, there are numerous references throughout the grammatical commentary sections to standard Hebrew grammar reference works (see the following bibliography). The student will want to note that most of these citations do not correspond to page numbers but rather to section numbers in each of the various reference works. Though more precise in terms of identifying the location of a reference, this system of citation may be more cumbersome at first for the beginning student. This system of citation is, however, a standard convention and represents the one employed in the appendices of works of this type. For this reason, the student will want to take some time to become familiar with the system. It should also be noted that because of the number of references to *Basics of Biblical Hebrew* (3rd edition) for the sake of review, these section citations appear without any prefix (such as *BBH*) to identify the work. While not required or necessary for using this reader, access to this grammar will facilitate review and reference to numerous grammatical issues, especially those related to beginning morphology and syntax.

Finally, a brief note is required regarding the use of this volume by students. The grammatical commentary following the parsing section in each text is not intended to function as a crutch or answer key for translation and parsing. The student who desires to benefit the most from this volume will work through the Hebrew text and parsing section before consulting or working through the grammatical commentary. Do not worry about making a mistake while working through the text and the parsing for the first time. You can make corrections as you review your answers when working through the grammatical commentary section.

A Comparison of the English and Hebrew Bible Arrangements

English Bible	Hebrew Bible
Pentateuch	**Law**
Genesis	Genesis
Exodus	Exodus
Leviticus	Leviticus
Numbers	Numbers
Deuteronomy	Deuteronomy
Historical Books	**Prophets**
Joshua	Joshua
Judges	Judges
Ruth	1-2 Samuel
1-2 Samuel	1-2 Kings
1-2 Kings	
1-2 Chronicles	Isaiah
Ezra	Jeremiah
Nehemiah	Ezekiel
Esther	Book of the Twelve
Poetry	**Writings**
Job	Psalms
Psalms	Job
Proverbs	Proverbs
Ecclesiastes	Ruth
Song of Songs	Song of Songs
	Ecclesiastes
Prophets	
Isaiah	Lamentations
Jeremiah	Esther
Lamentations	Daniel
Ezekiel	Ezra
Daniel	Nehemiah
12 Minor Prophets	1-2 Chronicles

Bibliography and Abbreviations

Accordance	Accordance Bible Software with the GRAMCORD Hebrew MT (Groves-Wheeler Westminster Hebrew Morphology) database. Distributed by Oaktree Software, Inc. (www.accordancebible.com)
Arnold-Choi	Arnold, Bill T. and John H. Choi. *A Guide to Biblical Hebrew Syntax*. Cambridge: Cambridge University Press, 2003.
BDB	Brown, F., S. R. Driver, and C. A. Briggs. *The New Brown-Driver-Briggs-Gesenius Hebrew and English Lexicon*. Peabody, MA: Hendrickson, 1996.
Chisholm	Chisholm, Robert B., Jr. *From Exegesis to Exposition: A Practical Guide to Using Biblical Hebrew*. Grand Rapids: Baker Academic, 1998.
GKC	Gesenius, W., E. Kautzsch, and E. A. Cowley. *Gesenius' Hebrew Grammar*. 2nd ed. Oxford: Clarenden, 1910.
Holladay	Holladay, W. L. *A Concise Hebrew and Aramaic Lexicon of the Old Testament*. Grand Rapids: Eerdmans, 1988.
Joüon-Muraoka	Joüon, Paul and T. Muraoka. *A Grammar of Biblical Hebrew*, 2 vols. Rome: Pontifical Biblical Institute, 1993.
HALOT	Köhler, L., W. Baumgartner, and J. Stamm. *The Hebrew and Aramaic Lexicon of the Old Testament*. Translated and edited under the supervision of M. E. J. Richardson. Study Edition. 2 vols. Leiden: Brill, 2001.
BBH	Pratico, Gary D. and Miles V. Van Pelt. *Basics of Biblical Hebrew: Grammar*. 3rd ed. Grand Rapids: Zondervan, 2019.
Scott	Scott, William R. *A Simplified Guide to BHS*. Berkeley, CA: BIBAL, 1987.
van der Merwe	van der Merwe, Christo, H., Jacobus A. Naude, and Jan Kroeze. *A Biblical Hebrew Reference Grammar*. 2nd ed. London: Bloomsbury T&T Clark, 2017.
VGBH	Van Pelt, Miles V. and Gary D. Pratico. *The Vocabulary Guide to Biblical Hebrew and Aramaic*. 2nd ed. Grand Rapids: Zondervan, 2019.

NIDOTTE	VanGemeren, W. A., ed. *The New International Dictionary of Old Testament Theology and Exegesis*. Grand Rapids: Zondervan, 1997.
Waltke-O'Connor	Waltke, Bruce K. and M. O'Connor. *An Introduction to Biblical Hebrew Syntax*. Winona Lake, IN: Eisenbrauns, 1990.
Wonneberger	Wonneberger, Reinhard. *Understanding BHS: A Manual for the Users of Biblia Hebraica Stuttgartensia*. 3rd rev. ed. Translated by Dwight R. Daniels. Subsidia Biblica 8. Rome: Pontifical Biblical Institute, 2001.

Abbreviations and Symbols

1	first person
2	second person
3	third person
Abs	Absolute
adj	adjective
adv	adverb
c	common
coll	collective
conj	conjunction
Cst	Construct
d	dual
dmstr	demonstrative
f	feminine
Hi	Hiphil
Hith	Hithpael
Hoph	Hophal
Imp	Imperfect
Impv	Imperative
Inf	Infinitive
interrog	interrogative
m	masculine
MT	Masoretic Text
n	noun
neg	negative
Ni	Niphal
p	plural
Pass	Passive
pers	personal
Pf	Perfect
Pi	Piel
pref	prefix
prep	preposition
pron	pronoun
Ptc	Participle
Pu	Pual
Q	Qal
rel	relative
s	singular
suff	suffix
WC	Waw Consecutive
֫	located over a Hebrew letter (אֶ֫רֶץ), identifies Hebrew words with penultimate (next-to-last syllable) stress

Translation 1

Genesis 1:1-5

In the Beginning

1 בְּרֵאשִׁית בָּרָא[1] אֱלֹהִים אֵת הַשָּׁמַיִם וְאֵת הָאָרֶץ 2 וְהָאָרֶץ
הָיְתָה תֹהוּ[2] וָבֹהוּ[3] וְחֹשֶׁךְ עַל־פְּנֵי תְהוֹם[4] וְרוּחַ אֱלֹהִים מְרַחֶפֶת[5]
עַל־פְּנֵי הַמָּיִם 3 וַיֹּאמֶר אֱלֹהִים יְהִי אוֹר וַיְהִי־אוֹר 4 וַיַּרְא אֱלֹהִים
אֶת־הָאוֹר כִּי־טוֹב וַיַּבְדֵּל[6] אֱלֹהִים בֵּין הָאוֹר וּבֵין הַחֹשֶׁךְ
5 וַיִּקְרָא אֱלֹהִים לָאוֹר יוֹם וְלַחֹשֶׁךְ קָרָא לָיְלָה וַיְהִי־עֶרֶב
וַיְהִי־בֹקֶר יוֹם אֶחָד

---

1. בָּרָא (Q) to create (48).
2. תֹּהוּ emptiness, wasteland, formlessness (20).
3. בֹּהוּ void, uninhabited area (3).
4. תְּהוֹם (cs) primeval ocean, deep, depth (36).
5. רָחַף (Pi) to hover (3).
6. בָּדַל (Ni) to separate oneself, withdraw; (Hi) divide, separate, set apart, make a distinction (between), single out (42).

Parse the following verbs from Genesis 1:1-5.

Genesis 1:1

בָּרָא ______________________________

Genesis 1:2

הָיְתָה ______________________________

מְרַחֶפֶת ______________________________

Genesis 1:3

וַיֹּאמֶר ______________________________

יְהִי ______________________________

וַיְהִי ______________________________

Genesis 1:4

וַיַּרְא ______________________________

וַיַּבְדֵּל ______________________________

Genesis 1:5

וַיִּקְרָא ______________________________

קָרָא ______________________________

Grammatical Commentary: Genesis 1:1-5

Genesis 1:1

בְּרֵאשִׁית The Hebrew Bible begins with a prepositional phrase. Here, the preposition בְּ is prefixed to the fs noun רֵאשִׁית (in [the] beginning). This construction is indefinite, though it is normally translated with the definite article.

בָּרָא This Qal Perfect 3ms verb is easy to identify. Remember that all III-א and III-ה verbs exhibit the Qamets-Qamets vowel pattern in the Perfect 3ms. This is also the lexical form (14.5.1; 14.7.1). In this verse, the verb is followed by its subject (אֱלֹהִים) and two definite direct objects (אֵת הַשָּׁמַיִם וְאֵת הָאָרֶץ). Both direct objects are marked with the definite direct object marker אֵת (God created the heavens and the earth).

Genesis 1:2

וְהָאָרֶץ הָיְתָה The conjunction וְ and the definite article are prefixed to the endingless fs noun אֶרֶץ, which functions as the subject of the verb הָיְתָה. The verb הָיְתָה is the Qal Perfect 3fs of הָיָה. In the Perfect 3fs form of III-ה verbal roots, the final ה of the verbal root is replaced by ת before the addition of the 3fs sufformative (14.7.3). The disjunctive Waw on וְהָאָרֶץ may be categorized as introductory (24.17.4). This part of the clause may be translated, "now the earth was…"

תֹהוּ וָבֹהוּ This construction consists of a pair of rare ms nouns that are joined by the conjunction וְ (spelled with Qamets in the pretonic position; see 5.7.4). These nouns constitute the predicate nominative of the preceding verb (הָיְתָה). One or more of the standard translations of this clause will be familiar to you, such as, "Now the earth was formless and empty" (NIV) or "the earth was without form and void" (RSV). Another possibility would be, "Now the earth was uninhabitable and uninhabited." This last translation preserves a measure of the assonance in the Hebrew expression תֹהוּ וָבֹהוּ.

וְחֹשֶׁךְ עַל־פְּנֵי תְהוֹם The combination of the ms noun חֹשֶׁךְ and the prepositional phrase that follows constitutes a verbless clause (23.8). The ms noun חֹשֶׁךְ is the subject. The prepositional phrase beginning with עַל constitutes the predicate (and darkness *was* over the surface of the deep). The preposition עַל is joined by Maqqef to the mp construct noun פָּנִים (lexical פָּנֶה) followed by the absolute noun תְּהוֹם.

וְרוּחַ אֱלֹהִים מְרַחֶפֶת The construct chain רוּחַ אֱלֹהִים, prefixed with the conjunction וְ, is followed by the Piel Participle fs of רָחַף (and the Spirit of God was hovering). With regard to the form of the Participle, the מְ prefix and Pathach under the first root letter identify the stem as Piel (30.11-12). The ת ֶ inflectional ending is one of two inflectional endings that appear with Hebrew Participles in the fs (22.3.2; Qamets He [ה ָ] is the other fs ending). The Daghesh Forte expected in the second consonant of the verbal root with the Piel stem is rejected by the guttural consonant ח. In this verb, the Pathach does not lengthen to Qamets with the rejection of the Daghesh Forte, according to the pattern of virtual doubling (31.8).

עַל־פְּנֵי הַמָּיִם This prepositional phrase is similar to עַל־פְּנֵי תְהוֹם appearing earlier in the verse. The only difference is the definite masculine dual noun הַמָּיִם in the absolute position. Note the pausal spelling (36.3.1) of מָיִם with Qamets instead of Pathach under the מ. In *BHS*, this form appears with Silluq under the מ (הַמָּֽיִם).

Genesis 1:3

יְהִי אוֹר The Qal Imperfect 3ms of הָיָה is followed by the singular noun אוֹר. The spelling יְהִי is the shortened form of יִהְיֶה (23.11.2). When prefixed with the Waw Consecutive (see below) or when the volitional nuance is intended, the short form of the III-ה verb is commonly used with the third and second persons. In this case, both the form (short) and the position of this verb in its clause (first or initial position) indicate the volitional nuance (*let* there be light).

וַיְהִי־אוֹר This expression is identical to יְהִי אוֹר except for the prefixing of the Waw Consecutive to the verb (and the presence of Maqqef). Once again, when prefixed with the Waw Consecutive, III-ה verbs prefer the short form in the third person (17.3.2). In the first person, the long form is preferred, as in וָאֶהְיֶה. With the prefixing of the Waw Consecutive, the form is not volitional, but rather past tense (and there was light).

Genesis 1:4

וַיַּרְא אֱלֹהִים In the absence of a sufformative, the Waw Consecutive and the preformative י identify the verb as Imperfect 3ms (and God saw). The root of this doubly weak verb is רָאָה. This form constitutes another example in which the 3ms III-ה verb prefers the short form when prefixed with the Waw Consecutive (יִרְאֶה is spelled וַיַּרְא with the Waw Consecutive).

כִּי־טוֹב The particle כִּי introduces a dependent verbless clause without an explicit subject. The ms adjective טוֹב constitutes the predicate (that *it was* good).

וַיַּבְדֵּל As with וַיַּרְא above, the Waw Consecutive and the preformative י without a sufformative identify the form as Imperfect 3ms. The Pathach under the Imperfect preformative and the Tsere stem vowel identify the stem as Hiphil. With the prefixing of the Waw Consecutive to the Hiphil Imperfect, the Hireq Yod stem vowel is spelled with Tsere (יַבְדִּיל is spelled וַיַּבְדֵּל with the Waw Consecutive). This is another example of the Waw Consecutive's preference for short forms in the third person (see וַיְהִי and וַיַּרְא above).

Genesis 1:5

וַיִּקְרָא אֱלֹהִים לָאוֹר יוֹם The combination of the verb קָרָא and the preposition לְ may be translated "to name" (*HALOT* 2:1129). The use of the idiom in this context translates as, "then God *named* the light 'day.'"

וְלַחֹשֶׁךְ קָרָא לָיְלָה This clause is joined to the preceding clause by the conjunction וְ. Again, the verb קָרָא is used with the preposition לְ with the nuance "to name" (and the darkness he *named* "night"). Note that the Imperfect with Waw Consecutive וַיִּקְרָא in the previous clause and the Qal Perfect קָרָא in this clause exhibit the same past tense translation value.

יוֹם אֶחָד The ms noun יוֹם and the ms adjective אֶחָד agree in gender, number, and (in)definiteness ("day one" or "one day").

Translation 2

Genesis 2:1-3

The Seventh Day

1 וַיְכֻלּוּ הַשָּׁמַיִם וְהָאָרֶץ וְכָל־צְבָאָם 2 וַיְכַל אֱלֹהִים בַּיּוֹם הַשְּׁבִיעִי

מְלַאכְתּוֹ אֲשֶׁר עָשָׂה וַיִּשְׁבֹּת בַּיּוֹם הַשְּׁבִיעִי מִכָּל־מְלַאכְתּוֹ אֲשֶׁר

עָשָׂה 3 וַיְבָרֶךְ אֱלֹהִים אֶת־יוֹם הַשְּׁבִיעִי וַיְקַדֵּשׁ אֹתוֹ כִּי בוֹ שָׁבַת

מִכָּל־מְלַאכְתּוֹ אֲשֶׁר־בָּרָא[1] אֱלֹהִים לַעֲשׂוֹת

---

1. בָּרָא (Q) to create (48).

Parse the following verbs from Genesis 2:1-3.

Genesis 2:1

וַיְכֻלּוּ ____________________________

Genesis 2:2

וַיְכַל ____________________________

עָשָׂה ____________________________

וַיִּשְׁבֹּת ____________________________

Genesis 2:3

וַיְבָרֶךְ ____________________________

וַיְקַדֵּשׁ ____________________________

שָׁבַת ____________________________

בָּרָא ____________________________

לַעֲשׂוֹת ____________________________

Grammatical Commentary: Genesis 2:1-3

Genesis 2:1

וַיְכֻלּוּ The preformative י and the sufformative וּ identify this verb as Imperfect 3mp from כָּלָה. The Vocal Shewa preformative vowel and the Daghesh Forte in the second root letter are diagnostic of the Piel and Pual stems in the Imperfect. The Qibbuts under the first root letter distinguishes this form as Pual. Note the loss of the Daghesh Forte of the Waw Consecutive in the Imperfect preformative (30.15).

וְכָל־צְבָאָם The conjunction וְ is prefixed to the ms construct noun כֹּל which is joined by Maqqef to the ms absolute noun צָבָא (with a 3mp pronominal suffix). This construct chain is considered definite because the absolute noun has a pronominal suffix (10.2.3). This construct chain, together with the two nouns הַשָּׁמַיִם and הָאָרֶץ, constitute the subject of the verb וַיְכֻלּוּ (and the heavens and the earth and all of their host were completed).

Genesis 2:2

וַיְכַל אֱלֹהִים In the absence of a sufformative, the preformative י identifies this verb as Imperfect 3ms. The Shewa under the Imperfect preformative and the Pathach under the first root letter are diagnostic of the Piel stem. As in verse 1, the verbal root is כָּלָה ([and] God finished). With the prefixing of the Waw Consecutive, the final vowel letter ה ֶ and the Daghesh Forte expected in the second root letter do not appear. In other words, יְכַלֶּה is spelled וַיְכַל with the Waw Consecutive. Once again, note the loss of the Daghesh Forte of the Waw Consecutive in the Imperfect preformative (30.15).

בַּיּוֹם הַשְּׁבִיעִי The preposition בְּ is prefixed to the definite noun (6.4.4) הַיּוֹם The ms ordinal number (11.6) שְׁבִיעִי follows and agrees with the noun in gender, number, and definiteness (on the seventh day).

מִכָּל־מְלַאכְתּוֹ The preposition מִן is prefixed to the ms construct form of כֹּל. This construction is joined by Maqqef to the fs absolute noun מְלָאכָה with a 3ms pronominal suffix. This prepositional phrase functions as the object of the verb וַיִּשְׁבֹּת (and [God] ceased *from all of his work*).

אֲשֶׁר עָשָׂה This relative clause begins with the relative pronoun אֲשֶׁר followed by the Qal Perfect 3ms of עָשָׂה. Its antecedent is the fs noun מְלַאכְתּוֹ (his work *which he had done*).

Genesis 2:3

וַיְבָרֶךְ The Imperfect preformative י without a sufformative identifies this verb as Imperfect 3ms (with Waw Consecutive). The Shewa preformative vowel is diagnostic of the Piel and Pual in the Imperfect. With the Qamets under the first root letter, the stem must be Piel. The guttural in the second root position rejects the Daghesh Forte of the Piel stem and the expected Pathach lengthens to Qamets according to the rule of compensatory lengthening (31.9-10). The Daghesh Forte in the Imperfect preformative is lost because the verb begins with the syllable יְ (30.15). Finally, in the Piel, the verbal root בֵּרַךְ translates with the simple action of the Qal (and [God] blessed).

וַיְקַדֵּשׁ אֹתוֹ Like וַיְבָרֶךְ at the beginning of this verse, וַיְקַדֵּשׁ is Piel Imperfect 3ms with Waw Consecutive. In this case, however, all of the Piel Imperfect strong verb diagnostics are present. The meaning of the Piel stem with the verbal root קָדַשׁ ("to be holy" in the Qal stem) is factitive (30.2.2), making the verb transitive (capable of taking a direct object). As a transitive verb, it is followed by the definite direct object marker אֵת with a 3ms pronominal suffix ("and he sanctified it" or "and he consecrated it"). In this verse, note that the object marker is spelled אֶת־ when followed by Maqqef and אֹת before a pronominal suffix beginning with, or consisting entirely of, a vowel (9.14). The antecedent of this 3ms pronominal suffix is the ms noun יוֹם (יוֹם הַשְּׁבִיעִי) that appears earlier in the verse.

אֲשֶׁר־בָּרָא אֱלֹהִים לַעֲשׂוֹת This relative clause begins with the relative pronoun אֲשֶׁר joined by Maqqef to the Qal Perfect 3ms of בָּרָא. The noun אֱלֹהִים is the subject of the verb. This construction is complemented by לַעֲשׂוֹת that follows. The combination of the preposition לְ and the וֹת ending help to identify this verb as Qal Infinitive Construct from the III-ה verbal root עָשָׂה. Recall that III-ה Infinitive Construct forms will always end in וֹת or ֹת (20.4). Additionally, the presence of the preposition לְ is common with the Infinitive Construct. In fact, almost sixty-nine percent (4,528 verbs) of all Infinitive Construct verbs in the Hebrew Bible (6,599 verbs) appear with the preposition לְ. Verse 3b may be translated idiomatically, "because on it *God* ceased from all of his work *which he had done in creation*."

Genesis 26:1-6

God's Promises to Isaac

1 וַיְהִי רָעָב בָּאָרֶץ מִלְּבַד הָרָעָב הָרִאשׁוֹן אֲשֶׁר הָיָה בִּימֵי
אַבְרָהָם וַיֵּלֶךְ יִצְחָק אֶל־אֲבִימֶלֶךְ מֶלֶךְ־פְּלִשְׁתִּים גְּרָרָה[1] 2 וַיֵּרָא
אֵלָיו יְהוָה וַיֹּאמֶר אַל־תֵּרֵד מִצְרָיְמָה שְׁכֹן בָּאָרֶץ אֲשֶׁר אֹמַר
אֵלֶיךָ 3 גּוּר בָּאָרֶץ הַזֹּאת וְאֶהְיֶה עִמְּךָ וַאֲבָרְכֶךָּ כִּי־לְךָ וּלְזַרְעֲךָ
אֶתֵּן אֶת־כָּל־הָאֲרָצֹת הָאֵל[2] וַהֲקִמֹתִי אֶת־הַשְּׁבֻעָה[3] אֲשֶׁר
נִשְׁבַּעְתִּי לְאַבְרָהָם אָבִיךָ 4 וְהִרְבֵּיתִי אֶת־זַרְעֲךָ כְּכוֹכְבֵי[4] הַשָּׁמַיִם
וְנָתַתִּי לְזַרְעֲךָ אֵת כָּל־הָאֲרָצֹת הָאֵל וְהִתְבָּרֲכוּ בְזַרְעֲךָ כֹּל גּוֹיֵי
הָאָרֶץ 5 עֵקֶב[5] אֲשֶׁר־שָׁמַע אַבְרָהָם בְּקֹלִי וַיִּשְׁמֹר מִשְׁמַרְתִּי
מִצְוֺתַי חֻקּוֹתַי וְתוֹרֹתָי 6 וַיֵּשֶׁב יִצְחָק בִּגְרָר

1. גְּרָר Gerar (10).
2. אֵל (cp dmstr) these (9). The demonstrative אֵל is an alternative form of the more common form אֵלֶּה.
3. שְׁבוּעָה oath; also spelled שְׁבֻעָה (30).
4. כּוֹכָב star; (mp) כּוֹכָבִים (37).
5. עֵקֶב (conj) because, on account of; (n) result, wages (15).

Parse the following verbs from Genesis 26:1-6.

Genesis 26:1

וַיְהִי ______________________

הָיָה ______________________

וַיֵּלֶךְ ______________________

Genesis 26:2

וַיֵּרָא ______________________

וַיֹּאמֶר ______________________

תֵּרֵד ______________________

שְׁכֹן ______________________

אֹמַר ______________________

Genesis 26:3

גּוּר ______________________

וְאֶהְיֶה ______________________

וַאֲבָרְכֶךָּ ______________________

אֶתֵּן ______________________

וַהֲקִמֹתִי ______________________

נִשְׁבַּעְתִּי ______________________

Genesis 26:4

וְהִרְבֵּיתִי ______________________

וְנָתַתִּי ______________________

וְהִתְבָּרְכוּ ______________________

Genesis 26:5

שָׁמַע ______________________________

וַיִּשְׁמֹר ______________________________

Genesis 26:6

וַיֵּשֶׁב ______________________________

Grammatical Commentary: Genesis 26:1-6

Genesis 26:1

וַיְהִי רָעָב בָּאָרֶץ The verbal form וַיְהִי is not the temporal modifier introducing a Perfect-Imperfect narrative sequence (17.4.3). It is a verb followed by its subject רָעָב and the prepositional phrase בָּאָרֶץ (and *there was* a famine in the land).

מִלְּבַד This form consists of the ms noun בַּד prefixed with the prepositions מִן and לְ. This entire construction is simply translated "besides."

הָרָעָב הָרִאשׁוֹן The ms noun רָעָב is prefixed with the definite article and followed by the ms ordinal number, also prefixed with the definite article. The ordinal number is in an attributive relationship (11.6.3) with the preceding noun (the first famine).

בִּימֵי אַבְרָהָם The form בִּימֵי is the construct plural of יָמִים which, in turn, is the absolute plural of יוֹם (day). In this construction, the preposition בְּ is prefixed to this mp construct noun. The Hireq Yod with the preposition is the result of the application of Rule of Shewa to a word that begins with the syllable יְ (4.11.2). The entire construct chain is definite because the absolute noun is the proper name אַבְרָהָם (in the days of Abraham).

וַיֵּלֶךְ The Imperfect preformative י without a sufformative identifies the Imperfect 3ms. It is prefixed with Waw Consecutive. The Tsere preformative vowel is diagnostic of the I-י (Type 1) Qal Imperfect (16.16.1). Though this verb inflects like a I-י verb, its root is actually הָלַךְ (16.7.2).

גְּרָרָה This is the proper noun גְּרָר (Gerar) with the directional ending (7.7).

Genesis 26:2

וַיֵּרָא In the absence of a sufformative, the Imperfect preformative י identifies this verb as Imperfect 3ms. It is prefixed with Waw Consecutive. In this form, the Tsere preformative vowel is not diagnostic of the I-י Qal Imperfect. The stem is Niphal and the verbal root is the doubly weak verb רָאָה. The נ of the Niphal stem can not assimilate into the guttural in first root position. This causes the compensatory lengthening of the Hireq preformative vowel to Tsere (25.7.1). Note that the verbal root רָאָה in the Niphal stem is translated "to appear" (and he appeared).

אַל־תֵּרֵד Remember that the negative particle אַל before an Imperfect verb expresses an immediate, specific, and non-durative prohibition (15.8.2). The Qal Imperfect verb תֵּרֵד preserves the expected spelling of a I-י (Type 1) weak verb (16.16.1; 16.7.1). In every form of the paradigm, the י in first root position drops off and the Imperfect preformative vowel is Tsere. Verbs of this type can be difficult to recognize because the initial י is lost, leaving only the second and third consonants of the verbal root. In this case, the key to reconstructing the verbal root is the Tsere preformative vowel.

מִצְרָיְמָה The proper noun מִצְרַיִם appears with the directional ending (ה ָ). Note the pausal spelling (36.3.1) with Qamets instead of Pathach under the consonant ר. In *BHS*, this form appears with Athnach under the ר (מִצְרָ֑יְמָה).

שְׁכֹן The vowel pattern of this strong verb (Shewa-Holem) may be either Qal Imperative ms or Qal Infinitive Construct. In this case, context requires the Imperative.

אֹמַר The Imperfect preformative vowel is Holem in I-א (Type 3) weak verbs (16.2; 16.3.2). While this pattern occurs with only six verbs, אָמַר is very common with 2,993 occurrences in the Imperfect. In this Qal Imperfect 1cs form, you would expect the א to be written twice, once for the preformative and once for the first consonant of the verbal root. It is, however, written only once. The א that is written is the Imperfect preformative for the 1cs. The first root consonant is not written in this form.

גּוּר Most Biconsonantal Imperatives (2ms) are quite easy to recognize because they preserve the distinctive medial vowel (letter) of the corresponding Imperfect forms. This form can also be an Infinitive Construct, but not in this context. Here, it is the Imperative 2ms of גּוּר.

בָּאָרֶץ הַזֹּאת The fs demonstrative adjective זֹאת is modifying the fs noun אֶרֶץ (8.6; 8.7.1). Both the preposition בְּ and the definite article are prefixed to the noun (in this land).

וְאֶהְיֶה The ה ֶ ending is helpful in the identification of this verb as the Qal Imperfect 1cs of הָיָה (16.14-15). This Imperfect verb is prefixed with the conjunction וְ (and I will be).

וַאֲבָרְכֶךָּ This Piel Imperfect verb is identified by the Hateph Pathach beneath the 1cs preformative and the Qamets beneath the first root consonant. This Qamets is the result of compensatory lengthening. The ר cannot take the distinctive Daghesh Forte of the Piel stem (33.7-8). This form also has a 2ms pronominal suffix and the conjunction וְ spelled with Pathach before a guttural with Hateph Pathach (5.8.5). A Waw Consecutive on this form would be spelled with Qamets (17.2.2).

וּלְזַרְעֲךָ This form consists of four parts. The conjunction וְ (spelled as וּ before Vocal Shewa [5.8.5b]) and the preposition לְ are prefixed to the ms Segholate noun זֶרַע. This form also appears with a 2ms pronominal suffix (and to your offspring [lit. seed]).

אֶתֵּן The preformative אֶ identifies this verb as Qal Imperfect 1cs. The Daghesh Forte in the ת represents the assimilated נ that is the first consonant of the verbal root נָתַן (16.14; 16.15.4).

הָאֲרָצֹת הָאֵל The form הָאֲרָצֹת is the fp of the Segholate noun אֶרֶץ with the vowel of the fp inflectional ending (וֹת) written defectively as Holem. It is prefixed with the definite article. The form אֵל is a variant or alternate form of the demonstrative אֵלֶּה (8.6.3). Here, it functions as a demonstrative adjective (8.7.1), modifying הָאֲרָצֹת and agreeing in gender, number, and definiteness (these lands).

וַהֲקִמֹתִי This Hiphil Perfect of the Biconsonantal קוּם with Waw Consecutive can be difficult to identify. The תִי ending is obviously the 1cs Perfect sufformative. The combination of the ה prefix and the defectively written Hireq Yod stem vowel identify the verb as a

Hiphil Perfect (27.14). In most Biconsonantal forms, the prefix vowel is Hateph Pathach (27.15.2). The Hiphil Perfect of this verb class takes a Holem Waw "connecting" vowel (here written defectively) between the verbal root and the Perfect sufformatives in all second and first person forms (and I will establish).

נִשְׁבַּעְתִּי Like the preceding form, the תִּי sufformative identifies this verb as Perfect 1cs. The נִ prefix is diagnostic of the Niphal Perfect. In the Niphal stem, the verbal root שָׁבַע is translated with the simple action of the Qal stem (I swore).

Genesis 26:4

וְהִרְבֵּיתִי The תִי sufformative identifies the verb as Perfect 1cs. The הִ prefix is diagnostic of the Hiphil stem. The Tsere Yod stem vowel identifies the verbal root as III-ה. This Perfect 1cs verb is also prefixed with Waw Consecutive (and I will increase).

כְּכוֹכְבֵי הַשָּׁמַיִם With the diagnostic Tsere Yod ending, כְּכוֹכְבֵי is the mp construct of כּוֹכָבִים prefixed with the preposition כְּ. Because the absolute noun in this construct chain is definite, the entire construction is considered definite (like the stars of [the] heaven)

וְנָתַתִּי The Qamets-Pathach vowel pattern and the תִּי sufformative identify this form as Qal Perfect 1cs (with Waw Consecutive). Note that the Daghesh in the תִּי sufformative is Forte and not Lene (3.5.1). This Daghesh Forte represents the assimilated נ that is the third consonant of the verbal root נָתַן (13.9).

וְהִתְבָּרְכוּ The הִתְ prefix and the Perfect sufformative וּ identify this form as Hithpael Perfect 3cp (with Waw Consecutive). The guttural ר rejects the Daghesh Forte of the Hithpael stem and the expected Pathach lengthens to Qamets under the first root letter (35.9.2).

Unfortunately, the translation of this Hithpael is not as easy as its identification. Should the phrase וְהִתְבָּרְכוּ בְזַרְעֲךָ כֹּל גּוֹיֵי הָאָרֶץ be translated passively, reflexively, or reciprocally? Each of these are well-attested meanings for the Hithpael stem. The difficulty of translation here is complicated by similar passages that record the divine promise of blessing to Abraham and Jacob using the Niphal of this same verb בָּרַךְ (Gen 12:3; 18:18; and 28:14). It would appear that בָּרַךְ is being used in these two verbal stems with no apparent distinction. Biblical scholars also disagree on how to translate these three promise texts in which the Niphal of בָּרַךְ is used. The decision of how to translate the Niphal or Hithpael of בָּרַךְ in these various promise passages is of great exegetical, hermeneutical, and theological significance (for a helpful introduction to the problem, see Chisholm, 83-85).

Genesis 26:5

עֵקֶב אֲשֶׁר	This construction is translated "because" (see *HALOT* 1:873).
שָׁמַע אַבְרָהָם בְּקֹלִי	The verb שָׁמַע followed by בְּקוֹל may be translated "to obey." The form בְּקֹלִי is the noun קוֹל (with defectively spelled Holem Waw) prefixed with the preposition בְּ and with a 1cs pronominal suffix. This expression may be translated "(because) Abraham obeyed me."

Genesis 35:9-15

God's Promises to Jacob

9 וַיֵּרָא אֱלֹהִים אֶל־יַעֲקֹב עוֹד בְּבֹאוֹ מִפַּדַּן[1] אֲרָם וַיְבָרֶךְ אֹתוֹ 10
וַיֹּאמֶר־לוֹ אֱלֹהִים שִׁמְךָ יַעֲקֹב לֹא־יִקָּרֵא שִׁמְךָ עוֹד יַעֲקֹב כִּי
אִם־יִשְׂרָאֵל יִהְיֶה שְׁמֶךָ וַיִּקְרָא אֶת־שְׁמוֹ יִשְׂרָאֵל 11 וַיֹּאמֶר לוֹ
אֱלֹהִים אֲנִי אֵל שַׁדַּי[2] פְּרֵה[3] וּרְבֵה גּוֹי וּקְהַל גּוֹיִם יִהְיֶה מִמֶּךָּ
וּמְלָכִים מֵחֲלָצֶיךָ[4] יֵצֵאוּ 12 וְאֶת־הָאָרֶץ אֲשֶׁר נָתַתִּי לְאַבְרָהָם
וּלְיִצְחָק לְךָ אֶתְּנֶנָּה וּלְזַרְעֲךָ אַחֲרֶיךָ אֶתֵּן אֶת־הָאָרֶץ 13 וַיַּעַל
מֵעָלָיו אֱלֹהִים בַּמָּקוֹם אֲשֶׁר־דִּבֶּר אִתּוֹ 14 וַיַּצֵּב יַעֲקֹב מַצֵּבָה[5]
בַּמָּקוֹם אֲשֶׁר־דִּבֶּר אִתּוֹ מַצֶּבֶת אָבֶן וַיַּסֵּךְ[6] עָלֶיהָ נֶסֶךְ וַיִּצֹק עָלֶיהָ

---

1. פַּדַּן Paddan (11).
2. שַׁדַּי (divine title) Almighty, Shaddai (48).
3. פָּרָה (Q) to bear fruit, be fruitful (29).
4. חֲלָצַיִם (md) loins, stomach, waist (11).
5. מַצֵּבָה sacred stone, pillar (33).
6. נָסַךְ (Q) to pour out, pour (cast) a metal image or statue; (Hi) pour out libations, offer a drink offering (25).

שָׁמֶן 15 וַיִּקְרָא יַעֲקֹב אֶת־שֵׁם הַמָּקוֹם אֲשֶׁר דִּבֶּר אִתּוֹ שָׁם
אֱלֹהִים בֵּית־אֵל

Parse the following verbs from Genesis 35:9-15.

Genesis 35:9

וַיֵּרָא ________________________________

בְּבֹאוֹ ________________________________

וַיְבָרֶךְ ________________________________

Genesis 35:10

וַיֹּאמֶר ________________________________

יִקָּרֵא ________________________________

יִהְיֶה ________________________________

וַיִּקְרָא ________________________________

Genesis 35:11

פְּרֵה ________________________________

רְבֵה ________________________________

יִהְיֶה ________________________________

יֵצֵאוּ ________________________________

Genesis 35:12

נָתַתִּי ________________________________

אֶתְּנֶנָּה ________________________________

אֶתֵּן ________________________________

Genesis 35:13

וַיַּ֫עַל ______________________________

דִּבֶּר ______________________________

Genesis 35:14

וַיַּצֵּב ______________________________

וַיַּסֵּךְ ______________________________

וַיִּצֹק ______________________________

Grammatical Commentary: Genesis 35:9-15

Genesis 35:9

וַיֵּרָא The Tsere preformative vowel and the Qamets under the first root letter identifies the verbal stem as a Niphal Imperfect of רָאָה. The Tsere vowel is the result of compensatory lengthening from Hireq because the ר in first root position cannot take the assimilated Nun of the Niphal. This spelling will take place in all I-Guttural verbs in the Niphal Imperfect, Imperative, Infinitive Construct, and one form of the Infinitive Absolute (25.7.1). In the Niphal, the verbal root רָאָה translates "to appear" (and [God] appeared).

בְּבֹאוֹ The Qal Infinitive Construct of בּוֹא (with a defectively written medial vowel letter) appears with the preposition בְּ and a 3ms pronominal suffix. The use of the preposition בְּ with the Infinitive Construct marks the temporal usage (20.12.5) and the 3ms pronominal suffix is functioning as the subject of the verbal action (when he came).

מִפַּדַּן אֲרָם The proper name פַּדַּן אֲרָם (Paddan Aram) is prefixed with the preposition מִן.

וַיְבָרֶךְ In the absence of a sufformative, the preformative י identifies this verb as Imperfect 3ms with Waw Consecutive. The Shewa preformative vowel is diagnostic of the Piel and Pual Imperfect (30.6; 32.6). The Qamets under the first root consonant distinguishes the form as a Piel. In the Pual of this verb, the vowel with the first root consonant would be Holem. The Qamets in the Piel Imperfect and the Holem in the Pual Imperfect are the result of compensatory lengthening (31.10; 33.8).

Genesis 35:10

שִׁמְךָ יַעֲקֹב This construction is a verbless clause (of identification). The subject is the ms noun שֵׁם with a 2ms pronominal suffix. The predicate is the proper noun יַעֲקֹב (your name *is* Jacob).

לֹא־יִקָּרֵא The negative particle לֹא is joined by Maqqef to the Niphal Imperfect 3ms of קָרָא. This form is recognizable as a Niphal Imperfect by the Hireq preformative vowel, the Daghesh Forte in the first root consonant (the assimilated נ of the Niphal) and the Qamets under the first root consonant (24.6-7).

כִּי אִם The combination of כִּי with אִם may be translated "but rather."

שְׁמֶךָ This is the ms noun שֵׁם with a 2ms pronominal suffix, just like שִׁמְךָ earlier in the verse. In this case, however, the construction is pausal and so the Shewa connecting vowel of the 2ms pronominal suffix changes to Seghol (36.3.3). In *BHS,* this form appears with Zaqef Qatan over the מ (שְׁמֶ֔ךָ).

וַיִּקְרָא אֶת־שְׁמוֹ The noun שֵׁם with a 3ms pronominal suffix is the direct object of the Qal Imperfect 3ms of קָרָא with Waw Consecutive. This clause may be translated "and he called his name" or "and he named him."

Genesis 35:11

אֲנִי אֵל שַׁדַּי This is a verbless clause (of identification). The 1cs personal pronoun אֲנִי is the subject and the proper name אֵל שַׁדַּי (of uncertain etymology) is the predicate ("I *am* God Almighty" or "I *am* El Shaddai").

פְּרֵה The ֵה ending usually identifies the Imperative 2ms of III-ה verbs in the Qal and derived stems, though the ending may mark other grammatical forms as well (18.5; 25.4; 27.8; 29.4; 31.4; 35.4). This form preserves the expected spelling of the Qal Imperative 2ms of פָּרָה.

וּרְבֵה As with the Imperative פְּרֵה, which immediately precedes, this III-ה verb exhibits the same distinctive form. The conjunction וְ is spelled as Shureq because it is prefixed to a word that begins with Vocal Shewa (5.7.2b). It is a common construction in Hebrew to link several Imperative verbs in succession. Context will determine whether or not they are related consequentially or sequentially (18.12.1).

גּוֹי וּקְהַל גּוֹיִם The ms noun גּוֹי and the construct chain וּקְהַל גּוֹיִם (prefixed with the conjunction וְ) constitute the subject of the verb יִהְיֶה that follows (a nation and an assembly of nations). The verb often agrees with only the first element of a compound subject.

מִמְּךָ This is the preposition מִן with a 2ms pronominal suffix (9.12).

מֵחֲלָצֶיךָ The preposition מִן is prefixed to the masculine dual noun חֲלָצַיִם with a 2ms pronominal suffix. The Tsere of the preposition is the result of compensatory lengthening (Hireq to Tsere) because the ח rejects the assimilation of the נ of the preposition (6.5.2b).

יֵצֵאוּ The preformative י and the sufformative וּ identify the form as Imperfect 3mp of יָצָא. The Tsere preformative vowel is diagnostic of the I-י (Type 1) Qal Imperfect (16.6). The subject of this verb is מְלָכִים (and kings *will come out* from your loins).

Genesis 35:12

וְאֶת־הָאָרֶץ In Hebrew, normal word order for a verbal sentence is normally understood as verb-subject-object (12.14; 23.1-5). Exceptions to this pattern are common. This verse begins with the definite direct object הָאָרֶץ which is marked by the definite direct object marker אֶת־ prefixed with the conjunction וְ.

אֲשֶׁר נָתַתִּי The relative pronoun אֲשֶׁר introduces a relative clause that modifies the accusative noun (הָאָרֶץ). The verb that follows is identified as Qal Perfect 1cs by the Qamets-Pathach vowel pattern and the sufformative תִּי. The third consonant of the verbal root (נ) has assimilated into the ת of the Perfect sufformative and is represented by the Daghesh Forte (which I gave).

לְךָ This form is the preposition לְ with a 2ms pronominal suffix. It functions as the indirect object of אֶתְּנֶנָּה which immediately follows.

אֶתְּנֶנָּה This verb is difficult to identify. The preformative אֶ signifies the Qal (or Niphal) Imperfect 1cs. This form is Qal with a 3fs pronominal Nun-suffix ֶנָּה (19.13). The antecedent of the pronominal suffix is the definite fs noun הָאָרֶץ which appears earlier in the verse. The Daghesh Forte in the תּ represents the assimilated first root consonant of the verb נָתַן (I will give it).

וּלְזַרְעֲךָ This form consists of four parts. The conjunction וְ (spelled וּ before Vocal Shewa [5.8.5b]) and the preposition לְ are prefixed to the Segholate ms noun זֶרַע. This form also appears with a 2ms pronominal suffix (and to your offspring [lit. seed]).

Genesis 35:13

וַיַּעַל This is the Qal Imperfect 3ms of עָלָה with Waw Consecutive. With the prefixing of Waw Consecutive, III-ה verbs are normally spelled without the final vowel letter in those Imperfect forms without a sufformative (יַעֲלֶה is spelled וַיַּעַל). The subject of this verb is אֱלֹהִים which appears after the prepositional phrase that follows this verbal construction.

מֵעָלָיו The preposition מִן is prefixed to the preposition עַל with a 3ms pronominal suffix. This construction is translated "from him" or "from before him."

אֲשֶׁר־דִּבֶּר The relative pronoun אֲשֶׁר is joined by Maqqef to the verb דִּבֶּר. This verb is identified as the Piel Perfect 3ms of דָּבַר by the Hireq under the first root consonant and the Daghesh Forte in the second root consonant (30.4).

אִתּוֹ This is the preposition אֵת with a 3ms pronominal suffix (9.14). Remember that the definite direct object marker אֵת with a 3ms pronominal suffix is spelled אֹתוֹ (him).

Genesis 35:14

וַיַּצֵּב The Pathach preformative vowel identifies the stem of this verb as Hiphil. The expected Hireq Yod stem vowel of the Hiphil has been shortened to Tsere with the prefixing of Waw Consecutive (יַצִּיב becomes וַיַּצֵּב). The Daghesh Forte in the צ identifies the verbal root as I-נ with the assimilation of the first root consonant to the second root consonant. The Hiphil of נָצַב translates as "to set up."

דִּבֶּר The subject of this Piel Perfect 3ms is ambiguous. It is either יַעֲקֹב or אֱלֹהִים. Based upon the similar construction in verse 15 below, it appears that אֱלֹהִים is to be understood as the subject of the verb in this instance.

מַצֶּבֶת אָבֶן This is a construct chain in apposition to the noun מַצֵּבָה earlier in the verse. Apposition is a grammatical construction in which two or more nouns are placed together and the second noun specifies, explains, or clarifies the first noun. מַצֶּבֶת is the fs construct spelling of מַצֵּבָה. Note the pausal spelling of the absolute noun אָבֶן (lexical form אֶבֶן). In *BHS*, this form appears with Athnak under the א (אָ֑בֶן). Seghol will change to Qamets in some Segholate nouns when in pause (36.3.2).

וַיַּסֵּךְ Like וַיַּצֵּב earlier in this verse, the stem of this Imperfect 3ms verb with Waw Consecutive is identified as Hiphil by the Pathach preformative vowel and the Tsere stem vowel. The verbal root is identified by the Daghesh Forte in the ס, representing the assimilated first root consonant of נָסַךְ. The י preformative and the absence of a sufformative identifies the form as 3ms.

עָלֶיהָ The preposition עַל occurs here with a 3fs (Type 2) pronominal suffix. The antecedent of the pronominal suffix is the fs noun מַצֵּבָה which appears earlier in the verse.

וַיִּצֹק The preformative י identifies this form as Imperfect 3ms. It is prefixed with the Waw Consecutive. The Hireq preformative vowel and the Holem stem vowel are the diagnostic spelling features of the Qal Imperfect. In this case, the identification of the verbal root יָצַק is difficult. The י of the verbal root has been lost.

שָׁמֶן The spelling of שֶׁמֶן with Qamets instead of Seghol is another example in this verse of pausal spelling (36.3.2) in a Segholate noun. In *BHS*, this form appears with Silluq under the שׁ (שָֽׁמֶן).

Genesis 35:15

וַיִּקְרָא The combination of the verb קָרָא and the verbal object שֵׁם in an expression like וַיִּקְרָא יַעֲקֹב אֶת־שֵׁם הַמָּקוֹם is literally translated "and Jacob *called the name* of the place." More idiomatically, this construction may be translated, "and Jacob *named* the place."

בֵּית־אֵל This is the proper name "Bethel," meaning "house of God."

Translation 5

Genesis 43:1-8

Jacob Sends Benjamin to Egypt

1 וְהָרָעָב כָּבֵד[1] בָּאָרֶץ 2 וַיְהִי כַּאֲשֶׁר כִּלּוּ לֶאֱכֹל אֶת־הַשֶּׁבֶר[2]
אֲשֶׁר הֵבִיאוּ מִמִּצְרָיִם וַיֹּאמֶר אֲלֵיהֶם אֲבִיהֶם שֻׁבוּ שִׁבְרוּ[3]־לָנוּ
מְעַט־אֹכֶל[4] 3 וַיֹּאמֶר אֵלָיו יְהוּדָה לֵאמֹר הָעֵד[5] הֵעִד בָּנוּ הָאִישׁ
לֵאמֹר לֹא־תִרְאוּ פָנַי בִּלְתִּי אֲחִיכֶם אִתְּכֶם 4 אִם־יֶשְׁךָ מְשַׁלֵּחַ
אֶת־אָחִינוּ אִתָּנוּ נֵרְדָה וְנִשְׁבְּרָה לְךָ אֹכֶל 5 וְאִם־אֵינְךָ מְשַׁלֵּחַ
לֹא נֵרֵד כִּי־הָאִישׁ אָמַר אֵלֵינוּ לֹא־תִרְאוּ פָנַי בִּלְתִּי אֲחִיכֶם
אִתְּכֶם 6 וַיֹּאמֶר יִשְׂרָאֵל לָמָה הֲרֵעֹתֶם לִי לְהַגִּיד לָאִישׁ הַעוֹד
לָכֶם אָח 7 וַיֹּאמְרוּ שָׁאוֹל שָׁאַל־הָאִישׁ לָנוּ וּלְמוֹלַדְתֵּנוּ[6] לֵאמֹר

---

1. כָּבֵד (adj) heavy, severe (41).
2. שֶׁ֫בֶר grain (9).
3. שָׁבַר (Q) to buy grain (for food) (21).
4. אֹ֫כֶל food (38).
5. עוּד (Hi) to warn, admonish, witness, be a witness, call as witness, testify (40).
6. מוֹלֶ֫דֶת relatives, offspring, native (land) (22).

הַעוֹד אֲבִיכֶם חַי הֲיֵשׁ לָכֶם אָח וַנַּגֶּד־לוֹ עַל־פִּי הַדְּבָרִים הָאֵלֶּה
הֲיָדוֹעַ נֵדַע כִּי יֹאמַר הוֹרִידוּ אֶת־אֲחִיכֶם 8 וַיֹּאמֶר יְהוּדָה
אֶל־יִשְׂרָאֵל אָבִיו שִׁלְחָה הַנַּעַר אִתִּי וְנָקוּמָה וְנֵלֵכָה וְנִחְיֶה וְלֹא
נָמוּת גַּם־אֲנַחְנוּ גַם־אַתָּה גַּם־טַפֵּנוּ[7]

Parse the following verbs from Genesis 43:1-8.

Genesis 43:2

וַיְהִי ________________________________

כִּלּוּ ________________________________

לֶאֱכֹל ________________________________

הֵבִיאוּ ________________________________

שֻׁבוּ ________________________________

שִׁבְרוּ ________________________________

Genesis 43:3

הָעֵד ________________________________

הֵעִד ________________________________

תִרְאוּ ________________________________

Genesis 43:4

מְשַׁלֵּחַ ________________________________

7. טַף children (41).

נֵרְדָה

וְנִשְׁבְּרָה

Genesis 43:5

נֵרֵד

אָמַר

Genesis 43:6

הֲרֵעֹתֶם

לְהַגִּיד

Genesis 43:7

שָׁאוֹל

שָׁאַל

וַנַּגֶּד

הֲיָדוֹעַ

נֵדַע

יֹאמַר

הוֹרִידוּ

Genesis 43:8

שִׁלְחָה

וְנָקוּמָה

וְנֵלֵכָה

וְנִחְיֶה

נָמוּת

Grammatical Commentary: Genesis 43:1-8

Genesis 43:1

וְהָרָעָב כָּבֵד A disjunctive Waw is prefixed to the noun רָעָב with the definite article. In its introductory usage (24.17.4), the disjunctive Waw may begin a new narrative or introduce a new idea or theme within a narrative. Here, at the beginning of 43:1, it introduces the narrative that records the second trip to Egypt taken by Joseph's brothers. One could also view this disjunctive Waw as introducing a parenthetical comment that is essential for understanding why the trip was necessary (24.17.1). In such contexts, the Waw is frequently translated as "now." The form כָּבֵד is commonly understood as a predicate adjective. It may also be interpreted as the Tsere-Stative verb כָּבֵד (13.10), inflected as a Qal Perfect 3ms (now the famine was severe).

Genesis 43:2

וַיְהִי The temporal modifier (Qal Imperfect 3ms of הָיָה with Waw Consecutive) signals a past tense narrative sequence (17.4.3).

כַּאֲשֶׁר כִּלּוּ The form כַּאֲשֶׁר (the relative pronoun with preposition כְּ) is frequently translated with a temporal nuance (when). The verb כִּלּוּ is Piel Perfect 3cp of כָּלָה. The Hireq under the first root letter and the Daghesh Forte in the second root are the diagnostic features of the Piel Perfect (31.4).

לֶאֱכֹל The preposition לְ prefixed to this verbal form helps to identify the Infinitive Construct. The form אֱכֹל preserves the diagnostic features of a I-א Qal Infinitive Construct (20.3.2). The Hateph Seghol under the first root letter is occasioned by the guttural א (when they had finished *eating*). In this context, the use of the Infinitive is complementary (20.12.4)

אֶת־הַשֶּׁבֶר The noun שֶׁבֶר (grain) is marked as the definite direct object of the Infinitive Construct.

אֲשֶׁר הֵבִיאוּ מִמִּצְרָיִם The relative pronoun אֲשֶׁר precedes the Hiphil Perfect 3cp of בּוֹא. The הֵ prefix and Hireq Yod stem vowel identify the Biconsonantal verb as Hiphil Perfect (27.14-15). With regard to מִמִּצְרָיִם, the preposition מִן is prefixed to the proper name מִצְרָיִם. Note the pausal spelling (36.3.1) of מִצְרַיִם with Qamets instead of Pathach under ר (which they brought out from Egypt). In *BHS*, this form appears with Athnach under the ר (מִמִּצְרָ֑יִם).

שֻׁבוּ Recognizing that the Qibbuts represents a defectively written Shureq, שֻׁבוּ is easy to identify as the Qal Imperative 2mp of the Biconsonantal verb שׁוּב (return).

שִׁבְרוּ־לָנוּ The Qal Imperative 2mp of שָׁבַר is joined by Maqqef to the preposition לְ with a 1cp pronominal suffix. This verb may be translated "to buy grain" in certain contexts. In this case, however, it should be translated simply "to buy" in light of מְעַט־אֹכֶל which follows (buy for us a little food).

Genesis 43:3

לֵאמֹר The form לֵאמֹר (Qal Infinitive Construct of אָמַר prefixed with the preposition לְ) frequently introduces direct quotations. Often, it is best handled in translation only with punctuation (and Judah said to them, "…). The comma and quotation marks represent the rendering of לֵאמֹר.

הָעֵד הֵעִד בָּנוּ הָאִישׁ These first two forms are difficult to identify. Recognition that both are constructed on the same verbal root suggests the construction in which an Infinitive Absolute precedes a Perfect or Imperfect verb (21.6.1). The verb הָעֵד is the Hiphil Infinitive Absolute of the Biconsonantal עוּד. The verb הֵעִד is the Hiphil Perfect 3ms of the same verb with Hireq in the place of Hireq Yod. The הֵ prefix and Hireq (Yod) stem vowel are diagnostic (27.14-15) of the Biconsonantal Hiphil Perfect. The subject of the verb (הָאִישׁ) appears at the end of the clause and the preposition בְּ marks the direct object of the verbal construction, "the man surely warned us" or "the man sternly warned us."

לֵאמֹר Having noted above that לֵאמֹר is often rendered with the use of English punctuation, the traditional translation "saying" fits well in this context.

לֹא־תִרְאוּ פָנַי The negative particle לֹא is joined to its verb by Maqqef. The preformative תִ (without Daghesh Lene when preceded by a vowel sound) and sufformative וּ identify the form as Qal Imperfect 2mp. The verbal root is רָאָה. Remember that, in the Imperfect, III-ה verbs drop the final ה vowel letter in those forms that take a sufformative (16.11.2). The form פָנַי is the direct object of the verb. It consists of the mp noun פָּנִים (without Daghesh Lene when preceded by a vowel) with a 1cs (Type 2) pronominal suffix (you shall not see my face).

בִּלְתִּי אֲחִיכֶם אִתְּכֶם The form בִּלְתִּי is the negative particle normally associated with the Infinitive Construct (20.11). In this case, however, it introduces an exceptive clause, and may be translated "unless." An exceptive clause is a dependent clause that presents an *exception* to the situation described in the main clause (van der Merwe, 41.4.6; Joüon-Muraoka, 173a). In this context, the exceptive clause introduced by בִּלְתִּי is a verbless clause. The subject (אֲחִיכֶם) is the ms noun אָח with a 2mp pronominal suffix. The Hireq Yod that appears between the noun and its pronominal suffix is a morphological peculiarity characteristic of certain monosyllabic nouns in the construct state (10.3.2e) or when taking pronominal suffixes (9.9). The predicate (אִתְּכֶם) is the preposition אֵת with a 2mp pronominal suffix (*unless* your brother *is* with you).

Genesis 43:4

אִם־יֶשְׁךָ Verses 4 and 5 provide two classical illustrations of conditional sentences using אִם followed by יֵשׁ in verse 4 and אִם followed by אֵין in verse 5 (21.9). In Hebrew, a conditional sentence consists of two clauses. The first clause states the condition and is called the protasis (the "if-clause"). The second clause states the consequence of the condition and is called the apodosis (the "then-clause"). The protasis of a conditional sentence will often begin with אִם (if) as in the beginning of both verses 4 and 5 (29.16.1). In verse 4, the protasis or "if-clause" begins with אִם (if), which is joined by Maqqef to the particle יֵשׁ with a 2ms pronominal suffix. In this case, the pronominal suffix functions as the subject of מְשַׁלֵּחַ which follows (if you are…)

מְשַׁלֵּחַ All of the distinctive points of spelling are present for the identification of this form as the Piel Participle ms of שָׁלַח (מְ prefix, Pathach under the first root consonant, and Daghesh Forte in the second root consonant [30.11-12]). Translate the Participle either as "(if you are) sending" or "(if you) send."

אֶת־אָחִינוּ אִתָּנוּ The form אָחִינוּ (ms noun אָח with a 1cp [Type 1] pronominal suffix) is the direct object of the Participle מְשַׁלֵּחַ. The form אִתָּנוּ is the preposition אֵת with a 1cp pronominal suffix (with us).

נֵרְדָה Though unmarked, this Qal Imperfect 1cp of יָרַד (with Paragogic ה) begins the apodosis (or "then-clause") of this conditional sentence (we will go down). The נ preformative identifies the Imperfect as 1cp and the Tsere preformative vowel is diagnostic of the I-י (Type 1) weak verb class.

וְנִשְׁבְּרָה לְךָ אֹכֶל Prefixed with the conjunction וְ, נִשְׁבְּרָה is Qal Imperfect 1cp (with Paragogic ה), and it continues the apodosis of the conditional sentence. This verb is followed by its indirect object לְךָ and direct object אֹכֶל (and we will buy food for you).

Genesis 43:5

וְאִם־אֵינְךָ Verse 5 provides another example of a conditional construction, beginning with אִם (to which the conjunction וְ has been prefixed) and followed by אֵין (lexical אַ֫יִן) with a 2ms pronominal suffix. As in verse 4, the protasis or "if-clause" begins with אִם (if) which is joined by Maqqef to the particle אֵין. Here, with a 2ms pronominal suffix, it translates "but if you are not" or "but if you do not." The suffix on אֵין is functioning as the subject of מְשַׁלֵּחַ which follows.

מְשַׁלֵּחַ This is the same form that appears in the conditional construction in verse 4 (Piel Participle ms of שָׁלַח). Translate the protasis either as "but if you are not sending (him)" or "but if you do not send (him)." Note that the object of מְשַׁלֵּחַ (him) must be supplied in translation.

לֹא נֵרֵד Again unmarked, the apodosis (or "then-clause") in this verse consists of the negative particle לֹא and the Qal Imperfect 1cp of יָרַד (we will not go down). The נ preformative identifies the Imperfect as 1cp and the Tsere preformative vowel identifies the weak verb class as I-י (16.7.1).

כִּי־הָאִישׁ אָמַר אֵלֵינוּ The conjunction כִּי should be translated with its causal value in this context (because). The form אֵלֵינוּ is the preposition אֶל with a 1cp pronominal suffix (because the man said to us).

לֹא־תִרְאוּ.... אִתְּכֶם This is precisely the same construction that appears at the end of verse 3 (see comments there).

Genesis 43:6

לָמָה הֲרֵעֹתֶם לִי The interrogative לָמָה (why?) is a combination of the preposition לְ and the interrogative pronoun מָה. The verb הֲרֵעֹתֶם is the Hiphil Perfect 2mp of the Geminate verb רָעַע. Though the form poses some difficulty for recognition, the הֲ prefix and 2mp sufformative תֶם (without Daghesh Lene when preceded by a vowel) suggest the Hiphil Perfect. The Holem (for Holem Waw) between the verbal root and Perfect sufformative is distinctive of Biconsonantal and Geminate verbs in the Perfect conjugation (why did you bring such calamity to me).

לְהַגִּיד לָאִישׁ In לְהַגִּיד, the הַ prefix and Hireq Yod stem vowel are diagnostic of the Hiphil Infinitive Construct (26.10). The presence of the preposition לְ also aids with the identification of this form as Infinitive Construct. In fact, as indicated in Gen 2:3, almost sixty-nine percent (4,528 verbs) of all Infinitive Construct verbs in the Hebrew Bible (6,599 verbs) appear with the preposition לְ. The Daghesh Forte in the ג represents the assimilated first root consonant (נָגַד). One of the primary uses of the Infinitive Construct is to explain, clarify, or complement a preceding statement or action (20.12.4). Here, the Infinitive is both clarifying and explaining Jacob's preceding comment. With the prepositional phrase לָאִישׁ functioning as the indirect object, translate this construction, "by telling the man."

הַעוֹד לָכֶם אָח The adverb עוֹד (yet, still, again) is prefixed with the interrogative particle (הֲ) and followed by the preposition לְ with a 2mp pronominal suffix. This combination serves as a dependent interrogative clause. Literally, this expression translates as "that still to you *was* a brother." Idiomatically, it may be rendered, "that you had another brother."

Genesis 43:7

שָׁאוֹל שָׁאַל הָאִישׁ With regard to the form שָׁאוֹל, the Qamets under the first root consonant and the Holem Waw stem vowel identify the form as the Qal Infinitive Absolute of שָׁאַל (21.4). The Qal Perfect 3ms of the same verbal root follows. This construction, intended to emphasize the verbal idea (21.6.1), is followed by its subject הָאִישׁ, "the man surely asked us" or, more idiomatically, "the man questioned us intensely."

וּלְמוֹלַדְתֵּנוּ This form consists of four parts. The noun מוֹלֶדֶת (relatives) is prefixed with the conjunction וְ and the preposition לְ. This noun also has a 1cp pronominal suffix (and about our relatives).

הַעוֹד אֲבִיכֶם חַי Introduced by לֵאמֹר, this first question begins with the adverb עוֹד prefixed with the interrogative particle (cf. הַעוֹד in verse 6). The construction אֲבִיכֶם חַי is a verbless clause. The subject is the ms noun אָב with a 2mp pronominal suffix and the predicate is the ms adjective חַי. With the interrogative particle and the adverb עוֹד, this clause translates as "is your father still alive?"

הֲיֵשׁ לָכֶם אָח This second question, also governed by לֵאמֹר, begins with the interrogative particle הֲ prefixed to the particle יֵשׁ. The particle יֵשׁ

(when followed by the preposition לְ) is frequently used with a nuance of possession (21.9). With the noun אָח, the construction should translate as "do you have another brother?"

וַנַּגֶּד־לוֹ The Waw Consecutive and the preformative נ identify this form as Imperfect 1cp (in *BHS*, the Daghesh Forte of the Waw Consecutive is missing in the Imperfect preformative). The Daghesh Forte in the ג represents the assimilated first root consonant (נָגַד). The Pathach preformative vowel is diagnostic of the Hiphil stem. Note that the expected Tsere stem vowel shortened to Seghol when the verb was joined to the following prepositional phrase by Maqqef, "and we told him" or "and we spoke to him."

עַל־פִּי The preposition עַל (on, upon) is joined by Maqqef to the construct form of the ms noun פֶּה (mouth). This construction should be translated, "according to."

הֲיָדוֹעַ נֵדַע This is another example of an Infinitive Absolute before a finite (Perfect or Imperfect) verb in order to emphasize the verbal idea (see שָׁאוֹל שָׁאַל earlier in this verse). The construction הֲיָדוֹעַ is the Qal Infinitive Absolute of יָדַע prefixed with the interrogative particle (הֲ). The form נֵדַע is the Qal Imperfect 1cp from the same verbal root. The Tsere preformative vowel is a diagnostic feature of the Qal Imperfect I-י (Type 1) weak verb (16.6-7). This verb's other weakness is III-ע which explains the Furtive Pathach in יָדוֹעַ and the Pathach stem vowel in נֵדַע (how were we to know?).

כִּי יֹאמַר Here כִּי introduces an object clause and should be translated as "that." A direct object clause of this type often follows a verb of perception or cognition ([how were we to know] *that* he would say).

הוֹרִידוּ אֶת־אֲחִיכֶם The ה prefix and the Shureq sufformative identify this form as either Hiphil Imperative 2mp or Hiphil Perfect 3cp. In this case, the verb is an Imperative. The verbal root יָרַד is identified by the Holem Waw prefix vowel, which is diagnostic of the I-י weak verb class (27.13.1). Followed by its direct object, this clause is translated, "bring down your brother."

Genesis 43:8

שִׁלְחָה הַנַּעַר אִתִּי שִׁלְחָה is the Qal Imperative 2ms of שָׁלַח with Paragogic ה (18.3.3). Note that this suffix may appear with the Imperative 2ms and with certain Imperfect forms (with or without Waw Consecutive) that do not take sufformatives. In this case, the alternate (or lengthened) form is not translated differently than the regular 2ms Imperative. The direct object הַנַּעַר and the prepositional phrase אִתִּי follow the verb (send the boy with me!).

וְנָקוּמָה The Imperative שִׁלְחָה is followed by three Imperfect verbs prefixed with the conjunction וְ. In this type of verbal sequence, the Imperfect verbs create a purpose or result clause often translated with "so that" (23.7.4). With this first Imperfect verb, the preformative consonant and vowel נָ identify the form as Qal Imperfect 1cp of the Biconsonantal verb קוּם. Like the Imperative it follows, this verb appears with a Paragogic ה (*so that* we may arise).

וְנֵלֵכָה Like the verb it follows, this verb is also Qal Imperfect 1cp with a Paragogic ה. The verbal root is recognizable as הָלַךְ by the Tsere under the preformative consonant, a diagnostic feature of I-י (Type 1) weak verbs in the Qal Imperfect. Remember that the verb הָלַךְ in the Imperfect (16.7.2) inflects just like a I-י (Type 1) verb (and *so that* we may go).

וְנִחְיֶה Like the preceding two verbs, this verb is also Qal Imperfect 1cp with the conjunction וְ. The verbal root is חָיָה (and *so that* we may live).

וְלֹא נָמוּת The conjunction וְ is prefixed to the negative particle לֹא followed by the Qal Imperfect 1cp of the Biconsonantal מוּת (and not die). With regard to the appearance of the Paragogic ה found with so many of the previous verbs in this verse, note that it does not normally appear with negated verbs, though such verbs may still carry the purpose or result nuance (and *so that* we may not die).

גַּם־טַפֵּנוּ Here, the conjunction גַּם (even, also) is joined by Maqqef to the Geminate ms noun טַף with a 1cp suffix pronominal (also our children).

Translation 6

Exodus 3:1-12

The Burning Bush

1 וּמֹשֶׁה הָיָה רֹעֶה אֶת־צֹאן יִתְרוֹ[1] חֹתְנוֹ[2] כֹּהֵן מִדְיָן[3] וַיִּנְהַג[4]
אֶת־הַצֹּאן אַחַר הַמִּדְבָּר וַיָּבֹא אֶל־הַר הָאֱלֹהִים חֹרֵבָה[5] 2 וַיֵּרָא
מַלְאַךְ יְהוָה אֵלָיו בְּלַבַּת[6]־אֵשׁ מִתּוֹךְ הַסְּנֶה[7] וַיַּרְא וְהִנֵּה הַסְּנֶה
בֹּעֵר בָּאֵשׁ וְהַסְּנֶה אֵינֶנּוּ אֻכָּל 3 וַיֹּאמֶר מֹשֶׁה אָסֻרָה־נָּא וְאֶרְאֶה
אֶת־הַמַּרְאֶה הַגָּדֹל הַזֶּה מַדּוּעַ לֹא־יִבְעַר הַסְּנֶה 4 וַיַּרְא יְהוָה כִּי
סָר לִרְאוֹת וַיִּקְרָא אֵלָיו אֱלֹהִים מִתּוֹךְ הַסְּנֶה וַיֹּאמֶר מֹשֶׁה מֹשֶׁה

---

1. יִתְרוֹ Jethro (9).
2. חֹתֵן father-in-law (21).
3. מִדְיָן Midian (59).
4. נָהַג (Q) to drive (flocks), lead, guide (30).
5. חֹרֵב Horeb (17).
6. לַבָּה flame (1). A word that occurs only one time in the Hebrew Bible is called a *hapax legomenon*. This unusual expression is a transliteration of the Greek ἅπαξ λεγόμενον, meaning "something said (only) once."
7. סְנֶה bush, briar, (species of) bramble (6).

וַיֹּאמֶר הִנֵּנִי 5 וַיֹּאמֶר אַל־תִּקְרַב הֲלֹם[8] שַׁל[9]־נְעָלֶיךָ[10] מֵעַל רַגְלֶיךָ
כִּי הַמָּקוֹם אֲשֶׁר אַתָּה עוֹמֵד עָלָיו אַדְמַת־קֹדֶשׁ הוּא 6 וַיֹּאמֶר
אָנֹכִי אֱלֹהֵי אָבִיךָ אֱלֹהֵי אַבְרָהָם אֱלֹהֵי יִצְחָק וֵאלֹהֵי יַעֲקֹב
וַיַּסְתֵּר מֹשֶׁה פָּנָיו כִּי יָרֵא מֵהַבִּיט אֶל־הָאֱלֹהִים 7 וַיֹּאמֶר יְהוָה
רָאֹה רָאִיתִי אֶת־עֳנִי[11] עַמִּי אֲשֶׁר בְּמִצְרָיִם וְאֶת־צַעֲקָתָם[12]
שָׁמַעְתִּי מִפְּנֵי נֹגְשָׂיו[13] כִּי יָדַעְתִּי אֶת־מַכְאֹבָיו[14] 8 וָאֵרֵד לְהַצִּילוֹ
מִיַּד מִצְרַיִם וּלְהַעֲלֹתוֹ מִן־הָאָרֶץ הַהִוא אֶל־אֶרֶץ טוֹבָה וּרְחָבָה[15]
אֶל־אֶרֶץ זָבַת[16] חָלָב[17] וּדְבָשׁ אֶל־מְקוֹם הַכְּנַעֲנִי וְהַחִתִּי וְהָאֱמֹרִי

---

8. הֲלֹם here, to here (12).
9. נָשַׁל (Q) to remove, loosen (7).
10. נַ֫עַל (fs) sandal, shoe (22).
11. עֳנִי poverty, affliction, misery (36).
12. צְעָקָה outcry, yelling (21).
13. נָגַשׂ (Q) to oppress, press, force to work, be a slave driver or taskmaster (23).
14. מַכְאוֹב pain, suffering (16).
15. רָחָב (adj) wide, spacious (20).
16. זוּב (Q) to flow (away) (42).
17. חָלָב milk (44).

וְהַפְּרִזִּי וְהַחִוִּי וְהַיְבוּסִי 9 וְעַתָּה הִנֵּה צַעֲקַת בְּנֵי־יִשְׂרָאֵל בָּאָה
אֵלָי וְגַם־רָאִיתִי אֶת־הַלַּחַץ[18] אֲשֶׁר מִצְרַיִם לֹחֲצִים[19] אֹתָם 10
וְעַתָּה לְכָה וְאֶשְׁלָחֲךָ אֶל־פַּרְעֹה וְהוֹצֵא אֶת־עַמִּי בְנֵי־יִשְׂרָאֵל
מִמִּצְרָיִם 11 וַיֹּאמֶר מֹשֶׁה אֶל־הָאֱלֹהִים מִי אָנֹכִי כִּי אֵלֵךְ
אֶל־פַּרְעֹה וְכִי אוֹצִיא אֶת־בְּנֵי יִשְׂרָאֵל מִמִּצְרָיִם 12 וַיֹּאמֶר
כִּי־אֶהְיֶה עִמָּךְ וְזֶה־לְּךָ הָאוֹת כִּי אָנֹכִי שְׁלַחְתִּיךָ בְּהוֹצִיאֲךָ
אֶת־הָעָם מִמִּצְרַיִם תַּעַבְדוּן אֶת־הָאֱלֹהִים עַל הָהָר הַזֶּה׃

Parse the following verbs from Exodus 3:1-12.

Exodus 3:1

הָיָה ______________________________

רֹעֶה ______________________________

וַיִּנְהַג ______________________________

וַיָּבֹא ______________________________

18. לַ֫חַץ oppression, affliction (12).

19. לָחַץ (Q) to squeeze, crowd, press, oppress, torment (19).

Exodus 3:2

וַיֵּרָא ______________________________

וַיַּרְא ______________________________

בֹּעֵר ______________________________

אֻכָּל ______________________________

Exodus 3:3

וַיֹּאמֶר ______________________________

אָסֻרָה ______________________________

וְאֶרְאֶה ______________________________

יִבְעַר ______________________________

Exodus 3:4

סָר ______________________________

לִרְאוֹת ______________________________

וַיִּקְרָא ______________________________

Exodus 3:5

תִּקְרַב ______________________________

שַׁל ______________________________

עוֹמֵד ______________________________

Exodus 3:6

וַיַּסְתֵּר ______________________________

יָרֵא ______________________________

מֵהַבִּיט ______________________________

Exodus 3:7

רָאֹה

רָאִיתִי

שָׁמַעְתִּי

נֹגְשָׂיו

יָדַעְתִּי

Exodus 3:8

וָאֵרֵד

לְהַצִּילוֹ

וּלְהַעֲלֹתוֹ

זָבַת

Exodus 3:9

בָּאָה

לֹחֲצִים

Exodus 3:10

לְכָה

וְאֶשְׁלָחֲךָ

וְהוֹצֵא

Exodus 3:11

אֵלֵךְ

אוֹצִיא

Exodus 3:12

אֶהְיֶה ______________________________

שְׁלַחְתִּיךָ ______________________________

בְּהוֹצִיאֲךָ ______________________________

תַּעַבְדוּן ______________________________

Grammatical Commentary: Exodus 3:1-12

Exodus 3:1

וּמֹשֶׁה This form is a proper name (Moses) with the conjunction וְ spelled as Shureq because it is prefixed to the consonant מ. The conjunction is spelled with Shureq before ב, מ, and פ and before words beginning with Vocal Shewa (5.7.2a).

הָיָה רֹעֶה The most distinctive spelling feature of a Qal active Participle (רֹעֶה) is the Holem with the first root consonant. The ה ֶ ending appears both in the Imperfect (only forms without sufformatives) and in the ms Participle of III-ה verbs. The appearance of הָיָה (Qal Perfect 3ms) with the Qal Participle requires the Participle to be translated in the past tense, "Moses *was* tending."

אֶת־צֹאן יִתְרוֹ This construct chain constitutes the direct object of רֹעֶה. It is definite (*the* flocks of Jethro) because the absolute noun (יִתְרוֹ) is a proper name.

חֹתְנוֹ The noun חֹתֵן (father-in-law) appears with the 3ms pronominal suffix.

כֹּהֵן מִדְיָן This definite construct chain is in apposition to יִתְרוֹ. Apposition is a grammatical construction in which two or more nouns are placed side by side and the second noun specifies, explains, or clarifies the first noun. The noun כֹּהֵן is technically a Qal Participle (ms) of the verbal root כָּהַן (to act as a priest). The proper noun מִדְיָן is the absolute noun (the priest of Midian).

וַיִּנְהַג The stem vowel on this Qal Imperfect verb is Pathach because the verbal root is II-Guttural. This weak verb class and III-ח/ע differ from the strong verb pattern primarily in the stem vowel. Strong verbs have Holem but these two weak verb classes (and some stative verbs) have Pathach. This is the Qal Imperfect 3ms of נָהַג with Waw Consecutive (and he led).

אַחַר הַמִּדְבָּר The preposition אַחַר is often translated "behind" but may also designate compass direction (to the west side of the wilderness). For this rare use of אַחַר, see van der Merwe, 39.2.1c; Waltke-O'Connor, 11.2.1.

וַיָּבֹא With the Waw Consecutive, the preformative י identifies this verbal form as Imperfect 3ms. The Qamets preformative vowel is diagnostic of the Biconsonantal weak verb class in the Qal stem. The Holem (changed from Holem Waw with the prefixing of the Waw Consecutive) identifies the root as בּוֹא (23.11.2).

חֹרֵבָה The proper name חֹרֵב appears with the directional ending ָה (7.7).

Exodus 3:2

וַיֵּרָא With the Waw Consecutive, the preformative י identifies this verbal form as Imperfect 3ms. The Tsere preformative vowel and the Qamets under the first root letter are diagnostic of the Niphal stem. The ר in the first root position cannot take the Daghesh Forte that represents the assimilated נ of the Niphal. When the ר rejects the Daghesh Forte, the Hireq preformative vowel lengthens to Tsere (compensatory lengthening). The verbal root is רָאָה and with the prefixing of the Waw Consecutive in the Imperfect, the final ֶה vowel letter normally drops off (יֵרָאֶה becomes וַיֵּרָא). In the Niphal stem, the verbal root רָאָה translates "to appear."

בְּלַבַּת־אֵשׁ The preposition בְּ is prefixed to a construct chain in which the construct and absolute nouns are joined by Maqqef (in a flame of fire). The lexical form of the construct noun לַבַּת is לַבָּה. Remember that the feminine singular ending ָה changes to ַת in the construct state (10.3.2b).

מִתּוֹךְ This preposition occurs 68 times in the Hebrew Bible and is constructed with the preposition מִן (from) prefixed to the construct form of the noun תָּוֶךְ (middle, center). Compare with בְּתוֹךְ (occurring 319 times) having the same basic meaning.

וַיַּרְא This Imperfect 3ms of the doubly weak verb רָאָה with Waw Consecutive may be either Qal (to see) or Hiphil (to show). In this context, it is Qal. Remember that Imperfect III-ה verbs (without sufformatives) are normally spelled without the final vowel letter (ֶה) when prefixed with the Waw Consecutive.

בֹּעֵר בָּאֵשׁ Literally, this construction (Qal Participle of בָּעַר followed by the definite noun אֵשׁ prefixed with the preposition בְּ) translates as "burning with fire" but simply "burning" would be an acceptable rendering.

אֵינֶנּוּ This form is the particle אַיִן with a 3ms pronominal suffix ֶנּוּ (for the spelling of the suffix, see 19.13). Together with the preceding noun (סְנֶה with the article and the conjunction), this expression translates as "but the bush was not . . ."

אֻכָּל The form אֻכָּל may be a Pual Participle ms from אָכַל (to eat, consume). Sometimes, the Pual Participle is spelled without the expected מְ prefix. For more on the spelling of this form, see Joüon-Muraoka, 58a-b, and GKC, 52s. This form may also be interpreted as a passive Qal Participle ms (see Waltke-O'Connor, 22.6c). Either "being consumed" or "consumed" would be an appropriate translation.

Exodus 3:3

אָסֻרָה־נָּא The particle נָא (here with conjunctive Daghesh; 32.11) may be used to mark any volitional verb. With the Imperfect 1cs preformative (א), the Paragogic ה, and its position in its clause, the form אָסֻרָה is easily identified as volition (23.11.1). The verbal root is סוּר with the vowel letter written defectively as Qibbuts ("let me turn aside" or "I will turn aside").

וְאֶרְאֶה Following the volitional form אָסֻרָה, the Qal Imperfect 1cs of רָאָה with the conjunction וְ expresses purpose ([let me turn aside] *in order to* see). For more on this construction, see 18.12.3; 23.7.4 or van der Merwe, 21.5.1.

אֶת־הַמַּרְאֶה הַגָּדֹל הַזֶּה The construction אֶת־הַמַּרְאֶה הַגָּדֹל הַזֶּה is the direct object of וְאֶרְאֶה. The adjective גָּדֹל is defectively spelled with Holem rather than Holem Waw (גָּדוֹל). In this attributive construction, both the adjective and the following demonstrative agree in gender, number, and definiteness with the noun מַרְאֶה. The syntax is precisely as expected with a noun followed by an attributive adjective and then the demonstrative adjective (this great sight).

לֹא־יִבְעַר In this case, translate the Imperfect of בָּעַר with the present tense (is not consumed).

Exodus 3:4

סָר Biconsonantal verbs (also called Hollow or II-ו/י), in all three classes, have Qamets in the Qal Perfect 3ms (14.12). This Qal Perfect 3ms form is from סוּר (he turned aside).

לִרְאוֹת The form רְאוֹת is distinctive in its spelling, preserving the pattern of a Qal Infinitive Construct in the III-ה weak verb class (20.4). While the וֹת ending may mark a number of verbal and non-verbal forms, it is a diagnostic spelling feature in III-ה Infinitive Construct forms (to see).

וַיֹּאמֶר The subject of וַיֹּאמֶר is אֱלֹהִים in the preceding clause.

מֹשֶׁה מֹשֶׁה The repetition of the prophet's name is a double vocative. The repetition of a name often communicates a sense of urgency and immediacy. See Gen 22:11 (וַיֹּאמֶר אַבְרָהָם אַבְרָהָם) for another example.

וַיֹּאמֶר הִנֵּנִי The subject of וַיֹּאמֶר is מֹשֶׁה. The construction הִנֵּנִי is the particle הִנֵּה with a 1cs pronominal suffix (13.15). Its use here indicates the immediate presence of the speaker with a sense of urgency, "I am here" or "here I am." See Isaiah 6:8 for another example.

Exodus 3:5

אַל־תִּקְרַב The use of the negative particle אַל before the Imperfect creates a prohibition that is immediate and specific, "do not approach" or "do not come near."

שַׁל An infrequent and nearly impossible verb to identify, this Qal Imperative 2ms has dropped the first consonant of the verbal root (נָשַׁל). The Imperative forms of certain I-נ verbs may simply drop the נ in first root position. These are often called short Imperatives because only two root consonants remain (18.5, footnote 5).

נְעָלֶיךָ This is the plural of the Segholate noun נַ֫עַל with a 2ms (Type 2) pronominal suffix.

רַגְלֶיךָ This is the plural of the Segholate noun רֶ֫גֶל with a 2ms (Type 2) pronominal suffix.

אֲשֶׁר אַתָּה עוֹמֵד עָלָיו Relatives clauses in Hebrew are frequently introduced by the particle אֲשֶׁר (who, that, which). Here, the 2ms independent personal pronoun אַתָּה precedes the Qal active Participle of עָמַד in which the distinctive Holem with the first root consonant is written as Holem Waw. Note the resumptive pronoun (9.19; see also Waltke-O'Connor, 19.3; Joüon-Muraoka, 158e-u; GKC, 138) with the preposition עַל at the end of this relative clause (עָלָיו) which is best left untranslated ([the place] on which you are standing).

אַדְמַת־קֹדֶשׁ הוּא The ending ת ַ identifies אַדְמַת as a fs construct form of the noun אֲדָמָה. The absolute noun in the chain is קֹדֶשׁ. The preferred translation of this particular construct chain (holy ground) is rendered as a noun with a modifying adjective. This construct chain, together with the following 3ms independent personal pronoun, constitutes a verbless clause of classification (it *is* holy ground). The antecedent of the pronoun הוּא is the ms noun מָקוֹם (with the definite article).

Exodus 3:6

אָבִיךָ Here, the 2ms pronominal suffix is prefixed to the singular noun אָב. There are a number of high frequency monosyllabic nouns that will add Hireq Yod to their stem before a pronominal suffix (9.9) or when in construct (10.3.2e). The construct chain אֱלֹהֵי אָבִיךָ translates as "the God of your father."

וַיַּסְתֵּר The Pathach preformative vowel and the Tsere stem vowel identify the verbal stem as Hiphil. The prefixing of the Waw Consecutive to this Hiphil Imperfect 3ms causes the expected Hireq Yod (יַסְתִּיר) to change to Tsere (וַיַּסְתֵּר).

פָּנָיו This is the noun פָּנִים (lexical form פָּנֶה) with a 3ms pronominal suffix. Though plural in form, this noun is translated as a singular (his face).

יָרֵא This is a Tsere-Stative verb which translates as "he was afraid." (13.10).

מֵהַבִּיט With the removal of the prefixed preposition מִן (spelled with Tsere as a result of compensatory lengthening; 6.5.2b), the הַ prefix and Hireq Yod stem vowel identify the stem as Hiphil. This form can only be the Infinitive Construct (26.10). The Daghesh Forte in the בּ represents the assimilated נ of the verbal root נָבַט. The phrase כִּי יָרֵא מֵהַבִּיט אֶל־הָאֱלֹהִים translates as "for he was afraid to look at God."

Exodus 3:7

רָאֹה רָאִיתִי These two forms are constructed from the same verbal root (רָאָה). This is the important construction in which an Infinitive Absolute precedes a Perfect or Imperfect verb to emphasize or intensify the verbal meaning (21.6.1). The form רָאֹה preserves the expected vowel pattern of a III-ה Infinitive Absolute (21.4.2) and, by now, the form רָאִיתִי should be easily recognized as the Qal Perfect 1cs of רָאָה with the diagnostic Hireq Yod stem vowel (most III-ה verbs were originally III-י). There are several ways to translate this construction with language like "surely," "certainly" or "indeed" (21.6.1). The translation, "I have surely seen," is perhaps best.

צַעֲקָתָם This is the noun צְעָקָה with a 3mp pronominal suffix. It functions as the definite direct object of the verb שָׁמַעְתִּי which immediately follows ([I have heard] their cry).

מִפְּנֵי נֹגְשָׂיו The form מִפְּנֵי is the preposition מִן prefixed to the construct plural of פָּנִים (lexical form פָּנֶה). The form נֹגְשָׂיו, with the diagnostic Holem with the first root consonant, is the Qal Participle mp (נֹגְשִׂים) with a 3ms pronominal suffix. The Participle is being used substantively as the object of the preposition. Given that the antecedent of the 3ms (Type 2) pronominal suffix is the collective noun עַם (עַמִּי), the suffix may be translated with the plural, as "*their* taskmasters."

יָדַעְתִּי As a verb of understanding (to know), this Qal Perfect may be translated with the present tense (I know).

מַכְאֹבָיו This form is the plural of מַכְאֹב with a 3ms (Type 2) pronominal suffix. As with נֹגְשָׂיו above, the suffix may be translated with the plural (*their* sufferings).

Exodus 3:8

וָאֵרֵד The distinctive vowel pattern (Tsere as both the preformative and stem vowel) identifies this Imperfect as I-י (16.7.1). When prefixed to the א preformative of the Imperfect 1cs, the Waw Consecutive is spelled with Qamets as a result of compensatory lengthening (I have come down).

לְהַצִּילוֹ With the removal of the preposition לְ and the 3ms pronominal suffix, the הַ prefix and the Hireq Yod stem vowel identify this verb as a Hiphil Infinitive Construct. The Daghesh Forte in the second root consonant (צ) identifies the verbal root as I-נ (נָצַל). The נ in first root position assimilates into the second root consonant as a Daghesh Forte (27.10; 27.11.2).

מִיַּד מִצְרָיִם This construction is a definite construct chain with the preposition מִן prefixed to the construct noun יַד (the construct spelling of יָד). As the absolute noun, the proper name מִצְרַ֫יִם makes the chain definite (from the hand of Egypt)

וּלְהַעֲלֹתוֹ Two prefixes (the conjunction וּ and the preposition לְ) and the 3ms pronominal suffix (וֹ) make the identification of this form a challenge. The הַ prefix and the ֹת (וֹת) ending identify the verb as a Hiphil Infinitive Construct of the III-ה verb עָלָה. Remember that III-ה Infinitive Construct forms end in וֹת (here with defective spelling of the Holem Waw). See 25.5.3 for a summary of endings on III-ה verbs.

הַהִוא In the Pentateuch, הִוא is the variant spelling of הִיא.

אֶל־מְקוֹם The preposition אֶל appears before the construct form of מָקוֹם.

הַכְּנַעֲנִי The absolute noun in the construct chain is הַכְּנַעֲנִי. It is the gentilic form of כְּנַעַן with the definite article. The entire construction may be translated "to the place of the Canaanites." A gentilic noun is "a noun that refers to a single member of a collective group, typically an ethnic or national group" (Arnold-Choi, 199), such as "Canaanite" or "Moabite."

Exodus 3:9

צַעֲקַת בְּנֵי־יִשְׂרָאֵל In the phrase צַעֲקַת בְּנֵי־יִשְׂרָאֵל there are two nouns in construct with the proper name יִשְׂרָאֵל in the absolute position. The form צַעֲקַת is the construct spelling of צְעָקָה and the form בְּנֵי is the construct spelling of the mp noun בָּנִים (lexical form בֵּן).

בָּאָה The verb בָּ֫אָה (with accent on the first syllable) is the Qal Perfect 3fs of בּוֹא (14.12). The form בָּאָ֫ה (accented on the final syllable) is the Qal Participle fs of the same verb (22.4.5). The form in this verse is the Qal Perfect 3fs.

אֵלָי Here, the preposition אֶל appears with a 1cs pronominal suffix. Note the pausal spelling (36.3.1) of this Type 2 pronominal suffix with Qamets instead of the expected Pathach. In *BHS*, this form appears with Athnach under the ל (אֵלָ֑י).

לֹחֲצִים The Holem vowel identifies this form as the Qal Participle of לָחַץ. The ִים ending marks this form as masculine plural. The Hateph

Pathach beneath the guttural in second root position is due to the fact that gutturals take Hateph vowels rather than Vocal Shewa.

אֹתָם The definite direct object marker appears with a 3mp pronominal suffix. The construct chain בְּנֵי־יִשְׂרָאֵל is the antecedent of this suffix.

Exodus 3:10

לְכָה This form is an alternate spelling (with Paragogic ה) of the Qal Imperative 2ms of הָלַךְ (18.3.3). The more common spelling of this form is לֵךְ with the loss of the first root consonant. Preceded by וְעַתָּה (and now), לְכָה is translated as a particle of entreaty (come!). The Paragogic ה appears frequently on first person volitional forms (אָסֻרָה in Exod 3:3), the Imperative (קוּמָה in Num 10:35), and even on Waw Consecutive forms (וָאֶעְבְּרָה in Judg 12:3).

וְאֶשְׁלָחֲךָ With the removal of the conjunction וְ and the 2ms pronominal suffix (ךָ ֲ), the Qal Imperfect 1cs of שָׁלַח is easy to recognize despite the spelling changes caused by the addition of the pronominal suffix (and I will send you).

וְהוֹצֵא The ה prefix and the Tsere stem vowel identify this verb as Hiphil Imperative (27.12). The Holem Waw identifies the verbal root as I-י or (27.13.1) יָצָא. Most I-י verbs were originally I-ו (25.11.1). In every conjugation of the Hiphil, the original ו reappears as Holem Waw after the verbal prefix or preformative, replacing the י in first root position.

בְּנֵי־יִשְׂרָאֵל A definite construct chain in apposition to עַמִּי. The absence of the Daghesh Lene in the first consonant of בְּנֵי is the result of this *begadkephat* consonant being preceded by a vowel, the Hireq Yod of עַמִּי which immediately precedes.

Exodus 3:11

אֵלֵךְ As with אֵרֵד at the beginning of verse 8 above, the Imperfect vowel pattern with Tsere as both the preformative and stem vowel identifies אֵלֵךְ as a verb that inflects like a I-י weak verb. In this case, however, the root is הָלַךְ which is inflected just like a I-י verb in the Qal Imperfect (16.6). The expression מִי אָנֹכִי כִּי אֵלֵךְ is translated "who am I that I should go?" The כִּי before this Imperfect verb introduces a clause that explains or expresses the outcome or consequence of מִי אָנֹכִי.

אוֹצִיא As with הוֹצֵא in verse 10 above, the Holem Waw with the Imperfect 1cs preformative consonant and the Hireq Yod stem vowel identify the verb as a I-י Hiphil Imperfect. Remember that most I-י verbs were originally I-ו. In the Hiphil, Hophal, and Niphal conjugations, the original Waw reappears as either a vowel letter (Holem Waw, Shureq) or as a consonantal Waw (27.12-13; 29.8-9). The expression וְכִי אוֹצִיא is translated "and that I should bring out." The particle כִּי is common after interrogatives.

Exodus 3:12

כִּי־אֶהְיֶה עִמָּךְ The particle כִּי has a remarkable range of uses. Here, it serves to introduce a direct quotation and should not be translated ([and he said,] "I will be with you"). The Qal Imperfect 1cs of הָיָה plays an important role in Exodus 6 with the identificantion of the divine name that appears in verse 14 (אֶהְיֶה אֲשֶׁר אֶהְיֶה and אֶהְיֶה).

כִּי אָנֹכִי שְׁלַחְתִּיךָ The particle כִּי preceding the 1cs independent personal pronoun is introducing a subordinate clause (אָנֹכִי שְׁלַחְתִּיךָ) that clarifies or explains the main clause וְזֶה־לְּךָ הָאוֹת. The entire construction is translated "and this will be the sign for you *that I have sent you*." The form שְׁלַחְתִּיךָ is the Qal Perfect 1cs of שָׁלַח with a 2ms pronominal suffix.

בְּהוֹצִיאֲךָ This is the third Hiphil I-י verb in this passage (see הוֹצֵא in verse 10 and אוֹצִיא in verse 11). Even before analyzing the spelling of the verb הוֹצִיא, the prepositional prefix and the pronominal suffix suggest an Infinitive Construct. The ה prefix and the Hireq Yod stem vowel identify the Infinitive Construct as Hiphil. The Holem Waw prefix vowel identifies the verbal root as I-י (27.12). In this usage, the preposition בְּ is translated with a temporal nuance (when) and the 2ms pronominal suffix is rendered as the subject of the verbal action (when you bring out).

תַּעַבְדוּן This Qal Imperfect 2mp of עָבַד follows the pattern of I-Guttural (Type 2) verbs (16.2-3). The נ at the end of this form is called a Paragogic נ. A Paragogic נ is a נ written in final form (ן) and added to the end of a verb (15.4.8; see also Waltke-O'Connor, 31.7.1; Joüon-Muraoka, 44e-f). The Paragogic נ is relatively rare, appearing only 325 times in the Hebrew Bible. It is most common in Deuteronomy (58 times), Isaiah (39 times), and Psalms (56 times). The Paragogic נ is most common on the Imperfect. It appears only 3 times on the Perfect and only on the 3cp form (Deut 8:3; 8:16; Isa 26:16). With the Imperfect, the Paragogic נ is most common on the

3mp (180 times) and 2mp (135 times) forms. Of the texts studied in this reader, the Paragogic ן appears 8 times (Exod 3:12; Deut 6:2, 3, 14; 11:22; Josh 24:15; 2 Kgs 17:37; Joel 3:1). The spelling of a verb with a Paragogic ן sometimes reflects the antiquity of the text. It may occur to promote euphony (to sound better), but it may also mark contrast or certainty compared to the corresponding form without Paragogic ן. The meaning of the Paragogic ן is subtle and will often depend on contextual considerations. It occurs frequently in pause.

Translation 7

Exodus 6:1-8

I Am Yahweh

1 וַיֹּאמֶר יְהוָה אֶל־מֹשֶׁה עַתָּה תִרְאֶה אֲשֶׁר אֶעֱשֶׂה לְפַרְעֹה כִּי
בְיָד חֲזָקָה יְשַׁלְּחֵם וּבְיָד חֲזָקָה יְגָרְשֵׁם[1] מֵאַרְצוֹ 2 וַיְדַבֵּר אֱלֹהִים
אֶל־מֹשֶׁה וַיֹּאמֶר אֵלָיו אֲנִי יְהוָה 3 וָאֵרָא אֶל־אַבְרָהָם אֶל־יִצְחָק
וְאֶל־יַעֲקֹב בְּאֵל שַׁדָּי[2] וּשְׁמִי יְהוָה לֹא נוֹדַעְתִּי לָהֶם 4 וְגַם
הֲקִמֹתִי אֶת־בְּרִיתִי אִתָּם לָתֵת לָהֶם אֶת־אֶרֶץ כְּנָעַן אֵת אֶרֶץ
מְגֻרֵיהֶם[3] אֲשֶׁר־גָּרוּ בָהּ 5 וְגַם אֲנִי שָׁמַעְתִּי אֶת־נַאֲקַת[4] בְּנֵי
יִשְׂרָאֵל אֲשֶׁר מִצְרַיִם מַעֲבִדִים אֹתָם וָאֶזְכֹּר אֶת־בְּרִיתִי 6 לָכֵן[5]
אֱמֹר לִבְנֵי־יִשְׂרָאֵל אֲנִי יְהוָה וְהוֹצֵאתִי אֶתְכֶם מִתַּחַת סִבְלֹת[6]

---

1. גָּרַשׁ (Q) to drive out, banish; (Pi) drive out (away) (45).
2. שַׁדַּי (divine title) Almighty, Shaddai (48); אֵל שַׁדַּי (uncertain etymology) "God Almighty."
3. מָגוֹר place of residence, temporary dwelling; (mp cstr) מְגוּרֵי (11).
4. נְאָקָה groaning (4).
5. לָכֵן This form is a combination of the preposition לְ and כֵּן (so, thus). It occurs 200 times in the Hebrew Bible and is best translated as "therefore."
6. סְבָלוֹת burden-bearing, compulsory labor (6).

מִצְרַיִם וְהִצַּלְתִּי אֶתְכֶם מֵעֲבֹדָתָם וְגָאַלְתִּי אֶתְכֶם בִּזְרוֹעַ נְטוּיָה
וּבִשְׁפָטִים[7] גְּדֹלִים 7 וְלָקַחְתִּי אֶתְכֶם לִי לְעָם וְהָיִיתִי לָכֶם
לֵאלֹהִים וִידַעְתֶּם כִּי אֲנִי יְהוָה אֱלֹהֵיכֶם הַמּוֹצִיא אֶתְכֶם מִתַּחַת
סִבְלוֹת מִצְרָיִם 8 וְהֵבֵאתִי אֶתְכֶם אֶל־הָאָרֶץ אֲשֶׁר נָשָׂאתִי
אֶת־יָדִי לָתֵת אֹתָהּ לְאַבְרָהָם לְיִצְחָק וּלְיַעֲקֹב וְנָתַתִּי אֹתָהּ לָכֶם
מוֹרָשָׁה[8] אֲנִי יְהוָה

Parse the following verbs from Exodus 6:1-8.

Exodus 6:1

וַיֹּאמֶר ______________________________

תִרְאֶה ______________________________

אֶעֱשֶׂה ______________________________

יְשַׁלְּחֵם ______________________________

יְגָרְשֵׁם ______________________________

Exodus 6:2

וַיְדַבֵּר ______________________________

7. שֶׁפֶט act of judgment, punishment; (mp) שְׁפָטִים (16).

8. מוֹרָשָׁה possession, property (9).

Exodus 6:3

וָאֵרָא

נוֹדַעְתִּי

Exodus 6:4

הֲקִמֹתִי

לָתֵת

גָּרוּ

Exodus 6:5

שָׁמַעְתִּי

מַעֲבִדִים

וָאֶזְכֹּר

Exodus 6:6

אֱמֹר

וְהוֹצֵאתִי

וְהִצַּלְתִּי

וְגָאַלְתִּי

נְטוּיָה

Exodus 6:7

וְלָקַחְתִּי

וְהָיִיתִי

וִידַעְתֶּם

הַמּוֹצִיא

Exodus 6:8

וְהֵבֵאתִי ______________________________

נָשָׂאתִי ______________________________

לָתֵת ______________________________

וְנָתַתִּי ______________________________

Grammatical Commentary: Exodus 6:1-8

Exodus 6:1

תִרְאֶה The ה ֶ ending is a diagnostic point of spelling for III-ה Imperfect verbal forms without a sufformative in the Qal and derived stems. With the preceding adverb (עַתָּה) ending in a vowel sound, the ת preformative gives up the Daghesh Lene that is expected in the initial *begadkephat* consonant.

אֶעֱשֶׂה This doubly weak verb (I-Guttural/III-ה) exhibits the distinctive points of spelling of both weak classes. As observed with תִרְאֶה, the ה ֶ ending is distinctive of III-ה Imperfect forms without a sufformative. The vowel pattern of Seghol under the Imperfect preformative and Hateph Seghol under the guttural in first root position is distinctive of I-Guttural (Type 1) verbs (16.2-3).

בְּיָד חֲזָקָה The preposition בְּ is prefixed to the noun יָד and followed by the fs attributive adjective of חָזָק. The construction translates as "with a strong hand."

יְשַׁלְּחֵם This III-ח Imperfect verb is identified as a Piel by the Shewa preformative vowel, the Daghesh Forte in the second consonant of the verbal root, and the Pathach under the first root consonant. With the 3mp object suffix, the verb translates as "he will send them out."

יְגָרְשֵׁם This verb is also Piel Imperfect 3ms with a 3mp pronominal suffix. In this case, however, the expected Pathach under the first root consonant has lengthened to Qamets (compensatory lengthening) because the guttural in the second root position rejects the Daghesh Forte of the Piel stem (31.9-10).

מֵאַרְצוֹ This form consists of the Segholate noun אֶרֶץ prefixed with the preposition מִן (6.5.2b) and a 3ms pronominal suffix.

Exodus 6:2

וַיְדַבֵּר One vowel definitively identifies the stem of this Imperfect verb, namely, the Pathach beneath the first root consonant. The Shewa preformative vowel occurs in both Piel and Pual; the Daghesh Forte in the second root consonant marks the Piel, Pual, and Hithpael. The Pathach identifies the stem as Piel. Note the absence of the Daghesh Forte of the Waw Consecutive in the Imperfect preformative consonant (30.15).

אֲנִי יְהוָה This is a verbless clause of identification (I am Yahweh). For studies of the verbless clause and the predicate nominative, see 23.8, Waltke-O'Connor, 8.4, and Arnold-Choi, 2.1.2.

Exodus 6:3

וָאֵרָא Following the Waw Consecutive (spelled with Qamets before the Imperfect 1cs preformative), the preformative א identifies this verb as Imperfect 1cs. The verbal root is רָאָה and the Tsere preformative vowel is diagnostic of the Niphal stem. The ר in first root position cannot assimilate the נ of the Niphal and so the expected Seghol beneath the א is lengthened to Tsere (25.6). The Niphal of רָאָה translates as "to appear."

בְּאֵל שַׁדָּי The preposition בְּ is prefixed to the proper name El Shaddai, a name or title of uncertain etymology, though sometimes translated "God Almighty."

וּשְׁמִי יְהוָה The conjunction וְ is prefixed to the noun שֵׁם with a 1cs pronominal suffix. The conjunction is spelled as Shureq because it is prefixed to a consonant with Vocal Shewa (5.7.2b). This disjunctive Waw should be translated contrastively (24.17.13). With the divine name, the phrase translates, "but [by] my name Yahweh."

לֹא נוֹדַעְתִּי The נ prefix and תִּי sufformative identify the verb as Niphal Perfect 1cs. The Holem Waw prefix vowel identifies the verb as I-(יָדַע) י, originally I-ו (25.10). In the Niphal Perfect and Participle, the original ו reappears as Holem Waw (25.11.2). As with the Niphal Imperfect of רָאָה above (וָאֵרָא), so here the Niphal of יָדַע expresses a passive nuance (literally, "I was not known [to them]").

Exodus 6:4

הֲקִמֹתִי The sufformative תִי marks the verb as a Perfect 1cs. The Hiphil stem is indicated by the ה prefix and defectively written Hireq Yod stem vowel (27.14). The Holem Waw "connecting" vowel is also written defectively. This connecting vowel helps to identify the verbal root as Biconsonantal (קוּם).

לָתֵת The preposition לְ is prefixed to תֵּת. This very difficult form is the Qal Infinitive Construct of נָתַן (20.5). Some I-נ verbs in the Qal Infinitive Construct preserve the first root consonant and the Shewa-Holem vowel pattern that is exhibited in the strong and many weak verb classes (קְטֹל). A number of I-נ verbs, however, have an alternate Infinitive Construct spelling in which the initial נ is lost and a ת is added to the end of the form as in the example סַעַת (from נָסַע). Here, the Infinitive Construct of נָתַן loses both its first and third consonants and adds the ת ending. The form is not uncommon with over 150 occurrences in the Hebrew Bible.

אֶרֶץ מְגֻרֵיהֶם This is a construct chain with the fs noun אֶרֶץ as the construct noun and the mp noun מְגוּרִים (lexical form מָגוּר) with a 3mp pronominal suffix as the absolute noun. Marked with the definite direct object marker, the construct chain is the direct object of לָתֵת.

אֲשֶׁר־גָּרוּ בָהּ The relative pronoun is joined with Maqqef to the Qal Perfect 3cp of גּוּר (14.12), followed by the preposition בְּ with a 3fs pronominal suffix (the land in which they sojourned). The antecedent of the 3fs suffix on the preposition is אֶרֶץ מְגֻרֵיהֶם.

Exodus 6:5

וְגַם אֲנִי שָׁמַעְתִּי Complementing the construction at the beginning of the previous verse (וְגַם הֲקִמֹתִי), the adverb (גַּם) and the 1cs independent personal pronoun impart a measure of emphasis to both the subject and the verbal action of שָׁמַעְתִּי (moreover I have heard). A string of first person verbs follows, emphasizing the dynamic quality of Yahweh's being as it manifests itself in his redemptive activity on behalf of his people.

מַעֲבִדִים This Hiphil Participle mp is identified by the מַ prefix and the defectively written Hireq Yod stem vowel beneath the second root consonant. The Hateph Pathach beneath the guttural in the first root position of עָבַד is expected in this form (27.2).

וָאֶזְכֹּר This Qal Imperfect of זָכַר with Waw Consecutive is the final form in a string of 1cs verbs which began with וָאֵרָא in verse 3, immediately following the divine self-revelation (אֲנִי יְהוָה) at the end of verse 2. God has appeared (וָאֵרָא), established (הֲקִמֹתִי), heard (שָׁמַעְתִּי) and remembered (וָאֶזְכֹּר). Then in verse 6, immediately following a repetition of the divine self-revelation (אֲנִי יְהוָה), the string of 1cs verbs continues, declaring what Yahweh will do on behalf of his oppressed people.

Exodus 6:6

אֱמֹר This spelling could be either a Qal Imperative ms of אָמַר (18.4) or a Qal Infinitive Construct of the same root (20.2). Context requires that it be identified as an Imperative.

אֲנִי יְהוָה This same verbless clause of identification appeared in verse 2 above.

וְהוֹצֵאתִי The תִּי sufformative identifies the form as Perfect 1cs. The ה prefix and Tsere stem vowel are diagnostic of the Hiphil stem. The Holem Waw prefix vowel identifies the verbal root as I-י (many I-י verbs were originally I-ו). This verb is also prefixed with Waw Consecutive (and I will bring out).

The Perfect with Waw Consecutive, among many functions, may express logical result. This usage is sometimes categorized as "consequential," that is, the Perfect with Waw Consecutive expresses or describes an action or circumstance that is the logical consequence of a previous action, statement, or situation (I am Yahweh and [therefore] I will bring you out). For more on the use of the Perfect with Waw Consecutive to express logical result or logical sequence, see Arnold-Choi, 3.5.2; van der Merwe, 21.3; Joüon-Muraoka, 119c.

סִבְלֹת This is the construct form of the rare noun סְבָלוֹת (forced labor).

וְהִצַּלְתִּי The הִ prefix and Pathach stem vowel are diagnostic of the Hiphil stem. These two points of spelling, together with the sufformative, clearly identify the form as a Hiphil Perfect 1cs with Waw Consecutive. The Daghesh Forte in the צ represents the assimilation of the נ which is the first consonant of the verbal root (27.10). With the direct object אֶתְכֶם that follows, the construction translates, "and I will deliver you."

מֵעֲבֹדָתָם The fs noun עֲבוֹדָה is prefixed with the preposition מִן and has a 3mp pronominal suffix (from their bondage).

וְגָאַלְתִּי This is another Qal Perfect 1cs verb with Waw Consecutive (and I will redeem you), declaring the nature of God's mighty and redemptive work for his covenant people.

בִּזְרוֹעַ נְטוּיָה The noun זְרוֹעַ is prefixed with the preposition בְּ and followed by the Qal Passive Participle fs of נָטָה (with an outstretched arm). The passive Participle is in an attributive relationship with זְרוֹעַ (22.7; 22.9.1).

Exodus 6:7

וְלָקַחְתִּי This is another Qal Perfect 1cs verb with Waw Consecutive. Though a weak verb (III-ח), the spelling of this Qal Perfect of לָקַח is the same as that of the strong verb.

לִי לְעָם The form לִי is the preposition לְ with a 1cs pronominal suffix. The second form is the noun עַם with the same preposition (and pausal spelling, 36.3.1). With the verb and direct object that precede (וְלָקַחְתִּי אֶתְכֶם), a literal translation of the clause is "and I will take you to (for) myself for a people." A more idiomatic translation would be "and I will take you for my people."

וְהָיִיתִי Despite its unusual appearance, the spelling of this Qal Perfect 1cs of הָיָה with Waw Consecutive follows the expected pattern of a III-ה Perfect verb (14.6; 14.17). Idiomatically, the clause וְהָיִיתִי לָכֶם לֵאלֹהִים translates, "and I will be your God." Note the unusual Tsere vowel of the preposition in לֵאלֹהִים (4.11.4).

וִידַעְתֶּם Recognition of this form (Qal Perfect 2mp of יָדַע) is hindered by the spelling of the Waw Consecutive. The conjunction is prefixed to a verb that begins with the syllable יְ (יְדַעְתֶּם). Normally, the conjunction would be spelled as Shureq since it is prefixed to a consonant with Vocal Shewa (5.7.2b). There is an exception to this rule. If the conjunction וְ is prefixed to a word that begins with the syllable יְ then these two syllables contract to וִי as in וִידַעְתֶּם (and you will know).

הַמּוֹצִיא With the removal of the definite article, the diagnostics of this Hiphil Participle are easily recognized. The מ prefix and Hireq Yod stem vowel identify both the stem (Hiphil) and the conjugation (Participle). The Holem Waw prefix vowel identifies the verbal root as I-י (27.12-13). This Participle is in an attributive relationship with יְהוָה אֱלֹהֵיכֶם ([Yahweh your God] who brought you out).

וְהֵבֵאתִי In the Hiphil stem, Biconsonantal verbs are often difficult to identify. The sufformative תִּי clearly identifies this forms as Perfect 1cs. The ה prefix and Tsere vowel are diagnostic of the Hiphil stem. The root of this Hiphil Perfect 1cs with Waw Consecutive is בּוֹא (and I will bring).

נָשָׂאתִי אֶת־יָדִי The verb נָשָׂא (to lift or raise) may appear with the noun יָד (hand) as its object with the meaning "to swear." The expression "to lift the hand" (the description of a customary oath procedure) in Hebrew is an idiom for the taking of an oath.

וְנָתַתִּי אֹתָהּ Only the identification of the verbal root is a challenge with this form. The Daghesh Forte in the final ת represents the assimilated third consonant of the verbal root (נָתַן). Followed by the definite direct object marker with 3fs suffix, this Perfect verb with Waw Consecutive translates, "I will give it."

אֲנִי יְהוָה The text concludes with the divine self-disclosure (verbless clause of identification), appearing a total of four times in verses 2, 6, 7, and 8.

Translation 8

Exodus 34:1-6

Yahweh Proclaims His Name

1 וַיֹּאמֶר יְהוָה אֶל־מֹשֶׁה פְּסָל[1]־לְךָ שְׁנֵי־לֻחֹת[2] אֲבָנִים כָּרִאשֹׁנִים
וְכָתַבְתִּי עַל־הַלֻּחֹת אֶת־הַדְּבָרִים אֲשֶׁר הָיוּ עַל־הַלֻּחֹת הָרִאשֹׁנִים
אֲשֶׁר שִׁבַּרְתָּ 2 וֶהְיֵה נָכוֹן לַבֹּקֶר וְעָלִיתָ בַבֹּקֶר אֶל־הַר סִינַי[3]
וְנִצַּבְתָּ לִי שָׁם עַל־רֹאשׁ הָהָר 3 וְאִישׁ לֹא־יַעֲלֶה עִמָּךְ וְגַם־אִישׁ
אַל־יֵרָא בְּכָל־הָהָר גַּם־הַצֹּאן וְהַבָּקָר אַל־יִרְעוּ אֶל־מוּל[4] הָהָר
הַהוּא 4 וַיִּפְסֹל שְׁנֵי־לֻחֹת אֲבָנִים כָּרִאשֹׁנִים וַיַּשְׁכֵּם מֹשֶׁה בַבֹּקֶר
וַיַּעַל אֶל־הַר סִינַי כַּאֲשֶׁר צִוָּה יְהוָה אֹתוֹ וַיִּקַּח בְּיָדוֹ שְׁנֵי לֻחֹת
אֲבָנִים 5 וַיֵּרֶד יְהוָה בֶּעָנָן וַיִּתְיַצֵּב[5] עִמּוֹ שָׁם וַיִּקְרָא בְשֵׁם יְהוָה

---

1. פָּסַל (Q) to carve, cut, hew (6).
2. לוּחַ (ms) tablet, plank; (mp) לֻחֹת (43).
3. סִינַי Sinai (35).
4. מוּל (prep) in front of, opposite (36).
5. יָצַב (Hith) to take one's stand, stand firm, station oneself, present oneself before, resist (48).

6 וַיַּעֲבֹר יְהוָה עַל־פָּנָיו וַיִּקְרָא יְהוָה יְהוָה אֵל רַחוּם[6] וְחַנּוּן[7] אֶרֶךְ
אַפַּיִם[8] וְרַב־חֶסֶד וֶאֱמֶת

Parse the following verbs from Exodus 34:1-6.

Exodus 34:1

וַיֹּאמֶר ______________________________

פְּסָל ______________________________

וְכָתַבְתִּי ______________________________

הָיוּ ______________________________

שִׁבַּרְתָּ ______________________________

Exodus 34:2

וֶהְיֵה ______________________________

נָכוֹן ______________________________

וְעָלִיתָ ______________________________

וְנִצַּבְתָּ ______________________________

Exodus 34:3

יַעֲלֶה ______________________________

יֵרָא ______________________________

יִרְעוּ ______________________________

---

6. רַחוּם (adj) compassionate (13).

7. חַנּוּן (adj) gracious, merciful (13).

8. אָרֵךְ (adj) long, slow (15); 13 times as אֶ֫רֶךְ־אַפַּ֫יִם (lit) "long of nose"; (idiom) "slow to anger" or "patient."

Exodus 34:4

וַיִּפְסֹל ______________________________

וַיַּשְׁכֵּם ______________________________

וַיַּעַל ______________________________

צִוָּה ______________________________

וַיִּקַּח ______________________________

Exodus 34:5

וַיֵּרֶד ______________________________

וַיִּתְיַצֵּב ______________________________

וַיִּקְרָא ______________________________

Exodus 34:6

וַיַּעֲבֹר ______________________________

Grammatical Commentary: Exodus 34:1-6

Exodus 34:1

פְּסָל־לְךָ In the spelling of this Qal Imperative 2ms of פָּסַל, the expected Holem has reduced to Qamets Hatuf (in a closed unaccented syllable) because the preposition לְ with a 2ms pronominal suffix has been joined to this Imperative by Maqqef. The two forms have become a single accented unit with the Imperative surrendering its primary accent to the preposition with suffix.

שְׁנֵי־לֻחֹת אֲבָנִים The cardinal number שְׁנֵי is the construct spelling of שְׁנַ֫יִם (11.2). The noun לֻחֹת (with defective spelling of both Shureq and Holem Waw) is the mp construct of לוּחַ. The absolute noun in the construct chain is אֲבָנִים (plural of the Segholate noun אֶ֫בֶן). The construction translates as "two stone tablets" or "two tablets of stone."

כָּרִאשֹׁנִים The preposition כְּ and the definite article (the article is identified by the Qamets beneath the preposition) are prefixed to the plural of רִאשׁוֹן (like the first).

וְכָתַבְתִּי This form is easy to identify as the Qal Perfect 1cs of כָּתַב with Waw Consecutive (and I will write).

עַל־הַלֻּחֹת The preposition עַל is joined by Maqqef to the plural noun לֻחֹת (lexical form לוּחַ) which is prefixed with the definite article (upon the tablets).

אֶת־הַדְּבָרִים This is the definite direct object of וְכָתַבְתִּי (and I will write [upon the tablets] the words....).

הָיוּ Despite its unusual appearance, the spelling of this Qal Perfect 3cp of הָיָה follows the expected pattern of a III-ה Perfect inflection (14.6; 14.17). The relative clause, beginning with אֲשֶׁר, translates as "which *were* upon the first tablets."

שִׁבַּרְתָּ The Hireq under the first root consonant and the Daghesh Forte in the second root consonant identify this form as the Piel Perfect of שָׁבַר. The Perfect sufformative תָּ is 2ms. All of the diagnostics of a Piel Perfect verb are present (30.3-4).

Exodus 34:2

וֶהְיֵה נָכוֹן The ה ֵ ending on וֶהְיֵה is distinctive for all III-ה 2ms Imperatives in the Qal and all derived stems (18.5; 18.6). This Imperative is Qal. The form נָכוֹן is difficult, though the נ prefix is helpful for stem identification. This is a Niphal Participle ms from the Biconsonantal verb כּוּן. The use of these two verbs is complementary (be ready).

וְעָלִיתָ The sufformative (תָ) identifies this verb as a Perfect 2ms. The Hireq Yod stem vowel identifies the verbal root as III-ה (עָלָה). The conjunction is the Waw Consecutive, creating an important sequence with the preceding Imperative. An Imperative may be followed by a Perfect verb with Waw Consecutive that takes the full force of the preceding Imperative in translation (be ready… and come up). In this sequence, the two forms are related in terms of consecution of action (18.13.6; 23.6.3).

וְנִצַּבְתָּ The נִ prefix is the prefix of the Niphal stem. The Daghesh Forte in the צ represents the assimilated נ of the verbal root (נָצַב). The תָּ sufformative identifies this form as Perfect 2ms. The sequence discussed above is continued with this Perfect verb with Waw Consecutive (be ready … and come up … and stand).

Exodus 34:3

וְאִישׁ לֹא־יַעֲלֶה עִמָּךְ Idiomatically, this clause is translated as "no man shall come up with you." The Qal Imperfect 3ms verb יַעֲלֶה exhibits the Pathach preformative vowel and Hateph Pathach beneath the guttural in first root position which is expected in I-Guttural (Type 2) verbs (16.2; 16.3.2). The ה ֶ ending is distinctive of III-ה Imperfect verbs (those forms without sufformatives) in the Qal and derived stems.

Note that twice in this verse the noun אִישׁ is used in constructions with the meaning of "nobody" or "no one." In the first clause, it appears with the negative particle לֹא; in the second clause it appears with the negative particle אַל.

וְגַם־אִישׁ Idiomatically, the clause וְגַם־אִישׁ אַל־יֵרָא בְּכָל־הָהָר is translated as "and also let no man be seen throughout all the mountain."

אַל־יֵרָא The verb יֵרָא (short form of יֵרָאֶה) is the Niphal Imperfect 3ms of רָאָה. The Tsere preformative vowel is the key to stem identification (25.6-7). The volitional nuance (*let* no man be seen) is indicated by the use of the negative particle אַל.

אַל־יִרְעוּ The negative particle אַל is joined by Maqqef to the Qal Imperfect 3mp of רָעָה (16.10).

Exodus 34:4

וַיַּשְׁכֵּם The Pathach preformative vowel and the Tsere stem vowel identify the stem as Hiphil. The prefixing of the Waw Consecutive changes the expected Hireq Yod stem vowel to Tsere (יַשְׁכִּים is spelled וַיַּשְׁכֵּם with the Waw Consecutive).

וַיַּעַל In the absence of the Shureq sufformative, the Waw Consecutive and the preformative י identify this verb as Imperfect 3ms. The verbal root of this Qal form is עָלָה. The spelling יַּעַל is the short spelling of יַעֲלֶה. Remember that with III-ה verbs, the Waw Consecutive is normally prefixed to the short form and not to the long form (23.11.2).

צִוָּה The Hireq under the first root consonant and the Daghesh Forte in the second root consonant identify the stem as Piel (31.4). With III-ה verbal roots, the Perfect 3ms ends in ה ָ .

וַיִּקַּח This is the Qal Imperfect 3ms of לָקַח with Waw Consecutive. It is important to remember that this verb inflects just like a I-נ weak verb (16.8; 16.9.2). The Daghesh Forte in the ק is the assimilated ל

of the verbal root. The Pathach stem vowel is due to the guttural consonant in the third root position.

Exodus 34:5

וַיֵּרֶד This is the Qal Imperfect 3ms of יָרַד with Waw Consecutive. The first root consonant has dropped out. The י that is written is the Imperfect preformative consonant. The Tsere preformative vowel identifies the form as belonging to the I-י weak verb class (16.7.1 16.16.1).

וַיִּתְיַצֵּב This form is easily identified as a Hithpael Imperfect 3ms of יָצַב with Waw Consecutive. The diagnostic spelling features are the יִתְ preformative and prefix, the Pathach beneath the first root consonant, and the Daghesh Forte in the second root consonant (34.5-6).

וַיִּקְרָא בְשֵׁם יְהוָה The verb קָרָא with בְשֵׁם (the noun שֵׁם with preposition בְּ) is translated, "to *proclaim* the name of Yahweh."

Exodus 34:6

וַיַּעֲבֹר The Pathach-Hateph Pathach vowel pattern with I-Guttural verbs occurs in both the Qal and Hiphil stems (16.2; 27.2). The Holem stem vowel identifies this verb as Qal. In the Hiphil, the stem vowel would be Tsere with the Waw Consecutive.

עַל-פָּנָיו In this construction, the preposition עַל is joined by Maqqef to the noun פָּנִים (lexical form פָּנֶה) with a 3ms (Type 2) pronominal suffix (idiomatically, "before him").

וַיִּקְרָא Though not stated, the subject of this Qal Imperfect 3ms of קָרָא with Waw Consecutive is Yahweh. It is Yahweh himself who twice proclaims the divine name and then, by way of apposition and exposition, sets forth five attributes of the divine character.

אֶרֶךְ אַפַּיִם The expression "long of nostrils [nose]" is a Hebrew idiom for patience. It is often translated as, "slow to anger" (15.11).

Translation 9

Leviticus 19:1-4

The Demand for Holiness

1 וַיְדַבֵּר יְהוָה אֶל־מֹשֶׁה לֵּאמֹר 2 דַּבֵּר אֶל־כָּל־עֲדַת בְּנֵי־יִשְׂרָאֵל
וְאָמַרְתָּ אֲלֵהֶם קְדֹשִׁים תִּהְיוּ כִּי קָדוֹשׁ אֲנִי יְהוָה אֱלֹהֵיכֶם 3
אִישׁ אִמּוֹ וְאָבִיו תִּירָאוּ וְאֶת־שַׁבְּתֹתַי תִּשְׁמֹרוּ אֲנִי יְהוָה אֱלֹהֵיכֶם
4 אַל־תִּפְנוּ אֶל־הָאֱלִילִים[1] וֵאלֹהֵי מַסֵּכָה[2] לֹא תַעֲשׂוּ לָכֶם אֲנִי
יְהוָה אֱלֹהֵיכֶם

Parse the following verbs from Leviticus 19:1-4.

Leviticus 19:1

וַיְדַבֵּר ______________________________

לֵּאמֹר ______________________________

Leviticus 19:2

דַּבֵּר ______________________________

וְאָמַרְתָּ ______________________________

תִּהְיוּ ______________________________

1. אֱלִיל worthlessness, idol (21).
2. מַסֵּכָה molten (metal) image, idol (26).

Leviticus 19:3

תִּירָאוּ ____________________

תִּשְׁמֹרוּ ____________________

Leviticus 19:4

תִּפְנוּ ____________________

תַּעֲשׂוּ ____________________

Grammatical Commentary: Leviticus 19:1-4

Leviticus 19:1

וַיְדַבֵּר The Shewa preformative vowel, Pathach beneath the first root consonant, and Daghesh Forte in the second root consonant identify this verb as Piel Imperfect 3ms. Note that the expected Daghesh Forte of the Waw Consecutive is missing in the Imperfect preformative because the form begins with the syllable יְ (30.15).

לֵאמֹר Though technically a Qal Infinitive Construct of אָמַר (prefixed with the preposition לְ), לֵאמֹר frequently introduces direct quotations and is best rendered with the use of punctuation, usually a comma and quotation marks (Yahweh said to Moses, "Speak..."). Note the presence of the conjunctive Daghesh in the preposition (32.11).

Leviticus 19:2

דַּבֵּר This form is the Piel Imperative 2ms of דָּבַר. The Pathach beneath the first root consonant and the Daghesh Forte in the second root consonant are diagnostic of the Piel Imperative. As with the Imperfect above (וַיְדַבֵּר), the Pathach is the definitive point of spelling for identifying the verbal stem (30.6-8).

אֶל־כָּל־עֲדַת בְּנֵי־יִשְׂרָאֵל This prepositional phrase, beginning with אֶל, is a construct chain with three nouns in the construct state and one absolute noun. The entire construct chain is definite because the absolute noun יִשְׂרָאֵל is a proper name. The form עֲדַת is the fs construct spelling of עֵדָה (literally, "to all of the congregation of the children of Israel").

וְאָמַרְתָּ This Qal Perfect 2ms of אָמַר with Waw Consecutive may be translated with the full force of the Imperative that begins the verse (17.6.3). This is one of several important verbal sequences with a volitional conjugation. In this sequence, the Imperative דַּבֵּר is followed by this Perfect with Waw Consecutive, relating the two forms in terms of consecution of action. Therefore, translate וְאָמַרְתָּ as an Imperative ([speak] … and say).

קְדֹשִׁים תִּהְיוּ The adjective קְדֹשִׁים is the mp of קָדוֹשׁ with defective writing of the Holem Waw. It is followed by the Qal Imperfect 2mp of הָיָה (16.14). The predicate adjective (קְדֹשִׁים) and the verb (תִּהְיוּ) translates as "you shall be holy."

כִּי קָדוֹשׁ אֲנִי The conjunction כִּי introduces a dependent clause describing the motive or ground for the preceding command. The expression קָדוֹשׁ אֲנִי is a verbless clause of classification (23.8.2) where the predicate קָדוֹשׁ precedes the subject אֲנִי (because I *am* holy).

יְהוָה אֱלֹהֵיכֶם The divine name is followed by אֱלֹהִים with 2mp pronominal suffix. The construction stands in apposition to אֲנִי (I Yahweh your God). For a description of apposition, see Gen 35:14 and Exod 3:1, 10.

Leviticus 19:3

אִמּוֹ This is the fs noun אֵם with a 3ms pronominal suffix. For the spelling of Geminate nouns with Daghesh Forte, see 4.8.4 and 9.15.

וְאָבִיו Here, the ms noun אָב appears with the conjunction וְ and a 3ms pronominal suffix. For the spelling of this noun with Hireq Yod, see 9.9.

תִּירָאוּ The Hireq Yod preformative vowel identifies the verb as I-י (יָרֵא). In terms of the Imperfect conjugation, I-י verbs may be spelled with one of two patterns. In the first pattern, the initial י is lost in every form of the paradigm and the class is identified by a Tsere preformative vowel in every form (16.7.1). In the second pattern, as exhibited in the verb תִּירָאוּ, the initial י of the verbal root is seemingly preserved as the vowel letter Hireq Yod (16.7.3). This form is the Qal Imperfect 2mp from יָרֵא which, in this context, should be translated, "you shall fear" or "you shall revere."

אִישׁ ... תִּירָאוּ The use of the ms noun אִישׁ (a singular) and the 2mp Imperfect (a plural) imparts a *distributive* nuance to the translation (*every one of you* shall revere his mother and his father).

וְאֶת־שַׁבְּתֹתַי The conjunction and definite direct object marker are joined by Maqqef to שַׁבָּתוֹת (the plural of שַׁבָּת) with a 1cs (Type 2) pronominal suffix. Note the defective writing of the Holem Waw in the fp ending.

תִּשְׁמֹרוּ The stem vowel has not reduced to Shewa as expected in this 2mp verb. Nevertheless, the verb is still easily identified as a Qal Imperfect of שָׁמַר. The preservation of the Holem stem vowel is because this form is pausal (36.3), appearing in *BHS* with Athnach under the מ (תִּשְׁמֹ֑רוּ). With the definite direct object that precedes, the clause translates as "and my Sabbaths you will keep."

Leviticus 19:4

אַל־תִּפְנוּ This is a prohibition (negative command) created with the negative particle אַל before the Qal Imperfect 2mp of פָּנָה (do not turn). In Hebrew, prohibitions are not created by negating the Imperative. Negative commands are expressed with the particles לֹא or אַל with the Imperfect (15.8; 18.9).

אֶל־הָאֱלִילִם The preposition אֶל is joined by Maqqef to the plural of אֱלִיל. This noun refers to idols or to pagan gods with the nuance of their worthlessness or insignificance.

וֵאלֹהֵי מַסֵּכָה Prefixed with the conjunction וְ, this construct chain is composed of אֱלֹהִים in its construct spelling and the noun מַסֵּכָה in the absolute state. This construct chain may be translated either "cast idols" or "molten gods." Note the spelling of the conjunction on the construct noun. Before a reduced or Hateph vowel, the conjunction is spelled with the corresponding short vowel of the Hateph vowel. When אֱלֹהִים occurs with the conjunction וְ it is spelled וֵאלֹהִים (5.7.3).

לֹא תַעֲשׂוּ לָכֶם The previous construct chain אֱלֹהֵי מַסֵּכָה is the direct object of this Qal Imperfect 2mp of עָשָׂה with the negative particle (you shall not make for yourselves molten gods).

Translation 10

Numbers 6:22-26

Aaron's Blessing

22 וַיְדַבֵּר יְהוָה אֶל־מֹשֶׁה לֵּאמֹר 23 דַּבֵּר אֶל־אַהֲרֹן וְאֶל־בָּנָיו
לֵאמֹר כֹּה תְבָרֲכוּ אֶת־בְּנֵי יִשְׂרָאֵל אָמוֹר לָהֶם

24 יְבָרֶכְךָ יְהוָה וְיִשְׁמְרֶךָ

25 יָאֵר[1] יְהוָה פָּנָיו אֵלֶיךָ וִיחֻנֶּךָּ

26 יִשָּׂא יְהוָה פָּנָיו אֵלֶיךָ וְיָשֵׂם לְךָ שָׁלוֹם

Parse the following verbs from Numbers 6:22-26.

Numbers 6:22

וַיְדַבֵּר ______________________________

לֵאמֹר ______________________________

Numbers 6:23

דַּבֵּר ______________________________

תְבָרֲכוּ ______________________________

אָמוֹר ______________________________

---

1. אור (Hi) to give light, shine, illuminate, light up (44).

Numbers 6:24

יְבָרֶכְךָ ______________________________

וְיִשְׁמְרֶךָ ______________________________

Numbers 6:25

יָאֵר ______________________________

וִיחֻנֶּךָּ ______________________________

Numbers 6:26

יִשָּׂא ______________________________

וְיָשֵׂם ______________________________

Grammatical Commentary: Numbers 6:22-26

Numbers 6:22

וַיְדַבֵּר The Hebrew of this verse is identical to that of Leviticus 19:1 (see that discussion for comment on the forms וַיְדַבֵּר and לֵאמֹר).

Numbers 6:23

דַּבֵּר The Pathach under the first root letter and the Daghesh Forte in the second root letter are the diagnostic features of the Piel stem. In this context, the Imperative 2ms is the correct identification, though the Infinitive Construct and the Infinitive Absolute share the same diagnostic spelling features.

כֹּה תְבָרֲכוּ This construction is the adverb כֹּה (thus) preceding the Piel Imperfect 2mp of בָּרַךְ. A Shewa preformative vowel in the Imperfect occurs most frequently in the Piel and Pual (rarely in the Qal). It is the Qamets beneath the first root consonant (compensatory lengthening from Pathach because the ר cannot take the Daghesh Forte of the Piel) that identifies the stem as Piel and not Pual (thus you will bless). Frequently, כֹּה is used to introduce speech or initiate a section of discourse.

אָמוֹר לָהֶם The verb אָמוֹר preserves the diagnostic vowel pattern of a Qal Infinitive Absolute (21.2-4). As one of its main uses, the Infinitive

Absolute may complement the main verb of a sentence and carry the temporal value of that verb (21.6.4). In this case, אָמוֹר complements the Piel Imperfect תְבָרְכוּ ([thus you will bless] … *by saying* to them).

Numbers 6:24

יְבָרֶכְךָ With יְהוָה as its subject, this verb is a Piel Imperfect 3ms of בָּרַךְ with a 2ms pronominal suffix. Just like the Piel Imperfect תְבָרֲכוּ in the previous verse, the Qamets beneath the first root consonant is diagnostic of the Piel stem. Note the loss of the Tsere stem vowel (reduced to Seghol) with the addition of the pronominal (object) suffix. Because this Imperfect verb begins its clause and it does not appear with the Waw Consecutive, it carries the volitional nuance (*may* the Lord bless you).

In verses 24-26, there are six Imperfect 3ms verbs (a pair in each verse, the second of which is joined to the first by the conjunction וְ), each of which appears at the beginning of its clause. When an Imperfect verb (without the Waw Consecutive) begins its clause, it is normally to be understood as volitional (23.7.3). As such, all six Imperfect verbs in these three verses are volitional.

וְיִשְׁמְרֶךָ The conjunction וְ is prefixed to the Qal Imperfect 3ms of שָׁמַר (and *may* he keep you). This verb continues the volitional nuance of the preceding verb at the beginning of this verse. Note the loss of the Holem stem vowel with the addition of the pronominal suffix (19.7). The stem vowel may also be reduced from Holem to Qamets Hatuf with the addition of the 2ms pronominal suffix.

Numbers 6:25

יָאֵר יְהוָה פָּנָיו אֵלֶיךָ Difficult to identify, יָאֵר is the short form of יָאִיר and identified as the Hiphil Imperfect 3ms of the Biconsonantal verb אוֹר (27.14). A Qamets preformative vowel is distinctive of both Biconsonantal (16.17; 27.14) and Geminate (16.12; 27.16) verbs in the Qal and Hiphil stems (*may* the Lord cause his face to shine toward you). Note that two of the six volitional Imperfect verbs appear with the short spelling of the verb. For an explanation of the short spelling of the Imperfect verb, see 23.11.2.

וִיחֻנֶּךָּ This form is not a Pual Imperfect despite its spelling. It is the Qal Imperfect 3ms from חָנַן with a 2ms pronominal suffix. The Qal Imperfect 3ms of a Geminate verbal root is יָחֹן (16.12). To this basic form, the 2ms suffix (ֶךָּ) is added. With the addition of the pronominal suffix, the Geminate consonant appears as a Daghesh Forte in the Nun. The addition of the pronominal suffix also causes the accent to shift. This shift in accent causes the Holem stem vowel to reduce to Qibbuts and the Qamets under the preformative to undergo propretonic reduction (Qamets to Vocal Shewa). The resulting form is יְחֻנֶּךָּ. The addition of the Conjunction וְ results in the application of the Rule of Shewa whereby וְיְ becomes וִי (4.11.2) and so the final form is וִיחֻנֶּךָּ. Few verbal forms will undergo so many complex changes.

Numbers 6:26

יִשָּׂא The Hireq preformative vowel and the Qamets stem vowel are diagnostic features of this III-א Qal Imperfect 3ms. The verbal root is identified by recognizing that the Daghesh Forte in the שׂ represents the assimilated first root consonant of נָשָׂא (16.4; 16.8).

פָּנָיו This form consists of the mp פָּנִים (lexical פָּנֶה) with a 3ms (Type 2) pronominal suffix. The expression יִשָּׂא יְהוָה פָּנָיו אֵלֶיךָ is literally translated, "*may* the Lord lift up his face to you."

וְיָשֵׂם The Qamets preformative vowel and the Tsere stem vowel identify the stem of this Imperfect 3ms as Hiphil. The Tsere also helps in the identification of the verbal root as the Biconsonantal שִׂים. The regular spelling of the Hiphil Imperfect 3ms of שִׂים is יָשִׂים. The short spelling is יָשֵׂם (23.11.2). Followed by לְךָ שָׁלוֹם, the clause translates as "and *may* he give you peace."

Translation 11

Deuteronomy 6:1-15

The Shema

1 וְזֹאת הַמִּצְוָה הַחֻקִּים וְהַמִּשְׁפָּטִים אֲשֶׁר צִוָּה יְהוָה אֱלֹהֵיכֶם
לְלַמֵּד אֶתְכֶם לַעֲשׂוֹת בָּאָרֶץ אֲשֶׁר אַתֶּם עֹבְרִים שָׁמָּה לְרִשְׁתָּהּ
2 לְמַעַן תִּירָא אֶת־יְהוָה אֱלֹהֶיךָ לִשְׁמֹר אֶת־כָּל־חֻקֹּתָיו וּמִצְוֹתָיו
אֲשֶׁר אָנֹכִי מְצַוֶּךָ אַתָּה וּבִנְךָ וּבֶן־בִּנְךָ כֹּל יְמֵי חַיֶּיךָ וּלְמַעַן
יַאֲרִכֻן[1] יָמֶיךָ 3 וְשָׁמַעְתָּ יִשְׂרָאֵל וְשָׁמַרְתָּ לַעֲשׂוֹת אֲשֶׁר יִיטַב לְךָ
וַאֲשֶׁר תִּרְבּוּן מְאֹד כַּאֲשֶׁר דִּבֶּר יְהוָה אֱלֹהֵי אֲבֹתֶיךָ לָךְ אֶרֶץ
זָבַת[2] חָלָב[3] וּדְבָשׁ 4 שְׁמַע יִשְׂרָאֵל יְהוָה אֱלֹהֵינוּ יְהוָה אֶחָד
5 וְאָהַבְתָּ אֵת יְהוָה אֱלֹהֶיךָ בְּכָל־לְבָבְךָ וּבְכָל־נַפְשְׁךָ
וּבְכָל־מְאֹדֶךָ 6 וְהָיוּ הַדְּבָרִים הָאֵלֶּה אֲשֶׁר אָנֹכִי מְצַוְּךָ הַיּוֹם

---

1. אָרַךְ (Hi) to make long, lengthen, extend (34).
2. זוּב (Q) to flow (away), suffer a discharge (42).
3. חָלָב milk (44).

עַל־לְבָבֶךָ 7 וְשִׁנַּנְתָּם[4] לְבָנֶיךָ וְדִבַּרְתָּ בָּם בְּשִׁבְתְּךָ בְּבֵיתֶךָ
וּבְלֶכְתְּךָ בַדֶּרֶךְ וּבְשָׁכְבְּךָ וּבְקוּמֶךָ 8 וּקְשַׁרְתָּם[5] לְאוֹת עַל־יָדֶךָ
וְהָיוּ לְטֹטָפֹת[6] בֵּין עֵינֶיךָ 9 וּכְתַבְתָּם עַל־מְזֻזוֹת[7] בֵּיתֶךָ וּבִשְׁעָרֶיךָ
10 וְהָיָה כִּי יְבִיאֲךָ יְהוָה אֱלֹהֶיךָ אֶל־הָאָרֶץ אֲשֶׁר נִשְׁבַּע לַאֲבֹתֶיךָ
לְאַבְרָהָם לְיִצְחָק וּלְיַעֲקֹב לָתֶת לָךְ עָרִים גְּדֹלֹת וְטֹבֹת אֲשֶׁר
לֹא־בָנִיתָ 11 וּבָתִּים מְלֵאִים כָּל־טוּב[8] אֲשֶׁר לֹא־מִלֵּאתָ וּבֹרֹת
חֲצוּבִים[9] אֲשֶׁר לֹא־חָצַבְתָּ כְּרָמִים וְזֵיתִים[10] אֲשֶׁר לֹא־נָטָעְתָּ
וְאָכַלְתָּ וְשָׂבָעְתָּ 12 הִשָּׁמֶר לְךָ פֶּן־תִּשְׁכַּח אֶת־יְהוָה אֲשֶׁר
הוֹצִיאֲךָ מֵאֶרֶץ מִצְרַיִם מִבֵּית עֲבָדִים 13 אֶת־יְהוָה אֱלֹהֶיךָ תִּירָא

---

4. שָׁנַן (Pi) to repeat, recite, teach (1).
5. קָשַׁר (Q) to bind, be in league together, conspire (against) (44).
6. טוֹטָפֹת (meaning uncertain) symbol, sign (later as "phylactery," a small box of Scripture verses worn as a sign of obedience to the covenant) (3).
7. מְזוּזָה doorpost, doorframe (19).
8. טוּב goodness, well-being, happiness (32).
9. חָצַב (Q) to quarry, hew (out), dig, dress (stones) (16).
10. זַ֫יִת olive tree, olive; (mp) זֵיתִים (38).

וְאֹתוֹ תַעֲבֹד וּבִשְׁמוֹ תִּשָּׁבֵעַ 14 לֹא תֵלְכוּן אַחֲרֵי אֱלֹהִים אֲחֵרִים
מֵאֱלֹהֵי הָעַמִּים אֲשֶׁר סְבִיבוֹתֵיכֶם 15 כִּי אֵל קַנָּא[11] יְהוָה אֱלֹהֶיךָ
בְּקִרְבֶּךָ פֶּן־יֶחֱרֶה אַף־יְהוָה אֱלֹהֶיךָ בָּךְ וְהִשְׁמִידְךָ מֵעַל פְּנֵי
הָאֲדָמָה

Parse the following verbs from Deuteronomy 6:1-15.

Deuteronomy 6:1

צִוָּה ______________________________

לְלַמֵּד ______________________________

לַעֲשׂוֹת ______________________________

עֹבְרִים ______________________________

לְרִשְׁתָּהּ ______________________________

Deuteronomy 6:2

תִּירָא ______________________________

לִשְׁמֹר ______________________________

מְצַוֶּךָּ ______________________________

יַאֲרִכֻן ______________________________

11. קַנָּא jealous (6).

Deuteronomy 6:3

וְשָׁמַעְתָּ ______________________________

וְשָׁמַרְתָּ ______________________________

יִיטַב ______________________________

תִּרְבּוּן ______________________________

דִּבֶּר ______________________________

זָבַת ______________________________

Deuteronomy 6:4

שְׁמַע ______________________________

Deuteronomy 6:5

וְאָהַבְתָּ ______________________________

Deuteronomy 6:6

וְהָיוּ ______________________________

Deuteronomy 6:7

וְשִׁנַּנְתָּם ______________________________

וְדִבַּרְתָּ ______________________________

בְּשִׁבְתְּךָ ______________________________

וּבְלֶכְתְּךָ ______________________________

וּבְשָׁכְבְּךָ ______________________________

וּבְקוּמֶךָ ______________________________

Deuteronomy 6:8

וּקְשַׁרְתָּם ______________________________

Deuteronomy 6:9

וּכְתַבְתָּם ______________________

Deuteronomy 6:10

וְהָיָה ______________________

יְבִיאֲךָ ______________________

נִשְׁבַּע ______________________

לָתֶת ______________________

בָנִיתָ ______________________

Deuteronomy 6:11

מְלֵאָת ______________________

חֲצוּבִים ______________________

חָצַבְתָּ ______________________

נָטָעְתָּ ______________________

וְאָכַלְתָּ ______________________

וְשָׂבָעְתָּ ______________________

Deuteronomy 6:12

הִשָּׁמֶר ______________________

תִּשְׁכַּח ______________________

הוֹצִיאֲךָ ______________________

Deuteronomy 6:13

תִּירָא ______________________

תַעֲבֹד ______________________

תִּשָּׁבֵעַ ______________________

Deuteronomy 6:14

תֵּלְכוּן ______________________________

Deuteronomy 6:15

יֶחֱרֶה ______________________________

וְהִשְׁמִידְךָ ______________________________

Grammatical Commentary: Deuteronomy 6:1-15

Deuteronomy 6:1

וְזֹאת The conjunction וְ is prefixed to the fs demonstrative pronoun **זֹאת** (8.6; 8.7.2). Followed by three definite nouns (one singular and two plurals), **זֹאת** functions as the subject of a verbless clause (and this *is*).

הַחֻקִּים Prefixed with the definite article with virtual doubling (5.4.2), **חֻקִּים** is the plural form of the Geminate noun **חֹק** (4.8.4)

אֲשֶׁר צִוָּה The relative pronoun **אֲשֶׁר** appears before the Piel Perfect 3ms of **צִוָּה**. The Piel Perfect is identified by the Hireq under the first root consonant and the Daghesh Forte in the second root consonant. The ה ָ ending is expected in the 3ms form of III-ה Perfect verbs in the Qal and derived stems. With **יְהוָה אֱלֹהֵיכֶם** as the subject of the verb, the clause is translated as "which Yahweh your God commanded."

לְלַמֵּד אֶתְכֶם The Pathach under the first root consonant and the Daghesh Forte in the second root consonant identify this form as Piel. The preposition לְ regularly appears with the Infinitive Construct. The direct object follows ([in order] to teach you).

לַעֲשׂוֹת The verb **עֲשׂוֹת** preserves the diagnostic vowel pattern for a III-ה Infinitive Construct in the Qal stem with a Vocal Shewa (or Hateph vowel with gutturals) under the first root consonant and an **וֹת** ending (20.4). Infinitive Constructs of III-ה verbs end in **וֹת** in all stems. Note the vocalization of the preposition לְ which takes the corresponding short vowel of the Hateph vowel beneath the guttural (6.4.2).

אֲשֶׁר אַתֶּם עֹבְרִים שָׁמָּה The relative pronoun אֲשֶׁר precedes the 2mp personal pronoun. The form עֹבְרִים is a I-Guttural Qal active Participle mp that inflects like a strong verb (22.4). שָׁמָּה is the adverb שָׁם with the directional ending (7.7). Literally, the construction translates, "which you are going over to there." Idiomatically, it may be rendered, "to which you are going over."

לְרִשְׁתָּהּ Some I-י and I-נ Qal Infinitive Construct verbs are difficult to recognize because they drop the first root consonant and add ת to the end of the form (20.5-6). This is one of those forms. With the preposition לְ and a 3fs pronominal suffix (הּ ָ), the Infinitive Construct is רֶ֫שֶׁת from the verb יָרַשׁ. With the I-י class, most verbs form the Infinitive Construct with this pattern, though some preserve the Shewa-Holem vowel pattern of the strong verb. The antecedent of the 3fs suffix is אֶ֫רֶץ (to possess it).

Deuteronomy 6:2

לְמַעַן תִּירָא The form לְמַעַן (מַעַן with the preposition לְ) with the Imperfect translates, "so that." The verb תִּירָא is the Qal Imperfect 2ms of the stative verb יָרֵא (so that you may fear). The Hireq Yod preformative vowel identifies the root as I-י (Type 2; 16.7.3).

לִשְׁמֹר The spelling of this Qal Infinitive Construct with the preposition לְ preserves the vowel pattern that is diagnostic of this conjugation's basic form (Shewa-Holem). In this context, the Infinitive Construct is complementary (20.12.4). It complements the preceding verb תִּירָא (so that you may fear … *by keeping*).

אֶת־כָּל־חֻקֹּתָיו The form חֻקִּים, used in the preceding verse, is the mp of חֹק. Here, the noun חֻקֹּת is the fp of חֻקָּה with a 3ms pronominal suffix (all his statutes).

וּמִצְוֹתָיו The conjunction וְ (spelled as Shureq before ב, מ, or פ) is prefixed to the fp form of מִצְוָה with a 3ms (Type 2) pronominal suffix (and his commandments).

וּבִנְךָ This is the noun בֵּן with the conjunction וְ and a 2ms pronominal suffix (and your son). With the addition of the suffix, the Tsere of בֵּן changes to Hireq.

וּבֶן־בִּנְךָ This construction begins with the conjunction וְ prefixed to a construct chain. The absolute noun appears with a 2ms pronominal suffix (and the son of your son).

כֹּל יְמֵי חַיֶּיךָ The form יְמֵי is the mp construct form of יָמִים (lexical form יוֹם) and חַיֶּיךָ is the plural noun חַיִּים with a 2ms (Type 2) pronominal suffix (all the days of your life).

יַאֲרִכֻן יָמֶיךָ The Imperfect preformative with Pathach and the guttural in first root position with Hateph Pathach could be either Qal (16.2-3) or Hiphil (27.2-3). In this case, the verbal stem must be Hiphil with the Hireq stem vowel (defective writing of Hireq Yod). The Shureq sufformative of the 3mp is also written defectively before the Paragogic נ. The subject of the verb is the plural noun יָמִים with a 2ms (Type 2) pronominal suffix (and so that your days may be long).

Deuteronomy 6:3

וְשָׁמַעְתָּ יִשְׂרָאֵל The Qal Perfect 2ms of שָׁמַע with Waw Consecutive is followed by the proper name יִשְׂרָאֵל functioning as a vocative, the case of direct address (and you will hear, O Israel).

וְשָׁמַרְתָּ לַעֲשׂוֹת The Qal Perfect 2ms of שָׁמַר with Waw Consecutive and the Qal Infinitive Construct of עָשָׂה with preposition לְ are complementary in translation (and be careful to do [them]).

אֲשֶׁר יִיטַב לְךָ Translate אֲשֶׁר as a conjunction of consequence with "so that." The verbal form יִיטַב is the Qal Imperfect 3ms of יָטַב (so that it may go well for you). As in the verb תִּירָא in verse 2, the Hireq Yod preformative vowel is the key to identifying the verbal root as I-י (16.7.3).

וַאֲשֶׁר תִּרְבּוּן מְאֹד Here as well, אֲשֶׁר should be translated "so that." The verb is Qal Imperfect 2mp of the III-ה verb רָבָה (16.10) with a Paragogic נ (and so that you may become very numerous).

דִּבֶּר The Hireq under the first root consonant and the Daghesh Forte in the second root consonant identify this form as Piel Perfect 3ms of דָּבַר.

אֱלֹהֵי אֲבֹתֶיךָ This is a construct chain in apposition to the divine name יְהוָה. The absolute noun is אָבוֹת (irregular plural of אָב) with a 2ms (Type 2) pronominal suffix (the God of your fathers).

זָבַת The form זָבַת is difficult to identify in this well-known description of the land. It is the Qal active Participle fs of the Biconsonantal verb זוּב (to flow). The spelling זָבָה (Qal Ptc fs of זוּב) changes to זָבַת in the construct state (10.3.2b).

Deuteronomy 6:4

שְׁמַע יִשְׂרָאֵל In the Qal Imperative 2ms, III-ע verbs have a Pathach stem vowel rather than the Holem stem vowel of the strong verb (18.4). As in יִשְׂרָאֵל at the beginning of verse 3, the proper name here is functioning as a vocative (Hear, O Israel).

יְהוָה אֱלֹהֵינוּ יְהוָה אֶחָד This first declaration of the Shema has several translation possibilities (Yahweh our God, Yahweh is one; Yahweh is our God, Yahweh is one; Yahweh is our God, Yahweh alone; Yahweh our God is Yahweh alone). The form אֶחָד is the cardinal number (one) in the masculine absolute state (11.2).

Deuteronomy 6:5

וְאָהַבְתָּ Though doubly weak, this Qal Perfect 2ms of אָהַב inflects like a strong verb in this form. With Waw Consecutive, it translates as "and you shall love."

בְּכָל־לְבָבְךָ This is the preposition בְּ prefixed to כֹּל and joined by Maqqef to the noun לֵבָב with a 2ms (Type 1) pronominal suffix (with all your heart). In this phrase and in the following two, בְּ translates as a preposition of means (*HALOT* 1:105).

וּבְכָל־נַפְשְׁךָ This is a similar construction to the one above but with the absolute noun נֶפֶשׁ (and with all your soul).

וּבְכָל־מְאֹדֶךָ Again, a similar construction but here with the absolute noun מְאֹד (and with all your might).

Deuteronomy 6:6

וְהָיוּ The Waw Consecutive is prefixed to the Qal Perfect 3cp of הָיָה. Though this triconsonantal root is doubly weak, it inflects regularly as a III-ה verb in most forms of the Qal Perfect paradigm.

הַדְּבָרִים הָאֵלֶּה The demonstrative אֵלֶּה is functioning as an attributive adjective in its relationship to the noun דְּבָרִים by agreeing in gender, number, and definiteness (these words).

אֲשֶׁר אָנֹכִי מְצַוְּךָ This relative clause begins with אֲשֶׁר. The relative pronoun is followed by the 1cs personal pronoun אָנֹכִי and the Piel Participle ms of צָוָה with a 2ms pronominal suffix ("which I am commanding you" or "which I command you"). A מ prefix marks Participles of the Piel, Pual, Hiphil, and Hophal stems. The מְ prefix marks the Participles of the Piel and Pual stems. A מְ prefix with Pathach under the first root consonant marks the Piel Participle. The Daghesh Forte in the second root consonant (וּ) is distinctive of both Piel and Pual stems.

הַיּוֹם The noun יוֹם with the definite article may be translated as either "this day" or "today."

Deuteronomy 6:7

וְשִׁנַּנְתָּם This Piel Perfect 2ms of שָׁנַן with a 3mp pronominal suffix and Waw Consecutive occurs only here in the Hebrew Bible (and you shall speak of them again and again). The stem is easily identified by the Hireq under the first root consonant, the Daghesh Forte in the second root consonant, and the Pathach stem vowel. The 2ms sufformative is also easily recognized with the removal of the 3mp pronominal suffix.

לְבָנֶיךָ In this construction, the preposition לְ is prefixed to the masculine plural noun בָּנִים (lexical form בֵּן) followed by a 2ms (Type 2) pronominal suffix (to your sons).

וְדִבַּרְתָּ בָּם Following the Waw Consecutive, the Hireq under the first root letter and the Daghesh Forte in the second root letter identify this verb as Piel Perfect (30.3-4). The sufformative תָּ is 2ms. The form בָּם is the preposition בְּ with a 3mp pronominal suffix (and you will speak of them).

בְּשִׁבְתְּךָ The combination of a prepositional prefix (בְּ, כְּ, or לְ) and a pronominal suffix with a verb frequently signals an Infinitive Construct, though this one is particularly difficult to identify. While some I-י verbs preserve the Shewa-Holem vowel pattern of the Qal Infinitive Construct, most will drop the initial י and add a final ת as in שֶׁ֫בֶת (20.6). With the addition of a suffix, the two Seghols become Hireq in a closed syllable. This construction is, therefore, the Qal Infinitive Construct of יָשַׁב with the preposition בְּ and a 2ms pronominal suffix. The preposition בְּ marks the temporal usage of the Infinitive Construct and the pronominal suffix is functioning as the subject of the verbal idea (when you sit).

בְּבֵיתֶךָ In this form, the noun בַּ֫יִת is prefixed with the preposition בְּ and has a 2ms pronominal suffix (in your house).

וּבְלֶכְתְּךָ This form consists of four elements. The conjunction וְ and the preposition בְּ are prefixed to the Qal Infinitive Construct of הָלַךְ

with a 2ms pronominal suffix. The verb הָלַךְ inflects just like a I-י verb, dropping the first root letter and adding ת at the end (לֶ֫כֶת). Once again, the preposition בְּ marks the temporal usage of the Infinitive Construct, and the pronominal suffix is functioning as the subject of the verbal idea (and when you walk).

וּבְשָׁכְבְּךָ With precisely the same prefixes and suffix as וּבְלֶכְתְּךָ, the verbal root of this Qal Infinitive Construct is שָׁכַב (and when you lie down). Note the Qamets Hatuf beneath the first consonant of the verbal root. This spelling is caused by the addition of the suffix. This initial closed syllable with Qamets Hatuf is a diagnostic spelling feature of the strong verb Infinitive Construct with pronominal suffix (20.9).

וּבְקוּמֶךָ This is a fourth Qal Infinitive Construct with the same prefixes and suffix. This time, the verbal root is the Biconsonantal verb קוּם (and when you arise).

Deuteronomy 6:8

וּקְשַׁרְתָּם The Waw Consecutive (spelled as Shureq before Vocal Shewa) is prefixed to the Qal Perfect 2ms of קָשַׁר with a 3mp pronominal suffix (and you will bind them).

עַל־יָדֶךָ The preposition עַל is joined by Maqqef to the noun יָד with a 2ms pronominal suffix (upon your hand).

וְהָיוּ In this form, the Waw Consecutive is prefixed to the Qal Perfect 3cp of הָיָה (see comments on this form above in verse 6).

לְטֹטָפֹת The preposition לְ is prefixed to the rare noun טוֹטָפוֹת ("as phylacteries" or "as frontlets"). The noun refers to one or two small leather boxes that contain slips inscribed with biblical texts. Traditionally, they are bound with a cord or leather strap and worn on the forehead (or on the left arm) during appointed times of prayer.

בֵּין עֵינֶיךָ The preposition בֵּין is followed by the dual noun עֵינַ֫יִם (lexical form עַ֫יִן) with a 2ms pronominal suffix (between your eyes).

Deuteronomy 6:9

וּכְתַבְתָּם This form is not Qal Perfect 2mp. The ending is not תֶּם. The Qal Perfect sufformative is 2ms (תָּ) and the verb has a 3mp pronominal suffix (and you will write them). The verbal root is כָּתַב and the form has a Waw Consecutive.

עַל־מְזוּזֹת בֵּיתֶךָ The preposition עַל is joined by Maqqef to the plural form of מְזוּזָה (doorpost). This noun appears in the fp construct state. The absolute noun in the construct chain is בַּ֫יִת with a 2ms pronominal suffix (upon the doorposts of your house).

וּבִשְׁעָרֶיךָ In this form, the conjunction וְ and the preposition בְּ are prefixed to the mp form of שַׁ֫עַר with a 2ms (Type 2) pronominal suffix (and upon your gates).

Deuteronomy 6:10

וְהָיָה כִּי יְבִיאֲךָ The temporal modifier וְהָיָה (Qal Perfect 3ms of הָיָה with Waw Consecutive) is followed by the conjunction כִּי translated with its temporal usage (when). With regard to יְבִיאֲךָ, the Hireq Yod identifies the stem of this Biconsonantal verb as Hiphil (27.14). The expected Qamets preformative vowel is reduced (propretonic reduction) to Shewa with the addition of the 2ms pronominal suffix. This is the Hiphil Imperfect 3ms of בּוֹא (when … brings you in).

נִשְׁבַּע This Niphal Perfect 3ms of שָׁבַע is identified by the נ prefix (24.4; 25.1). This verbal form appears in a relative clause beginning with אֲשֶׁר (which he swore). In the Niphal stem, this verbal root is translated with the simple, active voice of the Qal stem (24.2.4)

לַאֲבֹתֶיךָ The preposition לְ is prefixed to the irregular plural noun אָבוֹת (lexical form אָב) with a 2ms pronominal suffix (to your fathers).

לָתֶת This form is difficult to identify. It is the Qal Infinitive Construct of נָתַן with the preposition לְ (to give). Like other I-י verbs, this form drops the נ in first root position and adds a ת to the end of the verb (20.5). Additionally, the נ in third root position has dropped out.

לָךְ This prepositional phrase looks like a combination of the preposition לְ and the 2fs (Type 2) pronominal suffix. However, the pronominal suffix attached to this preposition is 2ms (לְךָ). When the 2ms pronominal suffix appears with a major disjunctive accent, its pausal spelling (לָ֑ךְ with the Athnach under the ל) looks like that of לְ with a 2fs pronominal suffix (36.3).

עָרִים גְּדֹלֹת וְטֹבֹת This expression constitutes the indefinite direct object of the Infinitive Construct לָתֶת (great and good cities). The fp noun

עָרִים (with mp grammatical ending) is modified by two adjectives (גְּדֹלֹת and טֹבֹת). Both are inflected in the feminine plural, in agreement with the "natural" gender of עָרִים (lexical form עִיר). Note the four instances of defective spelling in these two adjectives.

אֲשֶׁר לֹא־בָנִיתָ The relative pronoun אֲשֶׁר precedes the negated Qal Perfect 2ms of בָּנָה (which you did not build). The key to identifying the verbal root of this form is the Hireq Yod stem vowel (14.7.4). Remember that most III-ה verbs were originally I-י and the stem vowel of a form like בָנִיתָ is reminiscent of the original consonant in third root position.

Deuteronomy 6:11

וּבָתִּים Prefixed with the conjunction וְ (spelled as Shureq before ב, מ, or פ), בָּתִּים is the irregular mp form of בַּיִת (and houses).

מְלֵאִים כָּל־טוּב The form מְלֵאִים is the mp of the adjective מָלֵא (full), "[And houses] filled with every good thing."

אֲשֶׁר לֹא־מִלֵּאתָ The construction אֲשֶׁר לֹא plus the Perfect 2ms (cf. אֲשֶׁר לֹא־בָנִיתָ in verse 10) will be repeated three times in this verse. In this first case, the Hireq under the first root consonant and the Daghesh Forte in the second root consonant identify the verbal stem of מִלֵּאתָ as Piel (which you did not fill).

וּבֹרֹת חֲצוּבִים The conjunction וְ is prefixed to the defectively spelled (irregular) mp noun בּוֹרוֹת (lexical form בּוֹר). The form חֲצוּבִים is the Qal passive Participle mp of חָצַב (to hew [out], quarry, dig). This Qal passive Participle preserves the diagnostic vowel pattern of a I-Guttural verb with Hateph Pathach-Shureq (22.8-9). The Participle is being used attributively, "and cisterns hewn out" or "and cisterns that have been dug."

אֲשֶׁר לֹא־חָצַבְתָּ This is the second instance of the construction אֲשֶׁר לֹא plus Perfect 2ms. In this second case, the verbal stem is easily identifiable as Qal, "which you did not hew" or "which you did not dig."

כְּרָמִים וְזֵיתִים The mp form of the noun כֶּרֶם and the mp form of the noun זַיִת are joined by the conjunction וְ (vineyards and olive trees).

אֲשֶׁר לֹא־נָטָעְתָּ This is the third instance of the construction אֲשֶׁר לֹא plus Perfect 2ms. In this third case, the verbal stem is Qal with pausal spelling (which you did not plant).

וְאָכַלְתָּ וְשָׂבָעְתָּ This verse concludes with two Qal Perfect 2ms verbs. In each case, the verbs are prefixed with Waw Consecutive and should be translated imperfectively (i.e., and you will eat) and not perfectively like the preceding three Perfect 2ms verbs in the אֲשֶׁר clauses.

Deuteronomy 6:12

הִשָּׁמֶר לְךָ The הִ prefix, Qamets under the first root letter, and Daghesh Forte in the first root letter identify the stem as Niphal (24.8; 24.10). In the Niphal, the ה prefix appears in the Imperative and Infinitive Construct conjugations. The context in which this form appears (discourse and no prefixes or suffixes common with the Infinitive Construct) suggests the Niphal Imperative 2ms of שָׁמַר. The Imperative is often followed by the preposition לְ with a second person pronominal suffix that agrees in gender and number with the Imperative in order to emphasize the pronominal element, "*you* be careful" or "*you* be on your guard."

פֶּן־תִּשְׁכַּח The conjunction פֶּן (lest) is joined by Maqqef to the Qal Imperfect 2ms of שָׁכַח (lest you forget). The Pathach stem vowel is occasioned by the guttural consonant in third root position.

אֶת־יְהוָה The divine name is the direct object of the verb תִּשְׁכַּח.

אֲשֶׁר הוֹצִיאֲךָ The relative pronoun אֲשֶׁר precedes the Hiphil Perfect 3ms of יָצָא with 2ms suffix (who brought you out). The Hiphil stem is identified by the ה prefix and Hireq Yod stem vowel. The I-י verbal root is identified by the Holem Waw prefix vowel, which is present in every conjugation of the Hiphil I-י verb (27.12-13).

Deuteronomy 6:13

אֶת־יְהוָה אֱלֹהֶיךָ At the beginning of the verse, the divine name is marked as the direct object of the verb תִּירָא (Qal Imperfect 2ms of יָרֵא). Note that in all three clauses of this verse, the object precedes the Imperfect verb.

וְאֹתוֹ תַעֲבֹד The form וְאֹתוֹ is the object marker prefixed with the conjunction וְ and with a 3ms pronominal suffix (יְהוָה is the antecedent of the suffix). With regard to the verb, the Holem stem vowel identifies the 2ms Imperfect of עָבַד as Qal (and him you shall serve).

וּבִשְׁמוֹ Here, the noun שֵׁם is prefixed with the conjunction וְ and the preposition בְּ. The form also has a 3ms pronominal suffix (and by his name).

תִּשָּׁבֵעַ This Niphal Imperfect 2ms of שָׁבַע preserves the diagnostic spelling of a strong verb with the Hireq preformative vowel, Daghesh Forte in the first root letter (the assimilated נ of the Niphal), and Qamets under the first root letter (24.6-7). The verb שָׁבַע means "to swear" in the Niphal stem with the special nuance of making a statement, promise, or pledge with an oath (you will swear).

Deuteronomy 6:14

לֹא תֵלְכוּן The negative particle לֹא precedes the Qal Imperfect 2mp of הָלַךְ with a Paragogic נ. The ת preformative and Shureq sufformative identify the conjugation, person, gender, and number. The stem and verbal root are identified by the Tsere preformative vowel (16.7.1-2). Remember that הָלַךְ inflects just like I-י (Type 1) verbs (you shall not go after).

מֵאֱלֹהֵי הָעַמִּים The preposition מִן (6.5.2b) is prefixed to the construct form of אֱלֹהִים (gods). The absolute noun in this construct chain is the plural form of the Geminate noun עַם (4.8.4) with the definite article (from the gods of the peoples).

סְבִיבוֹתֵיכֶם This is the fp form of סָבִיב with a 2mp (Type 2) pronominal suffix. With the relative pronoun אֲשֶׁר, this verbless clause is translated "who are all around you."

Deuteronomy 6:15

כִּי אֵל קַנָּא The conjunction כִּי should be translated with a causal nuance (because, for), providing the reason for the prohibition against following after other gods at the beginning of verse 14. The noun אֵל is a very old Semitic term for deity and may refer to the high god El, to a god in the sense of a deity subordinate to Yahweh, and it may also refer to Yahweh himself (*HALOT* 1:48-50). The expression קַנָּא (jealous) is a rare adjective used with reference to God six times, appearing only in Exodus and Deuteronomy.

יְהוָה אֱלֹהֶיךָ The expressions אֵל קַנָּא (a jealous God) and יְהוָה אֱלֹהֶיךָ (Yahweh your God) form a verbless clause. The present tense of the verb "to be" must be supplied in English (Yahweh your God *is* a jealous God).

בְּקִרְבֶּךָ This is the noun קֶרֶב with the preposition בְּ and a 2ms pronominal suffix (in your midst).

פֶּן־יֶחֱרֶה The conjunction פֶּן (lest) precedes the Qal Imperfect 3ms of חָרָה (to become hot, angry). As a I-Guttural verb, the Seghol preformative vowel and the Hateph Seghol under the guttural in first root position are expected (16.2-3). The ה ֶ ending is diagnostic of III-ה Imperfect forms without a sufformative in every stem.

אַף־יְהוָה אֱלֹהֶיךָ This construct chain is the subject of the verb יֶחֱרֶה and is translated literally as "the nose of Yahweh your God." A literal translation of this clause is "lest the nose of Yahweh your God becomes hot." In Hebrew, a "hot nose" is an idiom for anger (15.11), and so this clause is translated idiomatically, "lest Yahweh becomes angry."

בָּךְ This is the preposition בְּ with a 2ms pronominal suffix (against you). Note the pausal spelling of this form (36.3). See לָךְ in 6:10 above.

וְהִשְׁמִידְךָ In this form, the Waw Consecutive is prefixed to the Hiphil Perfect 3ms of שָׁמַד with a 2ms pronominal suffix (and he will destroy you). The Hiphil stem and the Perfect conjugation are identified by the הִ prefix and the Hireq Yod stem vowel (26.3-4).

מֵעַל This is the preposition מִן prefixed to the preposition עַל ("from upon" or "from off").

פְּנֵי הָאֲדָמָה The form פְּנֵי is the mp construct spelling of פָּנִים (face). The form הָאֲדָמָה is the definite absolute noun (the face of the land). This construct chain is the object of the preposition מֵעַל.

Translation 12

Deuteronomy 11:18-23

Teach These Words to Your Children

18 וְשַׂמְתֶּם אֶת־דְּבָרַי אֵלֶּה עַל־לְבַבְכֶם וְעַל־נַפְשְׁכֶם וּקְשַׁרְתֶּם[1]
אֹתָם לְאוֹת עַל־יֶדְכֶם וְהָיוּ לְטוֹטָפֹת[2] בֵּין עֵינֵיכֶם 19 וְלִמַּדְתֶּם
אֹתָם אֶת־בְּנֵיכֶם לְדַבֵּר בָּם בְּשִׁבְתְּךָ בְּבֵיתֶךָ וּבְלֶכְתְּךָ בַדֶּרֶךְ
וּבְשָׁכְבְּךָ וּבְקוּמֶךָ 20 וּכְתַבְתָּם עַל־מְזוּזוֹת[3] בֵּיתֶךָ וּבִשְׁעָרֶיךָ 21
לְמַעַן יִרְבּוּ יְמֵיכֶם וִימֵי בְנֵיכֶם עַל הָאֲדָמָה אֲשֶׁר נִשְׁבַּע יְהוָה
לַאֲבֹתֵיכֶם לָתֵת לָהֶם כִּימֵי הַשָּׁמַיִם עַל־הָאָרֶץ 22 כִּי אִם־שָׁמֹר
תִּשְׁמְרוּן אֶת־כָּל־הַמִּצְוָה הַזֹּאת אֲשֶׁר אָנֹכִי מְצַוֶּה אֶתְכֶם
לַעֲשֹׂתָהּ לְאַהֲבָה אֶת־יְהוָה אֱלֹהֵיכֶם לָלֶכֶת בְּכָל־דְּרָכָיו
וּלְדָבְקָה־בוֹ 23 וְהוֹרִישׁ יְהוָה אֶת־כָּל־הַגּוֹיִם הָאֵלֶּה מִלִּפְנֵיכֶם
וִירִשְׁתֶּם גּוֹיִם גְּדֹלִים וַעֲצֻמִים[4] מִכֶּם

---

1. קָשַׁר (Q) to bind, be in league together, conspire (against) (44).
2. טוֹטָפֹת (meaning uncertain) symbol, sign (later as "phylactery," a small box of Scripture verses worn as a sign of obedience to the covenant) (3).
3. מְזוּזָה doorpost, doorframe (19).
4. עָצוּם (adj) mighty, numerous (31).

Parse the following verbs from Deuteronomy 11:18-23.

Deuteronomy 11:18

וְשַׂמְתֶּם ____________________

וּקְשַׁרְתֶּם ____________________

וְהָיוּ ____________________

Deuteronomy 11:19

וְלִמַּדְתֶּם ____________________

לְדַבֵּר ____________________

בְּשִׁבְתְּךָ ____________________

וּבְלֶכְתְּךָ ____________________

וּבְשָׁכְבְּךָ ____________________

וּבְקוּמֶךָ ____________________

Deuteronomy 11:20

וּכְתַבְתָּם ____________________

Deuteronomy 11:21

יִרְבּוּ ____________________

נִשְׁבַּע ____________________

לָתֵת ____________________

Deuteronomy 11:22

שָׁמֹר ____________________

תִּשְׁמְרוּן ____________________

מְצַוֶּה ____________________

לַעֲשֹׂתָהּ ____________________

לְאַהֲבָה ______________________

לָלֶכֶת ______________________

וּלְדָבְקָה ______________________

Deuteronomy 11:23

וְהוֹרִישׁ ______________________

וִירִשְׁתֶּם ______________________

Grammatical Commentary: Deuteronomy 11:18-23

Deuteronomy 11:18

וְשַׂמְתֶּם The sufformative תֶּם identifies the person, gender, and number of this Perfect verb. The key to identifying the verbal root is to remember your options and key diagnostic features. In this Qal Perfect 2mp form, there is no Hireq Yod stem vowel (III-ה), and no Holem Waw connecting vowel or Daghesh Forte in the second root consonant (Geminate). The only other type of weak verb having two root consonants in the Perfect conjugation is Biconsonantal. The root is שִׂים and the verb is prefixed with Waw Consecutive (and you will place).

אֶת־דְּבָרַי אֵלֶּה The direct object of וְשַׂמְתֶּם is the plural noun דְּבָרִים with a 1cs (Type 2) pronominal suffix. This noun is further modified by the demonstrative adjective אֵלֶּה. Translate idiomatically as either "these words of mine" or "these my words."

עַל־לְבַבְכֶם The preposition עַל is joined by Maqqef to the noun לֵבָב with a 2mp pronominal suffix (upon your heart).

וְעַל־נַפְשְׁכֶם The conjunction וְ and the preposition עַל are joined by Maqqef to the noun נֶ֫פֶשׁ with a 2mp pronominal suffix (and upon your soul).

וּקְשַׁרְתֶּם אֹתָם This verb is Qal Perfect 2mp from קָשַׁר with Waw Consecutive. It is followed by its direct object, a 3mp pronominal suffix attached to the definite direct object marker (and you shall bind them).

עַל־יֶדְכֶם The preposition עַל is joined by Maqqef to the noun יָד with a 2mp pronominal suffix (upon your hand). This noun is spelled with Seghol when it receives one of the so-called "heavy" suffixes.

וְהָיוּ Most Qal Perfect forms of הָיָה have an unusual appearance. However, this verb inflects regularly as a III-ה verb (14.17). This form is Qal Perfect 3cp of הָיָה with Waw Consecutive (and they shall be).

לְטוֹטָפֹת The preposition לְ is prefixed to the rare noun טוֹטָפֹת ("as phylacteries" or "as frontlets"). For a note on phylacteries, see commentary on Deut 6:8.

בֵּין עֵינֵיכֶם The preposition בֵּין is followed by the dual noun עֵינַ֫יִם (construct עֵינֵי) with a 2mp pronominal suffix (between your eyes).

Deuteronomy 11:19

וְלִמַּדְתֶּם The verbal stem of this Perfect 2mp with Waw Consecutive is identified by the Hireq under the first root consonant and Daghesh Forte in the second root consonant (30.3-4). The verbal stem is Piel (and you shall teach).

אֶת־בְּנֵיכֶם The mp noun בָּנִים (construct בְּנֵי) appears with a 2mp pronominal suffix, "to your sons" or "to your children."

לְדַבֵּר בָּם The Pathach under the first root letter and the Daghesh Forte in the second root letter are diagnostic of the Piel Imperative 2ms, Infinitive Construct, and Infinitive Absolute (30.7; 30.9). The presence of the preposition לְ prefixed to this verb identifies the form as the Infinitive Construct. Remember that almost seventy percent of Infinitive Construct verbal forms in the Hebrew Bible are prefixed with the preposition לְ. The verb is followed by its indirect object which is marked with the preposition בְּ (speaking of/about them).

בְּשִׁבְתְּךָ The text from בְּשִׁבְתְּךָ to the end of the verse preserves the language of Deut 6:7b. There are four Infinitive Construct forms prefixed with the preposition בְּ, indicating the temporal use of the Infinitives. The first two Infinitive Construct forms are followed by prepositional phrases, both of which begin with the בְּ preposition. If you need help, see the discussion of Deut 6:7 above for comments on morphology and grammatical form.

Deuteronomy 11:20

מְזוּזוֹת With the single exception of the spelling of מְזוּזוֹת (with Holem Waw instead of Holem), this verse is identical to Deut 6:9. If you need to review, see the discussion of Deut 6:9 above for comments on morphology and grammatical form.

Deuteronomy 11:21

לְמַעַן יִרְבּוּ יְמֵיכֶם The form יִרְבּוּ is the Qal Imperfect 3mp of the III-ה verb רָבָה (16.10-11). The subject of the verb is יְמֵיכֶם which is the plural noun יָמִים (construct יְמֵי) with a 2mp pronominal suffix. Beginning with לְמַעַן, this construction is translated, "so that your days may be numerous."

וִימֵי בְנֵיכֶם The construct noun in this construct chain is יְמֵי (the construct plural of יָמִים) with the conjunction וְ. Remember that if the conjunction וְ is prefixed to a word that begins with the syllable יְ then these two syllables contract to וִי as in this form (5.7.2b). The absolute noun בָּנִים appears with a 2mp (Type 2) pronominal suffix. This construction is translated "and the days of your children."

אֲשֶׁר נִשְׁבַּע יְהוָה The נִ prefix and Pathach stem vowel identify the verb after אֲשֶׁר as the Niphal Perfect 3ms of שָׁבַע (which Yahweh swore).

לַאֲבֹתֵיכֶם The mp noun אָבוֹת (construct אֲבוֹת) appears with the preposition לְ and a 2mp pronominal suffix (to your fathers). Remember that the Hebrew noun אָב (father) is irregular in that it takes the feminine plural inflectional ending (וֹת).

לָתֵת Despite its numerous occurrences in the Hebrew Bible, לָתֵת is always a difficult form to recognize. It is the Qal Infinitive Construct of נָתַן (to give) with the preposition לְ (20.5). Both I-י and I-נ verbs frequently form the Qal Infinitive Construct with the loss of the first root consonant and the addition of a ת to the end of the word.

כִּימֵי הַשָּׁמַיִם עַל־הָאָרֶץ Similar to וִימֵי earlier in the verse, כִּימֵי is the construct plural of the mp noun יָמִים with the preposition כְּ. This form exhibits the same vowel contraction that was detailed with וִימֵי (5.7.2b). The expression translates as "like the days of the heavens upon the earth." For a similar expression, see Ps 89:30[29].

Deuteronomy 11:22

כִּי אִם־שָׁמֹר תִּשְׁמְרוּן A conditional sentence consists of two clauses. The first clause states the condition and is called the *protasis* (the "if-clause"). The second clause states the consequence of the condition and is called the *apodosis* (the "then-clause"). The protasis of a conditional sentence will often begin with אִם (if) but it may also begin with כִּי, הֵן or אֲשֶׁר followed by a Perfect, Imperfect or Participle

(29.16.1). Here, the protasis begins with כִּי אִם (for if). The verb שָׁמֹר preserves the diagnostic vowel pattern (Qamets-Holem [Waw]) of the Qal Infinitive Absolute (21.2-3). The Infinitive precedes the Qal Imperfect 2mp of שָׁמַר with a Paragogic נ. A common use of the Infinitive Absolute before a finite (Perfect or Imperfect) verb is to give *emphasis* to the verbal idea (for if you *surely* observe).

אָנֹכִי מְצַוֶּה אֶתְכֶם The 1cs personal pronoun precedes the Piel Participle ms of צָוָה. The מְ prefix and Daghesh Forte in the second root consonant identify the Participle as either Piel or Pual. The Pathach beneath the first root consonant requires the Piel identification (31.4). The ה ֶ ending marks all III-ה Participles (ms only) in the Qal and derived stems, "I am commanding you" or "I command you."

לַעֲשֹׂתָהּ The preposition לְ is prefixed to the Qal Infinitive Construct of עָשָׂה with a 3fs pronominal suffix (to do [it]). Recall that the Infinitive Construct form of III-ה verbs ends in וֹת or (defectively) תֹ with Holem instead of Holem Waw (20.4).

לְאַהֲבָה אֶת־יְהוָה This Qal Infinitive Construct form is difficult to identify. The verbal root אָהַב is doubly weak, both I-א and II-Guttural. The form is prefixed with the preposition לְ and it also has an additional ה ָ suffix (Paragogic ה). This suffix appears approximately 60 times with the Infinitive Construct in the Hebrew Bible. It appears most frequently with אָהַב (13 times) and יָרֵא (14 times). It is also worth noting that approximately one-third (19 times) of all such forms appear in the book of Deuteronomy. The significance of the Paragogic ה on the Infinitive Construct is yet undetermined. This phrase is translated "to love Yahweh (your God)."

לָלֶכֶת This is the second appearance of the Qal Infinitive Construct of הָלַךְ in this passage (cf. וּבְלֶכְתְּךָ in verse 19). Here, the preposition לְ is prefixed to the Infinitive (to walk).

בְּכָל־דְּרָכָיו The preposition בְּ is prefixed to the construct noun כֹּל and joined by Maqqef to the plural noun דְּרָכִים (lexical form דֶּ֫רֶךְ) with a 3ms pronominal suffix (in all his ways).

וּלְדָבְקָה־בוֹ This Qal Infinitive Construct of דָּבַק appears with the preposition לְ and the ה ָ suffix (see לְאַהֲבָה above). The object of the verb follows and is marked by the preposition בְּ (and to cling to him).

Deuteronomy 11:23

וְהוֹרִישׁ יְהוָה The verb וְהוֹרִישׁ is Hiphil Perfect 3ms of יָרַשׁ with Waw Consecutive. The form is identified as Hiphil Perfect by the ה prefix and Hireq Yod stem vowel. The key to identifying the verbal root is the Holem Waw prefix vowel. Recall that most verbs now identified as I-י were originally I-ו and that in the Niphal (25.10-11), Hiphil (27.12-13), and Hophal (29.8-9) stems, the original ו reappears as either a vowel letter or as a consonant, replacing the י in first root position. In all conjugations of the Hiphil, the original ו reappears as Holem Waw as in וְהוֹרִישׁ. This Hiphil Perfect with Waw Consecutive begins the apodosis of the conditional sentence that began with כִּי אִם in verse 22 (then Yahweh will drive out).

מִלִּפְנֵיכֶם The mp noun פָּנִים is prefixed with the prepositions מִן and לְ with a 2mp pronominal suffix (from before you).

וִירִשְׁתֶּם This form is the Qal Perfect 2mp of יָרַשׁ with Waw Consecutive (and you will dispossess). The spelling of the Waw Consecutive exhibits the same pattern of vowel contraction that was observed twice in verse 21 (וִימֵי and כִּימֵי).

גּוֹיִם גְּדֹלִים וַעֲצֻמִים מִכֶּם The mp noun גּוֹיִם (with defectively written Hireq Yod) is followed by two mp adjectives (lexical forms גָּדוֹל and עָצוּם). These adjectives are the basis for comparison required by the preposition מִן with a 2mp pronominal suffix (6.6.1; 9.12). With the comparative use of מִן (6.6.1), the construction is translated as "nations *greater* and *mightier than* you."

Translation 13

Deuteronomy 31:1-8

Be Strong and Courageous

1 וַיֵּלֶךְ מֹשֶׁה וַיְדַבֵּר אֶת־הַדְּבָרִים הָאֵלֶּה אֶל־כָּל־יִשְׂרָאֵל

2 וַיֹּאמֶר אֲלֵהֶם בֶּן־מֵאָה וְעֶשְׂרִים שָׁנָה אָנֹכִי הַיּוֹם לֹא־אוּכַל

עוֹד לָצֵאת וְלָבוֹא וַיהוָה אָמַר אֵלַי לֹא תַעֲבֹר אֶת־הַיַּרְדֵּן הַזֶּה

3 יְהוָה אֱלֹהֶיךָ הוּא עֹבֵר לְפָנֶיךָ הוּא־יַשְׁמִיד אֶת־הַגּוֹיִם הָאֵלֶּה

מִלְּפָנֶיךָ וִירִשְׁתָּם יְהוֹשֻׁעַ הוּא עֹבֵר לְפָנֶיךָ כַּאֲשֶׁר דִּבֶּר יְהוָה

4 וְעָשָׂה יְהוָה לָהֶם כַּאֲשֶׁר עָשָׂה לְסִיחוֹן[1] וּלְעוֹג[2] מַלְכֵי הָאֱמֹרִי

וּלְאַרְצָם אֲשֶׁר הִשְׁמִיד אֹתָם 5 וּנְתָנָם יְהוָה לִפְנֵיכֶם וַעֲשִׂיתֶם

לָהֶם כְּכָל־הַמִּצְוָה אֲשֶׁר צִוִּיתִי אֶתְכֶם 6 חִזְקוּ וְאִמְצוּ[3] אַל־תִּירְאוּ

וְאַל־תַּעַרְצוּ[4] מִפְּנֵיהֶם כִּי יְהוָה אֱלֹהֶיךָ הוּא הַהֹלֵךְ עִמָּךְ לֹא

---

1. סִיחוֹן Sihon (37).
2. עוֹג Og (22).
3. אָמֵץ (Q) to be strong, be bold; (Pi) make firm, strengthen, harden someone's heart (41).
4. עָרַץ (Q) to tremble, be terrified, be in dread; (Hi) terrify, strike (inspire) with

יַרְפְּךָ[5] וְלֹא יַעַזְבֶךָּ 7 וַיִּקְרָא מֹשֶׁה לִיהוֹשֻׁעַ וַיֹּאמֶר אֵלָיו לְעֵינֵי
כָל־יִשְׂרָאֵל חֲזַק וֶאֱמָץ כִּי אַתָּה תָּבוֹא אֶת־הָעָם הַזֶּה אֶל־הָאָרֶץ
אֲשֶׁר נִשְׁבַּע יְהוָה לַאֲבֹתָם לָתֵת לָהֶם וְאַתָּה תַּנְחִילֶנָּה אוֹתָם 8
וַיהוָה הוּא הַהֹלֵךְ לְפָנֶיךָ הוּא יִהְיֶה עִמָּךְ לֹא יַרְפְּךָ וְלֹא יַעַזְבֶךָּ
לֹא תִירָא וְלֹא תֵחָת

Parse the following verbs from Deuteronomy 31:1-8.

Deuteronomy 31:1

וַיֵּלֶךְ ______________________________

וַיְדַבֵּר ______________________________

Deuteronomy 31:2

וַיֹּאמֶר ______________________________

אוּכַל ______________________________

לָצֵאת ______________________________

וְלָבוֹא ______________________________

אָמַר ______________________________

תַעֲבֹר ______________________________

Deuteronomy 31:3

עֹבֵר ______________________________

---

awe, be in terror (15).

5. רָפָה (Q) to sink, drop, relax, grow slack; (Hi) abandon, forsake, desert (46).

יַשְׁמִיד ______

וִירִשְׁתָּם ______

דִּבֶּר ______

Deuteronomy 31:4

וְעָשָׂה ______

עָשָׂה ______

הִשְׁמִיד ______

Deuteronomy 31:5

וּנְתָנָם ______

וַעֲשִׂיתֶם ______

צִוִּיתִי ______

Deuteronomy 31:6

חִזְקוּ ______

וְאִמְצוּ ______

תִּירְאוּ ______

תַּעַרְצוּ ______

הַהֹלֵךְ ______

יַרְפְּךָ ______

יַעַזְבֶךָּ ______

Deuteronomy 31:7

וַיִּקְרָא ______

וַיֹּאמֶר ______

חֲזַק ______

וֶאֱמָץ ______________________________

תָּבוֹא ______________________________

נִשְׁבַּע ______________________________

לָתֵת ______________________________

תַּנְחִילֶנָּה ______________________________

Deuteronomy 31:8

יִהְיֶה ______________________________

יַרְפְּךָ ______________________________

יַעַזְבֶךָּ ______________________________

תִירָא ______________________________

תֵחָת ______________________________

Grammatical Commentary: Deuteronomy 31:1-8

Deuteronomy 31:1

וַיֵּלֶךְ This triconsonantal verb with Waw Consecutive preserves only two root consonants. The Tsere under the Imperfect preformative is the clue to identifying this verb as belonging to the I-י (Type 1) weak verb class. The verbal root is הָלַךְ which, as you will recall, inflects just like a I-י verb.

וַיְדַבֵּר The Shewa under the Imperfect preformative, the Pathach under the first root consonant, and the Daghesh Forte in the second root consonant are the diagnostic features of this Piel Imperfect 3ms verb. Note that the Daghesh Forte of the Waw Consecutive is not present in the Imperfect preformative (30.15).

Deuteronomy 31:2

בֶּן־מֵאָה וְעֶשְׂרִים שָׁנָה Literally, this expression is translated "a son of one hundred and twenty years." Idiomatically, it may be translated, "one hundred and twenty years old." Note that the singular noun שָׁנָה is translated with the plural (years).

הַיּוֹם When prefixed with the definite article, the Hebrew noun **יוֹם** may be translated "this day" or "today" (*HALOT* 2:402).

לֹא־אוּכַל עוֹד The negative particle **לֹא** is joined by Maqqef to the Qal Imperfect 1cs of the stative verb **יָכֹל** (to be able). This verb is irregular in its Imperfect inflection with a Shureq preformative vowel in every form of the paradigm (16.21). With the adverb **עוֹד**, the negated verb translates as "I am no longer able."

לָצֵאת וְלָבוֹא Here, we recognize two Qal Infinitive Construct verbs, each prefixed with the preposition **לְ**. The first Infinitive (**צֵאת**) has dropped its first root letter and added **ת** to the end of the form. This phenomenon occurs with both I-**י** and I-**נ** weak verbal roots. In this case, the verbal root is **יָצָא**. The form **לָבוֹא** is easily identified as the Qal Infinitive Construct of the Biconsonantal **בּוֹא** (20.7). With **לֹא־אוּכַל**, the Infinitives translate as "I am no longer able *to go out and to come in*."

לֹא תַעֲבֹר An Imperfect 2ms with Pathach preformative vowel and Hateph Pathach beneath the guttural in first root position may be either Qal (16.2; 16.3.2) or Hiphil (27.2). The Holem stem vowel identifies this verb as Qal (you will not cross over).

אֶת־הַיַּרְדֵּן הַזֶּה Here, the object of the verb **תַעֲבֹר** is marked with the definite direct object marker (**אֶת־**) and modified with a demonstrative adjective (**הַזֶּה**). Note the definite article on the proper noun **יַרְדֵּן** (this Jordan).

Deuteronomy 31:3

יְהוָה אֱלֹהֶיךָ The verse begins with the subject of the Qal active Participle **עֹבֵר** (Yahweh your God).

הוּא עֹבֵר The 3ms independent personal pronoun (**הוּא**) precedes the Qal Participle ms, giving emphasis to the subject of the verbal action (Yahweh your God, *he himself* will go over).

לְפָנֶיךָ The noun **פָּנִים** appears with the preposition **לְ** and a 2ms pronominal suffix (before you).

הוּא־יַשְׁמִיד Again, the subject of the verbal action is given emphasis with the use of **הוּא** before the 3ms Hiphil Imperfect of **שָׁמַד** (he *himself* will destroy). The Hiphil stem is easy to identify with the Pathach preformative vowel and the Hireq Yod stem vowel.

מִלְּפָנֶיךָ This is the same prepositional construction as above (לְפָנֶיךָ) but with the preposition מִן prefixed (from before you).

וִירִשְׁתָּם Here, Waw Consecutive is prefixed to a Qal Perfect 2ms of יָרַשׁ with a 3mp pronominal suffix (so that you will dispossess them). The spelling of the conjunction with Hireq Yod represents the contraction of vowels when וְ is prefixed to the יְ preformative (5.7.2b). The 2ms sufformative is easily recognized with the removal of the 3mp suffix. The vowel changes in the verbal stem are expected with the addition of the suffix (19.4).

הוּא עֹבֵר לְפָנֶיךָ With הוּא as the subject of the Qal Participle ms, this is precisely the same construction used earlier in the verse to emphasize the subject of the verbal action (Joshua *he* will go over before you).

Deuteronomy 31:4

לְסִיחוֹן וּלְעוֹג The proper names סִיחוֹן (Sihon) and עוֹג (Og) are each prefixed with the preposition לְ and joined by the conjunction וְ.

מַלְכֵי הָאֱמֹרִי This construct chain begins with the mp construct form of מֶ֫לֶךְ. The absolute noun is the gentilic אֱמֹרִי with definite article (the kings of the Amorites). A gentilic noun is "a noun that refers to a single member of a collective group, typically an ethnic or national group" (Arnold-Choi, 199).

וּלְאַרְצָם This form is composed of four elements. The fs noun אֶ֫רֶץ is prefixed with the conjunction וְ (spelled as Shureq before Vocal Shewa; 5.7.2b) and the preposition לְ together with a 3mp (Type 1) pronominal suffix (and to their land).

אֲשֶׁר הִשְׁמִיד אֹתָם The relative pronoun אֲשֶׁר precedes the Hiphil Perfect 3ms of שָׁמַד (26.3-4), identified by the הִ prefix and the Hireq Yod stem vowel. The object marker with a 3mp pronominal suffix (אֹתָם) follows (when he destroyed them).

Deuteronomy 31:5

וּנְתָנָם The spelling of this Qal Perfect 3ms verbal stem has changed from נָתַן to נְתָן with the addition of the 3mp pronominal suffix (19.3). This change represents propretonic reduction in the first syllable (נְ) and lengthening of the pretonic vowel to Qamets (תָ). The Waw Consecutive with the Perfect is spelled as וּ before consonants with Vocal Shewa. With יְהוָה as the subject, this form translates as "and Yahweh will give them."

וַעֲשִׂיתֶם The Waw Consecutive on this Qal Perfect is spelled with Pathach because it takes the corresponding short vowel of the Hateph Pathach beneath the guttural in first root position (5.7.3). The Hireq Yod stem vowel identifies the verb as III-ה (and you will do).

צִוִּיתִי The sufformative תִּי identifies this verb as Perfect 1cs. The Hireq under the first root consonant and the Daghesh Forte in the second root consonant (וּ) are diagnostic of the Piel stem. The Hireq Yod stem vowel signals the III-ה verbal root צָוָה (I commanded).

Deuteronomy 31:6

חִזְקוּ וְאִמְצוּ Both of these Qal Imperative verbs preserve the expected spelling of the 2mp with Hireq in a closed syllable and the Shureq sufformative (18.3-4). Linked with the conjunction וְ, the construction translates as "be strong and be brave."

אַל־תִּירְאוּ Here, the negative particle אַל precedes an Imperfect, creating a prohibition. The Hireq Yod preformative vowel is one of two possible preformative vowels (the other is Tsere) that may occur in I-י Qal Imperfect verbs (16.6-7). The verb יָרֵא is stative (do not be afraid).

וְאַל־תַּעַרְצוּ Precisely the same construction as אַל־תִּירְאוּ above but with the verb עָרַץ (and do not be terrified).

מִפְּנֵיהֶם The preposition מִן is prefixed to the mp construct form of פָּנֶה with a 3mp pronominal suffix, "from before them" or "by them."

כִּי יְהוָה אֱלֹהֶיךָ הוּא הַהֹלֵךְ עִמָּךְ The conjunction כִּי (because) introduces the next clause with the proper name יְהוָה as the subject of the verbal action expressed by the Qal active Participle (ms) הַהֹלֵךְ. With the definite article, the Participle is being used substantively. The preceding 3ms independent personal pronoun emphasizes the subject of the verbal action (because Yahweh your God *it is he* who goes with you).

יַרְפְּךָ The Imperfect preformative consonant with Pathach identifies the stem and conjugation (Hiphil Imperfect). This 3ms verb has a 2ms pronominal suffix. The root is רָפָה (he will not abandon you).

יַעַזְבֶךָּ The 2ms pronominal suffix (ֶךָּ) on this Qal Imperfect 3ms of עָזַב is sometimes called a Nun-suffix because a נ has been assimilated into the consonant of the suffix and is represented by a Daghesh Forte (19.6). Nun-suffixes with the Imperfect are attested in several forms

(19.13). With the conjunction and negative particle, וְלֹא יַעַזְבֶךָּ translates as "and he will not abandon you."

Deuteronomy 31:7

חֲזַק וֶאֱמָץ At the beginning of verse 6, the verbs חָזַק and אָמַץ are inflected as Qal Imperatives. Here, both forms are 2ms because they are addressed to Joshua. The spelling of both Imperatives is as expected for these two weak verb classes, with Hateph vowels under the gutturals in first root position rather than Vocal Shewa (18.4).

אַתָּה תָּבוֹא The 2ms independent personal pronoun emphasizes the pronominal element of the Qal Imperfect 2ms of בּוֹא (you *yourself* shall go).

אֶת־הָעָם הַזֶּה The preposition אֵת is joined by Maqqef to the noun עַם with the definite article. Note the spelling change in the noun with the prefixing of the definite article (5.6). The demonstrative זֶה is functioning as an adjective, agreeing in gender, number and definiteness with the noun (with this people).

אֲשֶׁר נִשְׁבַּע יְהוָה The relative pronoun אֲשֶׁר introduces a relative clause with the Niphal Perfect 3ms of שָׁבַע (which Yahweh has sworn). The נִ prefix and Pathach stem vowel identify the verbal stem as Niphal (24.4-5).

לַאֲבֹתָם This is the noun אָב in its plural form (אָבוֹת) with the preposition לְ and a 3mp pronominal suffix (to their fathers). The Holem Waw of the plural ending has been written defectively as Holem.

לָתֵת This Qal Infinitive Construct of נָתַן (תֵּת) is one of Hebrew's most difficult verbal forms to identify (20.5) and it should be memorized. The verb has lost both its first and third root consonants. Apart from the preposition לְ which frequently marks Infinitive Construct verbs, and perhaps the final ת, the spelling offers little help in the identification of the form. With לָהֶם, the Infinitive translates as "to give to them."

וְאַתָּה תַּנְחִילֶנָּה אוֹתָם The ֶ֫נָּה on the form תַּנְחִילֶנָּה is the 3fs pronominal suffix (one of the Nun-suffixes with the Imperfect; 19.13). Its antecedent is the noun אֶ֫רֶץ. The Pathach preformative vowel and the Hireq Yod stem vowel are diagnostic features of the Hiphil stem. With the removal of the pronominal suffix, the Hiphil Imperfect 2ms of נָחַל is easily recognized. The subject of the verb is given emphasis by the 2ms independent personal pronoun (אַתָּה) that immediately precedes the verb. The form אוֹתָם is the definite direct object marker with a 3mp pronominal suffix, "you will put them in possession of it" or "you will cause them to possess it."

Deuteronomy 31:8

וְלֹא תֵחָת The verbal root of this Qal Imperfect 2ms is difficult to identify. With the Tsere preformative vowel, the I-י weak verb class would seem likely. In this case, however, it is not I-י, but the much less common (Type 3) Geminate חָתַת (16.12-13). Translate this construction, "do not be dismayed" or "do not be discouraged."

Translation 14

Joshua 24:14-18

Joshua's Challenge to Serve Yahweh

14 וְעַתָּה יְראוּ אֶת־יְהוָה וְעִבְדוּ אֹתוֹ בְּתָמִים וּבֶאֱמֶת וְהָסִירוּ
אֶת־אֱלֹהִים אֲשֶׁר עָבְדוּ אֲבוֹתֵיכֶם בְּעֵבֶר הַנָּהָר וּבְמִצְרַיִם וְעִבְדוּ
אֶת־יְהוָה 15 וְאִם רַע בְּעֵינֵיכֶם לַעֲבֹד אֶת־יְהוָה בַּחֲרוּ לָכֶם הַיּוֹם
אֶת־מִי תַעֲבֹדוּן אִם אֶת־אֱלֹהִים אֲשֶׁר־עָבְדוּ אֲבוֹתֵיכֶם אֲשֶׁר
בְּעֵבֶר [מֵעֵבֶר] הַנָּהָר וְאִם אֶת־אֱלֹהֵי הָאֱמֹרִי אֲשֶׁר אַתֶּם
יֹשְׁבִים בְּאַרְצָם וְאָנֹכִי וּבֵיתִי נַעֲבֹד אֶת־יְהוָה 16 וַיַּעַן הָעָם
וַיֹּאמֶר חָלִילָה[1] לָּנוּ מֵעֲזֹב אֶת־יְהוָה לַעֲבֹד אֱלֹהִים אֲחֵרִים 17 כִּי
יְהוָה אֱלֹהֵינוּ הוּא הַמַּעֲלֶה אֹתָנוּ וְאֶת־אֲבוֹתֵינוּ מֵאֶרֶץ מִצְרַיִם
מִבֵּית עֲבָדִים וַאֲשֶׁר עָשָׂה לְעֵינֵינוּ אֶת־הָאֹתוֹת הַגְּדֹלוֹת הָאֵלֶּה
וַיִּשְׁמְרֵנוּ בְּכָל־הַדֶּרֶךְ אֲשֶׁר הָלַכְנוּ בָהּ וּבְכֹל הָעַמִּים אֲשֶׁר

1. חָלִיל far be it! never! (21); חָלִילָה לָּנוּ "far be it from us!"

עֲבַרְנוּ בְּקִרְבָּם 18 וַיְגָרֶשׁ[2] יְהוָה אֶת־כָּל־הָעַמִּים וְאֶת־הָאֱמֹרִי

יֹשֵׁב הָאָרֶץ מִפָּנֵינוּ גַּם־אֲנַחְנוּ נַעֲבֹד אֶת־יְהוָה כִּי־הוּא אֱלֹהֵינוּ

Parse the following verbs from Joshua 24:14-18.

Joshua 24:14

יְראוּ ______

וְעִבְדוּ ______

וְהָסִירוּ ______

עִבְדוּ ______

Joshua 24:15

רַע ______

לַעֲבֹד ______

בַּחֲרוּ ______

תַּעֲבֹדוּן ______

יֹשְׁבִים ______

נַעֲבֹד ______

Joshua 24:16

וַיַּעַן ______

וַיֹּאמֶר ______

מֵעֲזֹב ______

---

2. גָּרַשׁ (Q) to drive out, banish; (Pi) drive out (away) (45).

לַעֲבֹד ________________________________

Joshua 24:17

הַמַּעֲלֶה ________________________________

עָשָׂה ________________________________

וַיִּשְׁמְרֵנוּ ________________________________

הָלַכְנוּ ________________________________

עָבַרְנוּ ________________________________

Joshua 24:18

וַיְגָרֶשׁ ________________________________

יֹשֵׁב ________________________________

נַעֲבֹד ________________________________

Grammatical Commentary: Joshua 24:14-18

Joshua 24:14

יְראוּ At first glance, the י at the beginning of this form might suggest the identification of יְראוּ as an Imperfect. In this case, however, the י is the first root consonant in this Qal Imperative 2mp of the stative verb יָרֵא (to be afraid).

וְעִבְדוּ This Qal Imperative 2mp of the I-Guttural verb עָבַד preserves the diagnostic vowel pattern of the strong verb, beginning with Hireq in a closed syllable (18.4).

בְּתָמִים וּבֶאֱמֶת Both תָמִים and אֱמֶת are prefixed with the preposition בְּ. These two prepositional phrases are functioning adverbially, complementing the two previous Imperatives יְראוּ and עִבְדוּ. As such, they may be translated idiomatically as adverbs (blamelessly and faithfully).

וְהָסִירוּ אֶת־אֱלֹהִים The הָ prefix and Hireq Yod stem vowel identify this form as a Hiphil Imperative belonging to the Biconsonantal weak verb class (27.14-15). The verbal root is סוּר. With the direct object אֶת־אֱלֹהִים,

the construction translates as "turn away from (the) gods" or "put away (the) gods."

בְּעֵ֫בֶר הַנָּהָר This phrase consists of עֵ֫בֶר with the preposition בְּ, followed by the noun נָהָר with the definite article (beyond the river). The river in the expression "beyond the river" or "on the other side of the river" is an allusion to the Euphrates River.

וּבְמִצְרַ֫יִם In this form, the conjunction וְ and preposition בְּ are prefixed to the proper name מִצְרַ֫יִם (and in Egypt). The conjunction וְ is spelled as Shureq before מ ,ב, or פ, and before Vocal Shewa.

Joshua 24:15

וְאִם Here, the conditional particle אִם marks the protasis (the "if" clause) of a conditional clause. The protasis of this conditional clause continues through אֶת־יְהוָה (if it is evil in your eyes to serve Yahweh . . .). The beginning of the apodosis (the "then" clause) is unmarked and begins with בַּחֲרוּ (*then* choose).

לַעֲבֹד Though עֲבֹד may be either Qal Imperative or Qal Infinitive Construct, the prefixed preposition (and, of course, context) requires identification of this form as an Infinitive Construct.

בַּחֲרוּ לָכֶם This pattern of spelling (Pathach beneath first root consonant and Hateph Pathach beneath ח in second root position) is present in both the fs and mp Qal Imperative forms of II-Guttural verbs (18.4). The Shureq sufformative indicates masculine plural. With לָכֶם to emphasize the subject, this expression translates as "choose for yourselves."

אֶת־מִי תַעֲבֹדוּן The definite direct object marker is joined by Maqqef to the interrogative pronoun מִי which functions as the direct object of the preceding clause בַּחֲרוּ לָכֶם הַיּוֹם (choose for yourselves this day). The direct object is followed by the Qal Imperfect 2mp of עָבַד with Paragogic נ (whom you will serve). For a good discussion of interrogatives in general and מִי in particular, see van der Merwe, 43.1-8. On the use of indefinite מִי in the accusative function, see Waltke- O'Connor, 18.2e. For a brief study of the Paragogic נ, see the comments on the verb תַּעַבְדוּן in Exodus 3:12.

וְאָנֹכִי וּבֵיתִי The conjunction וְ that is prefixed to אָנֹכִי is a disjunctive Waw (24.17.3). In this context, the disjunctive Waw on אָנֹכִי introduces a contrastive idea and should be translated as "but." Idiomatically, the construction may be rendered, "but as for me and my house."

נַעֲבֹד The verbal stem of this 1cp Imperfect of עָבַד is identified by the Holem. The verb is Qal (we will serve Yahweh). The נ preformative marks the verb as 1cp.

Joshua 24:16

וַיַּ֫עַן The form יַ֫עַן is the short or apocopated spelling of יַעֲנֶה (Qal Imperfect 3ms of עָנָה). When prefixed with the Waw Consecutive, 3ms III-ה verbs prefer the short spelling.

חָלִילָה לָּנוּ This expression consists of the negative interjection חָלִילָה, followed by the preposition לְ with a 1cp pronominal suffix (far be it from us!). Note the presence of the conjunctive Daghesh in the preposition (32.11).

מֵעֲזֹב אֶת־יְהוָה The preposition מִן with compensatory lengthening (מֵ) is prefixed to the Qal Infinitive Construct of עָזַב. The Infinitive preserves the diagnostic vowel pattern of the strong verb, though with Hateph Pathach and not Vocal Shewa under the guttural in first root position (20.2). Literally, the Infinitive and its direct object are translated as "from abandoning Yahweh." Idiomatically, the construction may be translated as "that we should abandon Yahweh."

לַעֲבֹד אֱלֹהִים אֲחֵרִים With the preposition לְ, the Qal Infinitive Construct of עָבַד expresses *intention* in this context (20.12.1). This Infinitive Construct is followed by the indefinite direct object אֱלֹהִים אֲחֵרִים (to serve other gods).

Joshua 24:17

הַמַּעֲלֶה This Hiphil Participle ms of עָלָה with the definite article is being used substantively in this כִּי clause (the one who brought us out).

אֶת־הָאֹתוֹת הַגְּדֹלוֹת הָאֵלֶּה This construction is the direct object of the verb עָשָׂה. The fp adjective גְּדֹלוֹת (lexical form גָּדוֹל) agrees with the noun it modifies in gender, number, and definiteness. The demonstrative adjective אֵלֶּה also agrees with the noun in the same categories (these great signs). Note the two instances when Holem Waw is written defectively as Holem (אֹתוֹת and גְּדֹלוֹת).

וַיִּשְׁמְרֵנוּ This Qal Imperfect of שָׁמַר has a 1cp pronominal suffix (ֵ֫נוּ) and Waw Consecutive. The absence of a sufformative and the י preformative identify the verb as 3ms (and he protected us).

אֲשֶׁר הָלַכְנוּ בָהּ The relative pronoun אֲשֶׁר precedes the Qal Perfect 1cp verb, which in turn, is followed by the preposition בְּ with a 3fs pronominal suffix. Literally, this relative clause is translated as "which we went in it." Translated idiomatically, it may be rendered as "in which we went."

וּבְכֹל הָעַמִּים The conjunction וְ (spelled as Shureq) and the preposition בְּ are prefixed to כֹּל. Note the Daghesh Forte in the Geminate consonant of עַם (4.8.4). Translate the preposition בְּ as "among" in this context (and among all the peoples).

בְּקִרְבָּם This is the preposition בְּ prefixed to the noun קֶ֫רֶב with a 3mp pronominal suffix (in their midst).

Joshua 24:18

וַיְגָרֶשׁ The Shewa beneath the Imperfect preformative identifies the stem of this verb as either Piel (30.6) or Pual (32.6). The Qamets beneath the first root letter identifies this verb as Piel. The Daghesh Forte expected in the second root consonant is rejected by the semi-guttural ר which caused the Pathach to lengthen to Qamets under the first root letter (31.9-10). Additionally, the Daghesh Forte of the Waw Consecutive is absent from the Imperfect preformative (30.15) and the Tsere stem vowel has changed to Seghol with the prefixing of the Waw Conversive (17.3.1). With יְהוָה as subject, the Piel translates as "Yahweh drove out."

אֶת־כָּל־הָעַמִּים וְאֶת־הָאֱמֹרִי Both direct objects of וַיְגָרֶשׁ are marked with the definite direct object marker אֶת־ (all the peoples and the Amorites). Some translators will subordinate the second direct object to the first and translate וְאֶת־הָאֱמֹרִי in apposition to אֶת־כָּל־הָעַמִּים (all the nations, including the Amorites [NIV]; all the peoples, the Amorites [ESV]).

גַּם־אֲנַחְנוּ נַעֲבֹד The conjunction גַּם is joined to the 1cp personal pronoun by Maqqef and is translated, "therefore" in this context. The pronoun אֲנַחְנוּ emphasizes the subject of נַעֲבֹד (therefore, we will serve...).

Judges 3:7-11

Yahweh Delivers Israel with Othniel

7 וַיַּעֲשׂוּ בְנֵי־יִשְׂרָאֵל אֶת־הָרַע בְּעֵינֵי יְהוָה וַיִּשְׁכְּחוּ אֶת־יְהוָה
אֱלֹהֵיהֶם וַיַּעַבְדוּ אֶת־הַבְּעָלִים וְאֶת־הָאֲשֵׁרוֹת[1] 8 וַיִּחַר־אַף יְהוָה
בְּיִשְׂרָאֵל וַיִּמְכְּרֵם בְּיַד כּוּשַׁן רִשְׁעָתַיִם[2] מֶלֶךְ אֲרַם נַהֲרָיִם[3]
וַיַּעַבְדוּ בְנֵי־יִשְׂרָאֵל אֶת־כּוּשַׁן רִשְׁעָתַיִם שְׁמֹנֶה שָׁנִים 9 וַיִּזְעֲקוּ
בְנֵי־יִשְׂרָאֵל אֶל־יְהוָה וַיָּקֶם יְהוָה מוֹשִׁיעַ לִבְנֵי יִשְׂרָאֵל וַיּוֹשִׁיעֵם
אֵת עָתְנִיאֵל[4] בֶּן־קְנַז[5] אֲחִי כָלֵב[6] הַקָּטֹן מִמֶּנּוּ 10 וַתְּהִי עָלָיו
רוּחַ־יְהוָה וַיִּשְׁפֹּט אֶת־יִשְׂרָאֵל וַיֵּצֵא לַמִּלְחָמָה וַיִּתֵּן יְהוָה בְּיָדוֹ
אֶת־כּוּשַׁן רִשְׁעָתַיִם מֶלֶךְ אֲרָם וַתָּעָז[7] יָדוֹ עַל כּוּשַׁן רִשְׁעָתָיִם
11 וַתִּשְׁקֹט[8] הָאָרֶץ אַרְבָּעִים שָׁנָה וַיָּמָת עָתְנִיאֵל בֶּן־קְנַז

---

1. אֲשֵׁרָה Asherah (pagan goddess), cultic pole; (fp) אֲשֵׁרִים and אֲשֵׁרוֹת (40).
2. כּוּשַׁן רִשְׁעָתַיִם (proper name) Cushan-Rishathaim (4).
3. אֲרַם נַהֲרַיִם (proper name) Aram Naharaim (5).
4. עָתְנִיאֵל (proper name) Othniel (7).
5. קְנַז (proper name) Kenaz (11).
6. כָּלֵב (proper name) Caleb (36).
7. עָזַז (Q) to be strong, prevail (against), defy (11).
8. שָׁקַט (Q) to be quiet, be peaceful, be at peace; (Hi) give (keep) peace (42).

Parse the following verbs from Judges 3:7-11.

Judges 3:7

וַיַּעֲשׂוּ ______________________________

וַיִּשְׁכְּחוּ ______________________________

וַיַּעַבְדוּ ______________________________

Judges 3:8

וַיִּחַר ______________________________

וַיִּמְכְּרֵם ______________________________

וַיַּעַבְדוּ ______________________________

Judges 3:9

וַיִּזְעֲקוּ ______________________________

וַיָּקֶם ______________________________

מוֹשִׁיעַ ______________________________

וַיּוֹשִׁיעֵם ______________________________

Judges 3:10

וַתְּהִי ______________________________

וַיִּשְׁפֹּט ______________________________

וַיֵּצֵא ______________________________

וַיִּתֵּן ______________________________

וַתָּעָז ______________________________

Judges 3:11

וַתִּשְׁקֹט ______________________________

וַיָּמָת ______________________________

Grammatical Commentary: Judges 3:7-11

Judges 3:7 — This short narrative text records the account of Othniel, the first judge in the book of Judges. It consists of sixteen contiguous Waw Consecutive clauses with no intervening subordinate clauses.

וַיַּעֲשׂוּ This verb is doubly weak, both I-Guttural and III-ה (16.15.2). The Pathach preformative vowel and Hateph Pathach under the first root letter are diagnostic of Qal (and Hiphil) I-Guttural verbs (16.2-3). In the Imperfect of III-ה verbs, the loss of the final ה vowel letter occurs in all forms that take a sufformative (2fs, 3mp, 3fp, 2mp, 2fp).

אֶת־הָרַע This is the direct object of the verb וַיַּעֲשׂוּ. Preceded by the definite direct object marker and prefixed with the definite article, the adjective רַע is used substantively in this context, "evil" or "that which was evil."

בְּעֵינֵי יְהוָה The preposition בְּ is prefixed to the dual construct form עֵינֵי (eyes of). Since the absolute noun יְהוָה is a proper name, and therefore definite, the entire construct chain is definite (in the eyes of Yahweh).

אֱלֹהֵיהֶם The mp noun אֱלֹהִים appears with a 3mp (Type 2) pronominal suffix (their God).

וַיַּעַבְדוּ As with the verb וַיַּעֲשׂוּ above, the Pathach preformative vowel and the Pathach under the first root letter (2fs, 3mp, 2mp) are diagnostic of Qal (and Hiphil) Imperfect I-Guttural verbs. In this case, וַיַּעַבְדוּ is Qal Imperfect 3mp of עָבַר with Waw Consecutive.

אֶת־הַבְּעָלִים וְאֶת־הָאֲשֵׁרוֹת The verb וַיַּעַבְדוּ takes two objects, both of which are marked with the definite direct object marker אֶת־.

Judges 3:8

וַיִּחַר The verbal root חָרָה is weak in each of its three root letters. In this Qal Imperfect 3ms form, the short form of the verb (יִּחַר) is used with the Waw Consecutive (17.3.2). The long form (יֶחֱרֶה) follows the I-Guttural (Type 1) pattern with the distinctive III-ה ending (ה ֶ).

אַף יְהוָה This definite construct chain is translated literally as "the nose [nostril] of Yahweh." אַף יְהוָה is the subject of the verb וַיִּחַר and together they may be rendered,"the nose of Yahweh became hot." In Hebrew, a "hot nose" is a figure of speech denoting anger. A more idiomatic translation would be, "Yahweh became angry" or "the anger of Yahweh burned" (NIV).

בְּיִשְׂרָאֵל The preposition בְּ is prefixed to the proper name יִשְׂרָאֵל. In this context, the translation of the preposition בְּ is "against." This is called the "adversative" use of the preposition בְּ (Arnold-Choi, 4.1.5d) and it is common with certain verbs.

וַיִּמְכְּרֵם This is the Qal Imperfect 3ms of מָכַר with Waw Consecutive and a 3mp pronominal suffix. The addition of the pronominal suffix has caused the expected Holem stem vowel to reduce to Vocal Shewa.

בְּיַד The preposition בְּ is prefixed to the fs construct noun יַד (into the hand of).

שְׁמֹנֶה שָׁנִים The ms cardinal number שְׁמֹנֶה appears with the irregular feminine plural noun שָׁנִים (lexical form שָׁנָה). Note that the cardinal number שְׁמֹנֶה does not agree with the noun it refers to in grammatical gender or number (11.2.3). The expression שְׁמֹנֶה שָׁנִים may be translated, "for eight years." The addition of the preposition "for" is required by English style and suggested by the position of this expression at the end of its clause. In Hebrew, modifiers such as this are frequently placed at the end their clause.

Judges 3:9

וַיִּזְעֲקוּ This verbal form is the Qal Imperfect 3mp of the II-Guttural verb זָעַק with Waw Consecutive. The only change in spelling when compared to the strong verb is the Hateph Pathach beneath the guttural consonant in second root position (16.4). Remember that gutturals cannot take Vocal Shewa but must instead take reduced or Hateph vowels.

וַיָּקֶם The form וַיָּקֶם is the Hiphil Imperfect 3ms of קוּם with Waw Consecutive. When prefixed with the Waw Consecutive, the Hiphil Imperfect form יָקִים is spelled with the short form יָקֵם (17.3.2; 23.11.2).

מוֹשִׁיעַ The מ prefix is diagnostic of the Participle conjugation. The Holem Waw prefix vowel is diagnostic of the I-י (originally I-ו) weak verb class. The Hireq Yod stem vowel is diagnostic of the Hiphil stem. With the lack of any inflectional ending, this form must be the Hiphil Participle ms of יָשַׁע. In its clause, מוֹשִׁיעַ is functioning substantively as the (indefinite) object of the verb וַיָּקֶם (Yahweh raised up *a deliverer*).

וַיּוֹשִׁיעֵם As with מוֹשִׁיעַ in this same verse, the Holem Waw preformative vowel and the Hireq Yod stem vowel identify this form as Hiphil from the I-י weak verb class. The Imperfect preformative and the Waw Consecutive of this form are easy to identify. With the 3mp pronominal suffix, this word is translated, "and he [Yahweh] saved them." The antecedent of the 3mp suffix is בְּנֵי יִשְׂרָאֵל and the subject of the verb is יְהוָה from the preceding clause. Most translations, perhaps incorrectly, render וַיּוֹשִׁיעֵם as either a relative clause (who saved/delivered them [KJV, RSV, ESV, NIV]) or an infinitive phrase (to deliver them [NASB]) with Othniel as the subject of the verbal action.

אֵת עָתְנִיאֵל This is perhaps best understood as a prepositional phrase with the proper name עָתְנִיאֵל functioning as the object of the preposition. In its clause, beginning with וַיּוֹשִׁיעֵם, this construction should be translated, "and he [Yahweh] delivered them *with Othniel*." With this translation, Yahweh is the primary agent and Othniel is the secondary instrument of deliverance. Note that almost all English translations render Othniel as the primary agent of deliverance.

אֲחִי כָלֵב This definite construct chain is in apposition to עָתְנִיאֵל. The construct spelling of the ms noun אָח (brother) is a bit unusual. Remember that certain singular monosyllabic nouns will add Hireq Yod to their stem in the spelling of their construct form (10.3.2e). In this instance, the Hireq Yod of אֲחִי is not a 1cs pronominal suffix. The definite absolute noun is a proper name (the brother of Caleb).

הַקָּטֹן מִמֶּנּוּ The definite ms adjective הַקָּטֹן is modifying אֲחִי. Because a construct chain cannot be broken, an adjective modifying a construct noun will occur after the construct chain (10.2.6). The prepositional phrase מִמֶּנּוּ consists of the preposition מִן and a 3ms pronominal suffix (9.13.2). This is an example of the comparative use of מִן (6.6.1) and is translated as "younger than him" or simply "younger." The entire expression, beginning with אֵת עָתְנִיאֵל, should be translated, "with Othniel ... Caleb's younger brother."

Judges 3:10

וַתְּהִי עָלָיו The Qal Imperfect 3fs of הָיָה is prefixed with the Waw Consecutive. Recall that with III-ה, Biconsonantal, and Hiphil Imperfect verbs, the Waw Consecutive is normally prefixed to a short form of the verb. With III-ה verbs, the final ה vowel letter of the long form (תִּהְיֶה) does not appear in the construction of the short form (תְּהִי). With the preposition עַל and 3ms (Type 2) pronominal suffix, this construction is translated, "[the Spirit of Yahweh] was upon him."

רוּחַ־יְהוָה This definite construct chain is the subject of the verb וַתְּהִי in its clause. The verb is 3fs because רוּחַ is an (endingless) fs noun (4.7.1).

וַיֵּצֵא The Waw Consecutive and Imperfect preformative identify this form as Imperfect 3ms. The Tsere preformative vowel further identify this form as belonging to the I-י weak verb class (יָצָא) and the Qal stem (16.7.1).

לַמִּלְחָמָה The fs noun מִלְחָמָה is prefixed with the definite article and the preposition לְ. Recall that when an inseparable preposition (בְּ, כְּ, or לְ) is prefixed to a word with the definite article, the consonant of the preposition will replace the ה of the definite article (6.4.4). With וַיֵּצֵא this construction is translated, "he went out to war."

וַיִּתֵּן יְהוָה בְּיָדוֹ As with וַיֵּצֵא above, the Waw Consecutive and Imperfect preformative identify וַיִּתֵּן as Imperfect 3ms. The Daghesh Forte in the ת represents the assimilated נ of the verbal root נָתַן and the Tsere stem vowel is diagnostic of certain weak verbs in the Qal Stem (I-י and נָתַן). With the verbal subject יְהוָה followed by the prepositional phrase בְּיָדוֹ, this portion of the clause is translated, "Yahweh gave into his hand."

וַתָּעָז יָדוֹ The Waw Consecutive and Imperfect preformative identify this form as Imperfect 3fs or 2ms. The presence of the (endingless) fs noun יָד (with a 3ms pronominal suffix) as the verbal subject makes the 3fs identification correct. With regard to the identification of the verbal root, the Qamets preformative vowel is diagnostic of both Geminate and Biconsonantal weak verb classes in the Qal stem (the stem vowel is Qamets Hatuf). In this case, the verbal root is the Geminate עָזַז.

Judges 3:11

וַתִּשְׁקֹט הָאָרֶץ The form וַתִּשְׁקֹט is the Qal Imperfect 3fs with Waw Consecutive of the stative verb שָׁקַט. Following וַתִּשְׁקֹט is its (endingless) fs subject הָאָרֶץ.

אַרְבָּעִים שָׁנָה The adverbial expression אַרְבָּעִים שָׁנָה is translated, "for forty years" (see שְׁמֹנֶה שָׁנִים in verse 8 above). Note how cardinal numbers, such as אַרְבָּעִים (mp), do not always appear to correspond in gender or number with the noun to which they are related.

וַיָּמָת Similar in form to וַתָּעָז in verse 10, the Waw Consecutive and Imperfect preformative identify this form as Imperfect 3ms. With regard to the identification of the verbal root, the Qamets preformative vowel is diagnostic of both Geminate and Biconsonantal weak verb classes in the Qal stem (this stem vowel is Qamets Hatuf). In this case, the verbal root is the Biconsonantal מוּת.

עָתְנִיאֵל בֶּן־קְנַז The proper name עָתְנִיאֵל is the subject of the verb וַיָּמָת and the definite construct chain בֶּן־קְנַז stands in apposition to עָתְנִיאֵל (then Othniel, the son of Kenaz, died).

Judges 10:10-15

Cry to the Gods Whom You Have Chosen

10 וַיִּזְעֲקוּ בְּנֵי יִשְׂרָאֵל אֶל־יְהוָה לֵאמֹר חָטָאנוּ לָךְ וְכִי עָזַבְנוּ
אֶת־אֱלֹהֵינוּ וַנַּעֲבֹד אֶת־הַבְּעָלִים 11 וַיֹּאמֶר יְהוָה אֶל־בְּנֵי יִשְׂרָאֵל
הֲלֹא מִמִּצְרַיִם וּמִן־הָאֱמֹרִי וּמִן־בְּנֵי עַמּוֹן וּמִן־פְּלִשְׁתִּים 12
וְצִידוֹנִים[1] וַעֲמָלֵק[2] וּמָעוֹן[3] לָחֲצוּ[4] אֶתְכֶם וַתִּצְעֲקוּ אֵלַי וָאוֹשִׁיעָה
אֶתְכֶם מִיָּדָם 13 וְאַתֶּם עֲזַבְתֶּם אוֹתִי וַתַּעַבְדוּ אֱלֹהִים אֲחֵרִים
לָכֵן לֹא־אוֹסִיף לְהוֹשִׁיעַ אֶתְכֶם 14 לְכוּ וְזַעֲקוּ אֶל־הָאֱלֹהִים אֲשֶׁר
בְּחַרְתֶּם בָּם הֵמָּה יוֹשִׁיעוּ לָכֶם בְּעֵת צָרַתְכֶם 15 וַיֹּאמְרוּ
בְּנֵי־יִשְׂרָאֵל אֶל־יְהוָה חָטָאנוּ עֲשֵׂה־אַתָּה לָנוּ כְּכָל־הַטּוֹב בְּעֵינֶיךָ
אַךְ הַצִּילֵנוּ נָא הַיּוֹם הַזֶּה

---

1. צִידֹנִי Sidonian (16).
2. עֲמָלֵק Amalek (39).
3. מָעוֹן Maon (6).
4. לָחַץ (Q) to squeeze, crowd, press, oppress, torment (19).

Parse the following verbs from Judges 10:10-15.

Judges 10:10

וַיִּזְעֲקוּ ____________________

חָטָאנוּ ____________________

עָזַבְנוּ ____________________

וַנַּעֲבֹד ____________________

Judges 10:11

וַיֹּאמֶר ____________________

Judges 10:12

לָחֲצוּ ____________________

וַתִּצְעֲקוּ ____________________

וָאוֹשִׁיעָה ____________________

Judges 10:13

עֲזַבְתֶּם ____________________

וַתַּעַבְדוּ ____________________

אוֹסִיף ____________________

לְהוֹשִׁיעַ ____________________

Judges 10:14

לְכוּ ____________________

וְזַעֲקוּ ____________________

בְּחַרְתֶּם ____________________

יוֹשִׁיעוּ ____________________

Judges 10:15

וַיֹּאמְרוּ ______________________________

חָטָאנוּ ______________________________

עֲשֵׂה ______________________________

הַצִּילֵנוּ ______________________________

Grammatical Commentary: Judges 10:10-15

Judges 10:10

וַיִּזְעֲקוּ In this II-Guttural Qal Imperfect 3mp verb with Waw Consecutive, only one point of spelling differs from that of a strong verb - the Hateph Pathach beneath the guttural in second root position.

חָטָאנוּ The verb חָטָא is doubly weak (I-Guttural and III-א). Its weakness as a I-Guttural verb occasions only a modest change in spelling and only in the 2mp and 2fp forms (14.2). Its weakness as a III-א verb occasions major changes throughout the paradigm when compared to the spelling of a strong verb. This Qal Perfect 1cp exhibits some of those changes (14.4-5). In this case, the stem vowel has changed from Pathach to Qamets and, because of the quiescent א, the expected Shewa under the third root consonant is no longer present. In this context, חָטָאנוּ is best translated with the English perfect tense (we have sinned).

לָךְ This is the preposition לְ with a 2ms pronominal suffix. The suffix is the object of the preposition and the antecedent of the suffix is the divine name (to [against] you). By all appearances, however, the suffix exhibits the spelling of the 2fs rather than the 2ms as required by context. The antecedent יְהוָה is obviously 2ms. One would expect agreement in gender and number between the pronominal suffix and its antecedent. The suffix is indeed masculine though it appears to be feminine. The reason for this spelling is that לָךְ is the pausal spelling of לְךָ (36.3).

A pausal form is a different (alternate) spelling of a word that may occur at one of the major points of pause in the recitation of the text (36.3). The symbol known as Athnach (לֵאמֹ֑ר) marks the end of the first major division in a verse. The symbol known as Silluq (הַבְּעָלִֽים) marks the end of the second major division in a verse and usually appears under the accented syllable of the last word in the verse. For a discussion of Hebrew accents, see Scott, 23-34 or Joüon-Muraoka, 15a-o. Of importance for the form under consideration (לָךְ) is that a word in pause may exhibit various changes in spelling as in לְךָ to לָךְ. There is no special meaning when a pausal spelling occurs but the student must be aware of the different spelling. Perhaps more importantly, there is a risk of erroneous interpretation or mistaken understanding if a reader does not recognize the spelling of a form in pause.

It is also important to note that not all pausal forms are marked with Athnach or Silluq. This is the case with לָךְ in Judg 10:10. Here, the pausal form in *BHS* is marked with a Zaqef Qatan (לָ֔ךְ, the two vertical dots above the consonant of the preposition). See also 1 Chr 17:10; 2 Chr 1:7).

וְכִי עָזַבְנוּ The second main clause of the verse begins with כִּי prefixed with the conjunction וְ and then followed by the Qal Perfect 1cp of עָזַב (and because we have forsaken).

וַנַּעֲבֹד The Pathach preformative vowel and the Hateph Pathach under the first root letter of this I-Guttural verb mark this form as either Qal or Hiphil. The Holem stem vowel identifies the verb as Qal (with Hiphil, the stem vowel would be Tsere). The preformative נ identifies this form as Imperfect 1cp.

אֶת־הַבְּעָלִים This direct object of וַנַּעֲבֹד is the mp of the Segholate noun בַּ֫עַל preceded by the definite direct object marker (we have served the Baals).

Judges 10:11

הֲלֹא This form is composed of the interrogative particle (8.10) prefixed to the negative particle לֹא. The verb negated by this negative particle is וָאוֹשִׁיעָה and does not appear until near the end of verse 12.

Judges 10:12

וְצִידוֹנִים וַעֲמָלֵק וּמָעוֹן This verse begins with three proper names, each with a different spelling of the conjunction וְ as required by the first syllable. צִידוֹנִים is a mp proper name (Sidonians). The forms עֲמָלֵק and מָעוֹן are the names of the ancestors of the Amalekites and the Maonites. It is not uncommon for an ancestral name to stand for a people, so עֲמָלֵק and מָעוֹן may be translated "Amalekites" and

"Maonites" respectively. The three proper nouns constitute the compound subject of לָחֲצוּ followed by its direct object אֶתְכֶם (the Sidonians and the Amalekites and the Maonites oppressed you).

וַתִּצְעֲקוּ אֵלַי With Waw Consecutive, the Qal Imperfect 2mp of צָעַק is followed by the preposition אֶל with a 1cs pronominal (object) suffix (and you cried out to me).

וָאוֹשִׁיעָה אֶתְכֶם This is the Hiphil Imperfect 1cs of יָשַׁע with Waw Consecutive and Paragogic ה (and I delivered you). The Waw Consecutive is spelled with Qamets because the Imperfect 1cs preformative rejects the Daghesh Forte of the Waw Consecutive and the Pathach lengthens to Qamets (compensatory lengthening). The Holem Waw following the Imperfect preformative is diagnostic of the I-י (27.12-13) weak verb class (יָשַׁע) and the Hireq Yod stem vowel is diagnostic of the Hiphil stem. The Paragogic ה is relatively rare with the Imperfect with Waw Consecutive, occurring only 104 times in the Hebrew Bible, primarily on first person forms. This ending may be related to the identical suffix appearing with the Imperfect (23.11) and lengthened Imperative (18.3.3). Finally, note that the Hireq Yod stem vowel of the Hiphil Imperfect normally changes to Tsere with the prefixing of the Waw Consecutive. In this case, that change did not take place.

מִיָּדָם In this form, the noun יָד is prefixed with the preposition מִן and suffixed with a 3mp pronominal suffix (from their hand).

Judges 10:13

וְאַתֶּם עֲזַבְתֶּם אוֹתִי This clause begins with a disjunctive Waw (24.17) prefixed to the 2mp personal pronoun followed by the Qal Perfect 2mp of עָזַב (yet you have abandoned me). Note the spelling of the definite direct object marker with the 1cs suffix. It is spelled with Holem Waw instead of Holem. This spelling occurs 361 times in the Hebrew Bible. The more common spelling with Holem occurs 1,034 times.

וַתַּעַבְדוּ The spelling of this Qal Imperfect 2mp of עָבַד with Waw Consecutive is as expected for this I-Guttural verb (16.2). In those forms of the Imperfect paradigm that have a sufformative consisting of a vowel (2fs, 3mp, and 2mp), the vowel under the first root letter is Pathach instead of Hateph Pathach. With the indefinite direct object אֱלֹהִים אֲחֵרִים, the construction translates as "and you served other gods."

לָכֵן Composed of the preposition לְ prefixed to כֵּן, לָכֵן frequently introduces a response to a previous statement and translates "therefore," as in this context. For study of the particle כֵּן (and its compound forms), see Arnold and Choi, 4.2.10; Waltke-O'Connor, 39.3.4e.

לֹא־אוֹסִיף לְהוֹשִׁיעַ אֶתְכֶם The negative particle לֹא precedes the Hiphil Imperfect 1cs of the I-י verb יָסַף. The diagnostic points of spelling for the identification of the stem and root are the same as those for the form וָאוֹשִׁיעָה in the preceding verse (27.12-13). Having now encountered two Hiphil I-י verbs in this passage alone, you should have little difficulty identifying לְהוֹשִׁיעַ as the Hiphil Infinitive Construct of יָשַׁע prefixed with the preposition לְ. The verb יָסַף is complementing the Infinitive and imparting the nuance of continuing to do something or, in this construction with the negative particle, not continuing to do something, "I will no longer deliver you" or "I will deliver you no more." It is important to be aware of this special and common usage of the verb יָסַף as a verbal complement (to do, to do more, to do again).

Arnold and Choi (4.3.3g) call this complementary use of two verbs "verbal hendiadys," that is, the conjoining of two or more verbs into a construction that refers to a single idea. They acknowledge what is perhaps the more common explanation of this type of construction as an adverbial use of the finite (Perfect or Imperfect) verbal forms of certain roots (commonly יָסַף) as in this verse (see Joüon-Muraoka, 177b). The Biconsonantal verb שׁוּב is also be used in this way.

Judges 10:14

לְכוּ The vowel pattern of this form is characteristic of the Qal Imperative 2mp in certain irregular or doubly weak verbs (18.6). Apart from familiarity with the common verb הָלַךְ, it would be difficult to identify the root of לְכוּ. You must remember that the verb הָלַךְ inflects just like the Type 1 class of I-י verbs in the Imperfect and Imperative (16.16; 18.6).

וְזַעֲקוּ It is a characteristic spelling pattern of a II-Guttural Qal Imperative to have Pathach under the first root consonant and Hateph Pathach under the guttural in second position (18.4). With the Shureq sufformative, this Imperative is 2mp.

אֶל־הָאֱלֹהִים אֲשֶׁר בְּחַרְתֶּם בָּם Translate this construction, "to the gods whom you have chosen." The form בָּם is the preposition בְּ with a 3mp pronominal suffix. The verb בָּחַר will sometimes mark its direct object with בְּ rather than with the definite direct object marker. In English, the accusative nuance of the relative clause אֲשֶׁר בְּחַרְתֶּם בָּם is communicated with the relative pronoun "whom" (the objective case of "who").

הֵמָּה יוֹשִׁיעוּ לָכֶם The 3mp personal pronoun precedes the Hiphil Imperfect 3mp of יָשַׁע. This is the third Hiphil form of יָשַׁע in these few verses, and in each case the root (יָשַׁע) is identified by the preformative vowel (Holem Waw) and the verbal stem (Hiphil) is identified by the Hireq Yod stem vowel. With the prepositional phrase לָכֶם, this clause translates as "they will deliver you."

בְּעֵת צָרַתְכֶם This is a construct chain prefixed with the preposition בְּ. The construct noun עֵת is spelled with Tsere in both its absolute and construct forms. The absolute noun in this chain is צָרָה with a 2mp pronominal suffix. Recall that when a feminine singular noun ending in ָה receives a pronominal suffix, the ָה is replaced by ַת as in צָרַתְכֶם (in the time of your distress).

Judges 10:15

וַיֹּאמְרוּ There are six I-א Qal Imperfect verbs that have a Holem preformative vowel: אָמַר (to say), אָכַל (to eat), אָבַד (to perish), אָחַז (to seize), אָפָה (to bake), and אָבָה (to be willing). Apart from these six, I-א verbs in the Qal Imperfect inflect like I-Guttural Type 1 verbs (16.2-3).

עֲשֵׂה־אַתָּה לָּנוּ In the Qal and derived stems of III-ה verbs, the Imperative 2ms form ends in ֵה (18.5). The form עֲשֵׂה is the Qal Imperative 2ms of עָשָׂה. Joined to the Imperative by Maqqef, the 2ms personal pronoun emphasizes the pronominal element of the Imperative (*you* do to us).

כְּכָל־הַטּוֹב בְּעֵינֶיךָ In this construction, the preposition כְּ (according to) is prefixed to the noun כֹּל and joined by Maqqef to the ms adjective טוֹב with the definite article. It is translated literally as "according to all the good in your eyes" or idiomatically as "what seems right to you."

אַךְ הַצִּילֵנוּ נָא The adverb אַךְ (only) precedes the Hiphil Imperative 2ms of נָצַל with a 1cp pronominal suffix. The הַ prefix and Hireq Yod stem vowel identify the verb as a Hiphil Imperative. The root is identified by the Daghesh Forte in the צ which represents the assimilated נ that is the first root consonant (27.10-11). The word נָא is the particle of entreaty (only *please* deliver us).

1 Samuel 15:10-24

To Obey Is Better Than Sacrifice

10 וַיְהִי דְּבַר־יְהוָה אֶל־שְׁמוּאֵל לֵאמֹר 11 נִחַמְתִּי כִּי־הִמְלַכְתִּי
אֶת־שָׁאוּל לְמֶלֶךְ כִּי־שָׁב מֵאַחֲרַי וְאֶת־דְּבָרַי לֹא הֵקִים וַיִּחַר
לִשְׁמוּאֵל וַיִּזְעַק אֶל־יְהוָה כָּל־הַלָּיְלָה 12 וַיַּשְׁכֵּם שְׁמוּאֵל לִקְרַאת
שָׁאוּל בַּבֹּקֶר וַיֻּגַּד לִשְׁמוּאֵל לֵאמֹר בָּא־שָׁאוּל הַכַּרְמֶלָה[1] וְהִנֵּה
מַצִּיב לוֹ יָד וַיִּסֹּב וַיַּעֲבֹר וַיֵּרֶד הַגִּלְגָּל[2] 13 וַיָּבֹא שְׁמוּאֵל
אֶל־שָׁאוּל וַיֹּאמֶר לוֹ שָׁאוּל בָּרוּךְ אַתָּה לַיהוָה הֲקִימֹתִי אֶת־דְּבַר
יְהוָה 14 וַיֹּאמֶר שְׁמוּאֵל וּמֶה קוֹל־הַצֹּאן הַזֶּה בְּאָזְנָי וְקוֹל הַבָּקָר
אֲשֶׁר אָנֹכִי שֹׁמֵעַ 15 וַיֹּאמֶר שָׁאוּל מֵעֲמָלֵקִי[3] הֱבִיאוּם אֲשֶׁר
חָמַל[4] הָעָם עַל־מֵיטַב[5] הַצֹּאן וְהַבָּקָר לְמַעַן זְבֹחַ לַיהוָה אֱלֹהֶיךָ

---

1. כַּרְמֶל Carmel (7).
2. גִּלְגָּל Gilgal (40).
3. עֲמָלֵקִי Amalekite (12).
4. חָמַל (Q) to have compassion (for), have pity (on), spare (41).
5. מֵיטָב best (part of something) (6).

וְאֶת־הַיּוֹתֵר[6] הֶחֱרַמְנוּ 16 וַיֹּאמֶר שְׁמוּאֵל אֶל־שָׁאוּל הֶרֶף[7]
וְאַגִּידָה לְּךָ אֵת אֲשֶׁר דִּבֶּר יְהוָה אֵלַי הַלָּיְלָה ויאמרו [וַיֹּאמֶר] לוֹ
דַּבֵּר 17 וַיֹּאמֶר שְׁמוּאֵל הֲלוֹא אִם־קָטֹן אַתָּה בְּעֵינֶיךָ רֹאשׁ
שִׁבְטֵי יִשְׂרָאֵל אָתָּה וַיִּמְשָׁחֲךָ יְהוָה לְמֶלֶךְ עַל־יִשְׂרָאֵל
18 וַיִּשְׁלָחֲךָ יְהוָה בְּדָרֶךְ וַיֹּאמֶר לֵךְ וְהַחֲרַמְתָּה אֶת־הַחַטָּאִים[8]
אֶת־עֲמָלֵק[9] וְנִלְחַמְתָּ בוֹ עַד כַּלּוֹתָם אֹתָם 19 וְלָמָּה לֹא־שָׁמַעְתָּ
בְּקוֹל יְהוָה וַתַּעַט[10] אֶל־הַשָּׁלָל וַתַּעַשׂ הָרַע בְּעֵינֵי יְהוָה
20 וַיֹּאמֶר שָׁאוּל אֶל־שְׁמוּאֵל אֲשֶׁר שָׁמַעְתִּי בְּקוֹל יְהוָה וָאֵלֵךְ
בַּדֶּרֶךְ אֲשֶׁר־שְׁלָחַנִי יְהוָה וָאָבִיא אֶת־אֲגַג[11] מֶלֶךְ עֲמָלֵק
וְאֶת־עֲמָלֵק הֶחֱרַמְתִּי 21 וַיִּקַּח הָעָם מֵהַשָּׁלָל צֹאן וּבָקָר רֵאשִׁית

---

6. יוֹתֵר the rest, surplus, profit, advantage (9).
7. רָפָה (Q) to sink, drop, relax, grow slack; (Hi) abandon, forsake, desert, leave (someone) alone (46).
8. חַטָּא (adj) sinful; (n) sinner; (mp) חַטָּאִים (19).
9. עֲמָלֵק Amalek (39).
10. עִיט (Q) to swoop, pounce, hurl insults (with shrieks) (2).
11. אֲגַג Agag (8).

הַחֵרֶם[12] לִזְבֹּחַ לַיהוָה אֱלֹהֶיךָ בַּגִּלְגָּל 22 וַיֹּאמֶר שְׁמוּאֵל הַחֵפֶץ[13]
לַיהוָה בְּעֹלוֹת וּזְבָחִים כִּשְׁמֹעַ בְּקוֹל יְהוָה הִנֵּה שְׁמֹעַ מִזֶּבַח טוֹב
לְהַקְשִׁיב[14] מֵחֵלֶב אֵילִים 23 כִּי חַטַּאת־קֶסֶם[15] מֶרִי[16] וְאָוֶן
וּתְרָפִים[17] הַפְצַר[18] יַעַן מָאַסְתָּ אֶת־דְּבַר יְהוָה וַיִּמְאָסְךָ מִמֶּלֶךְ
24 וַיֹּאמֶר שָׁאוּל אֶל־שְׁמוּאֵל חָטָאתִי כִּי־עָבַרְתִּי אֶת־פִּי־יְהוָה
וְאֶת־דְּבָרֶיךָ כִּי יָרֵאתִי אֶת־הָעָם וָאֶשְׁמַע בְּקוֹלָם

12. חֵ֫רֶם something set apart for destruction, something banned, devoted thing (29).
13. חֵ֫פֶץ delight, desire, pleasure, joy (38).
14. קָשַׁב (Hi) give (pay) attention, listen carefully or attentively (46).
15. קֶ֫סֶם divination, prediction (11).
16. מְרִי rebellion (23).
17. תְּרָפִים images, statues, idols (15).
18. פָּצַר (Q) to urge (someone), coerce, push, press (7).

Parse the following verbs from 1 Samuel 15:10-24.

1 Samuel 15:10

וַיְהִי ______________________________

לֵאמֹר ______________________________

1 Samuel 15:11

נִחַמְתִּי ______________________________

הִמְלַכְתִּי ______________________________

שָׁב ______________________________

הֵקִים ______________________________

וַיִּחַר ______________________________

וַיִּזְעַק ______________________________

1 Samuel 15:12

וַיַּשְׁכֵּם ______________________________

לִקְרַאת ______________________________

וַיֻּגַּד ______________________________

בָּא ______________________________

מַצִּיב ______________________________

וַיִּסֹּב ______________________________

וַיַּעֲבֹר ______________________________

וַיֵּרֶד ______________________________

1 Samuel 15:13

וַיָּבֹא ______________________________

בָּרוּךְ ______________________________

הֲקִימֹתִי

1 Samuel 15:14

שְׁמַע

1 Samuel 15:15

הֱבִיאוּם

חָמַל

זְבֹחַ

הֶחֱרַמְנוּ

1 Samuel 15:16

הֶרֶף

וְאַגִּידָה

דִּבֶּר

דַּבֵּר

1 Samuel 15:17

וַיִּמְשָׁחֲךָ

1 Samuel 15:18

וַיִּשְׁלָחֲךָ

לֵךְ

וְהַחֲרַמְתָּה

וְנִלְחַמְתָּ

כַּלּוֹתָם

1 Samuel 15:19

שָׁמַעְתָּ

וַתַּעַט ______________________________

וַתַּעַשׂ ______________________________

1 Samuel 15:20

שָׁמַעְתִּי ______________________________

וָאֵלֵךְ ______________________________

שְׁלָחַנִי ______________________________

וָאָבִיא ______________________________

הֶחֱרַמְתִּי ______________________________

1 Samuel 15:21

וַיִּקַּח ______________________________

לִזְבֹּחַ ______________________________

1 Samuel 15:22

כִּשְׁמֹעַ ______________________________

שְׁמֹעַ ______________________________

לְהַקְשִׁיב ______________________________

1 Samuel 15:23

הַפְצַר ______________________________

מָאַסְתָּ ______________________________

וַיִּמְאָסְךָ ______________________________

1 Samuel 15:24

חָטָאתִי ______________________________

עָבַרְתִּי ______________________________

יָרֵאתִי ______________________________

וָאֶשְׁמַע ______________________________

Grammatical Commentary: 1 Samuel 15:10-24

1 Samuel 15:10

וַיְהִי דְּבַר־יְהוָה This Qal Imperfect 3ms of הָיָה with Waw Consecutive is followed by a definite construct chain functioning as the subject of the verb, "the word of Yahweh was" or "the word of Yahweh came."

לֵאמֹר The Qal Infinitive Construct of אָמַר is used to mark the beginning of quoted speech or direct discourse. Oftentimes, this construction is best translated by an English comma and quotation marks.

1 Samuel 15:11

נִחַמְתִּי The sufformative תִּי identifies this form as Perfect 1cs. The Hireq under the first root consonant is diagnostic of the Piel stem, "I regret" or "I am sorry." The guttural ח in second root position has rejected the Daghesh Forte of the Piel stem and exhibits virtual doubling (31.7-8).

כִּי־הִמְלַכְתִּי The conjunction כִּי is joined by Maqqef to the Hiphil Perfect 1cs of מָלַךְ. The הִ prefix and Pathach stem vowel identify the verbal stem as Hiphil. The Hiphil of מָלַךְ means "to make someone king" or "to install someone as king" and it is often followed by לְמֶלֶךְ as it is here. The proper name שָׁאוּל is the direct object (that I made Saul king).

כִּי־שָׁב מֵאַחֲרַי The verb שָׁב may be either the Qal Perfect 3ms or Qal Participle ms of the Biconsonantal שׁוּב (14.12; 22.4.5). The context requires that it be identified as a Perfect. The construction מֵאַחֲרַי is the preposition מִן (מֵ) prefixed to the preposition אַחַר followed by a 1cs pronominal suffix (literally, "because he has turned from after me;" idiomatically, "because he has turned from following me."

וְאֶת־דְּבָרַי The construction דְּבָרַי (דְּבָרִים with 1cs pronominal suffix) is marked as the direct object of the verb הֵקִים that follows (and my words).

לֹא הֵקִים The הֵ prefix and the Hireq Yod stem vowel identify this form as Hiphil Perfect 3ms of the Biconsonantal root קוּם. In the Hiphil Perfect of קוּם, the third person forms (singular and plural) have the הֵ prefix. Second and first person forms have הֲ (27.14). Every form of the paradigm has the Hireq Yod stem vowel (he has not carried out).

וַיִּחַר לִשְׁמוּאֵל With the Waw Consecutive, the Qal Imperfect 3ms of חָרָה is spelled with the short form of the verb (יֶחֱרֶה is spelled יִחַר with the Waw Consecutive). The verb חָרָה can mark the subject of its verbal action with the preposition לְ (and Samuel became angry).

1 Samuel 15:12

וַיַּשְׁכֵּם שְׁמוּאֵל In the absence of a sufformative, the Waw Consecutive and the Imperfect preformative identify this verb as Imperfect 3ms. The Pathach preformative vowel and Tsere stem vowel are diagnostic of the Hiphil stem. When prefixed with the Waw Consecutive, Hiphil Imperfect verbs with Hireq Yod stem vowels (יַשְׁכִּים) normally change to Tsere (וַיַּשְׁכֵּם). The proper name שְׁמוּאֵל is functioning as the subject of the verb (and Samuel rose early).

לִקְרַאת This is the preposition לְ prefixed to the Qal Infinitive Construct of קָרָא translated, "to meet" (20.2, footnote 2).

וַיֻּגַּד לִשְׁמוּאֵל In the absence of a sufformative, the Waw Consecutive and Imperfect preformative identify this verb as Imperfect 3ms. The Qibbuts preformative vowel and Pathach stem vowel identify the verb as a Hophal. The key to identifying the verbal root is the Daghesh Forte in the ג (the second root consonant). This is the assimilated נ which is the first consonant of the verbal root (29.6-7). Followed by לִשְׁמוּאֵל, this Hophal Imperfect translates as "and it was told to Samuel."

בָּא־שָׁאוּל Like שָׁב in verse 11, בָּא may be either Qal Perfect 3ms or Qal Participle ms of בּוֹא. In this context, בָּא is the Qal Perfect.

הַכַּרְמֶלָה This is the proper name כַּרְמֶל with the definite article and the directional ending (to Carmel).

מַצִּיב לוֹ The מַ prefix and Hireq Yod stem vowel identify this verb as a Hiphil Participle (ms). The verbal root is נָצַב. The first root consonant (נ) has assimilated into the second root consonant (צ) and is represented by a Daghesh Forte (he set up for himself).

יָד In this context, the noun יָד should be translated as "monument" (*HALOT* 1:388).

וַיִּסֹּב Again, in the absence of a sufformative, the Waw Consecutive and Imperfect preformative identify this verb as Imperfect 3ms. The Hireq preformative vowel and Holem stem vowel are diagnostic of the Qal stem. With this form, the verbal root is difficult to identify.

It is the Geminate verb סָבַב (and he turned). In terms of inflection, this verb follows the alternate (Type 2) Geminate pattern (16.12-13).

וַיֵּרֶד הַגִּלְגָּל The Waw Consecutive and Imperfect preformative identify this verb as Imperfect 3ms. The Tsere preformative vowel is diagnostic of the Qal stem and the I-י class of weak verbs (יָרַד). The proper name גִּלְגָּל appears with the definite article (and he went down to Gilgal).

1 Samuel 15:13

וַיָּבֹא שְׁמוּאֵל The prefixing of Waw Consecutive to the Qal Imperfect 3ms of the Biconsonantal verb בּוֹא (יָבוֹא) normally occasions the reduction of the stem vowel from Holem Waw to Holem as in this form (and Samuel came).

בָּרוּךְ אַתָּה לַיהוָה The vowel pattern of בָּרוּךְ (Qamets-Shureq) is the diagnostic spelling of a Qal passive Participle (22.7-8). This form is masculine singular. Followed by the 2ms personal pronoun and the divine name with the preposition לְ, this construction is translated as "blessed are you by Yahweh."

הֲקִימֹתִי הֵקִים in verse 11 is the Hiphil Perfect 3ms of קוּם. In the Hiphil Perfect paradigm of קוּם, third person forms have the הֵ prefix and Hireq Yod stem vowel (27.14-15). The second and first person forms of this paradigm have the ה prefix but with Hateph Pathach (הֲ) and the Hireq Yod stem vowel. Also distinctive of the third and second person forms of this weak verb class is the Holem or Holem Waw connecting vowel as in this form הֲקִימֹתִי (I have performed).

1 Samuel 15:14

וּמֶה Here, the conjunction וּ is prefixed to the interrogative pronoun מָה (8.9).

קוֹל־הַצֹּאן הַזֶּה This is the construct chain קוֹל־הַצֹּאן with the demonstrative adjective זֶה. The construct noun קוֹל should be translated as "sound." With the interrogative pronoun, this construction is translated as "What is this sound of the flocks?" The NIV renders the interrogative clause, "what then is this bleating of sheep…?"

בְּאָזְנָי This form is the dual of the noun אֹזֶן prefixed with the preposition בְּ and the 1cs pronominal suffix with pausal spelling (in my ears). In *BHS*, this form appears with Athnach under the נ (בְּאָזְנָֽי).

וְקוֹל הַבָּקָר The RSV renders this construct chain, "and the lowing of the oxen." Literally, it is translated as "and the sound of the cattle..."

אֲשֶׁר אָנֹכִי שֹׁמֵעַ This relative clause consists of the relative pronoun אֲשֶׁר followed by the 1cs personal pronoun and the Qal active Participle ms of שָׁמַע with the diagnostic Holem following the first root consonant (22.4.2). The clause is translated, "which I hear" or "which I am hearing."

1 Samuel 15:15

מֵעֲמָלֵקִי Here, the preposition מִן is prefixed to the gentilic form of עֲמָלֵק. Both the name of the ancestor (עֲמָלֵק) and its gentilic form may stand for the people (from the Amalekites).

הֱבִיאוּם The ה prefix and Hireq Yod stem vowel identify this form as a Hiphil Perfect. The Shureq sufformative marks it as 3cp and the form also has a 3mp pronominal suffix. A Tsere is expected with the ה prefix, but the addition of the suffix has occasioned the reduction of the vowel to Hateph Seghol (27.14). The verbal root is בּוֹא (they have brought them).

אֲשֶׁר חָמַל הָעָם The relative pronoun אֲשֶׁר may be used as a conjunction to express the reason for something and so may be translated as "for" or "because" (*because* the people spared).

עַל־מֵיטַב הַצֹּאן וְהַבָּקָר The preposition עַל is joined by Maqqef to the construct form of the rare noun מֵיטָב and followed by two definite absolute nouns. This entire prepositional phrase is the object of the verb חָמַל. The verb חָמַל can mark its object with the preposition עַל. In this context, the preposition is not translated ([because the people spared] the best of the sheep and the cattle).

לְמַעַן זְבֹחַ The word מַעַן always appears with the preposition לְ and may be used as either a conjunction or preposition. With the Qal Infinitive Construct (זְבֹחַ), the construction לְמַעַן is used as a conjunction and translated, "in order to" (in order to sacrifice).

הֶחֱרַמְנוּ The ה prefix is diagnostic of the Hiphil stem and the נוּ sufformative is Perfect 1cp. The spelling of this form is as expected for the I-Guttural class of weak verbs (27.2-3). The הֶ prefix with Pathach stem vowel is present in all second and first person forms, singular and plural. With its direct object immediately preceding, the verb is translated as "and what was left (over) we completely destroyed."

1 Samuel 15:16

הֶרֶף Difficult to identify, הֶרֶף is a short Hiphil Imperative ms of רָפָה. The form has been shortened from הַרְפֵּה (stop!). In fact, in the Hiphil Imperative ms of III-ה verbal roots (without a pronominal suffix), short forms (24 times) are more common than long forms (15 times).

וְאַגִּידָה לְּךָ The preformative א with Pathach and the Hireq Yod stem vowel identify this verb as Hiphil Imperfect 1cs with the conjunction וְ and Paragogic ה. The verbal root is נָגַד with the assimilation of the first root consonant (נ) into the second root consonant (ג). This verb is followed by לְּךָ with a conjunctive Daghesh in the ג (32.11). When an Imperfect verb follows and Imperative verb, the Imperfect verb may be prefixed with the conjunction וְ (not Waw Consecutive) and translated "so that" (23.7.4), "Stop, *so that* I can tell you."

אֵת אֲשֶׁר דִּבֶּר יְהוָה The relative clause beginning with אֲשֶׁר (what Yahweh has said) is the direct object of the verb וְאַגִּידָה. It is marked by the definite direct object marker אֵת.

הַלָּיְלָה In this context, the definite article on לַ֫יְלָה imparts greater specificity (this night, tonight). Note the pausal spelling of לָ֫יְלָה. In *BHS*, this form appears with Athnach under the ל (הַלָּ֑יְלָה).

דַּבֵּר The Pathach beneath the first root consonant and the Daghesh Forte in the second root consonant definitively identify this verb as the Piel Imperative 2ms of דָּבַר (speak!).

1 Samuel 15:17

הֲלוֹא The interrogative particle הֲ is prefixed to the negative particle לֹא with the full or *plene* writing of the vowel (Holem Waw for Holem).

אִם־קָטֹן אַתָּה בְּעֵינֶיךָ The particle אִם is translated as "even though" in this context (*HALOT* 1:61). With the 2ms personal pronoun following, קָטֹן must be identified as the adjective and not the stative verb (even though you are small in your own eyes).

רֹאשׁ שִׁבְטֵי יִשְׂרָאֵל אָתָּה This verbless clause begins with a construct chain composed of two construct nouns (רֹאשׁ and שִׁבְטֵי) and one absolute noun (יִשְׂרָאֵל) functioning as the predicate. The subject is the 2ms personal pronoun אָתָּה (note the pausal spelling of אָתָּה with Athnach under the ת in *BHS*). In this context, this verbless clause is translated, "Are you not the head of the tribes of Israel?" The interrogative and negative nuances in this translation are picked up from the form הֲלוֹא toward the beginning of the verse.

וַיִּמְשָׁחֲךָ In the absence of a sufformative, the Waw Consecutive and the preformative identify this form as Imperfect 3ms. It has a 2ms pronominal suffix. The Hireq preformative vowel is diagnostic of the Qal stem. Note the Qamets beneath the שׁ. If the verb has a Pathach stem vowel, the Pathach is not reduced but lengthened to Qamets before the 2ms pronominal suffix (19.7.2). With יְהוָה as subject, the verb is translated as "Yahweh anointed you."

1 Samuel 15:18

וַיִּשְׁלָחֲךָ With the addition of the 2ms pronominal suffix on this Qal Imperfect 3ms of שָׁלַח, the Pathach stem vowel (expected because the verb is III-ח) is lengthened to Qamets (19.7.2).

בְּדָרֶךְ In this context, the noun דֶּרֶךְ has the nuance of an undertaking of particular significance ([Yahweh sent you] on a mission).

לֵךְ This Qal Imperative ms of הָלַךְ inflects like a I-י (Type 1) verb. An alternate spelling of this form is לְכָה with Paragogic ה (18.5-6).

וְהַחֲרַמְתָּה The ה prefix and the תָּה sufformative identify this form as Hiphil Perfect 2ms (תָּה is an alternate spelling of the 2ms sufformative תָּ that appears 152 times in the Hebrew Bible). The verb is prefixed with Waw Consecutive. Most often, I-Guttural Hiphil Perfects have Seghol under the ה prefix and Hateph Seghol under the guttural in first root position. The verb חָרַם exhibits the Seghol-Hateph Seghol pattern but also the pattern of Pathach under the ה prefix and Hateph Pathach under the guttural as it is here. This sequence of Imperative and converted Perfect translates, "go and destroy…"

אֶת־הַחַטָּאִים This is the direct object of the Hiphil Perfect verb that precedes. This form is the mp of the noun חַטָּא (the sinners).

וְנִלְחַמְתָּ בוֹ The נ prefix and Pathach stem vowel identify this verb as a Niphal Perfect. The sufformative is 2ms. Note that the preposition בְּ marks its direct object. The antecedent of the 3ms pronominal suffix on the preposition is עֲמָלֵק but context allows for the translation, "and fight against *them*." The Perfect with Waw Consecutive carries the full force of the Imperative as did the Hiphil of חָרַם (17.6.3).

עַד כַּלּוֹתָם With the removal of the 3mp pronominal suffix on כַּלּוֹת, the form is easily identified as a Piel Infinitive Construct of כָּלָה (31.4). The Pathach beneath the first root consonant and Daghesh Forte in the second root consonant are the diagnostic points of spelling. The וֹת ending is characteristic of all III-ה Infinitive Constructs in the Qal and derived stems. The 3mp pronominal suffix is functioning as the subject of the verbal action. Translating the preposition עַד with its temporal value, the construction is translated as "until they are consumed."

1 Samuel 15:19

וַתַּעַט אֶל־הַשָּׁלָל In the absence of a sufformative, the Waw Consecutive and Imperfect preformative identify this verb as Qal Imperfect 3fs or 2ms. Context, especially the 2ms Perfect verb שָׁמַעְתָּ, identify וַתַּעַט as 2ms and not 3fs. The verbal root is the Biconsonantal עִיט (you swooped down upon the plunder).

וַתַּעַשׂ הָרַע Like וַתַּעַט above, this is the Qal Imperfect 2ms of עָשָׂה with Waw Consecutive. With III-ה verbs, the Waw Consecutive is normally prefixed to the short form (תַּעַשׂ) and not the regular or long form (תַּעֲשֶׂה). The a-type vowel pattern is occasioned by the verb's weakness as I-Guttural (16.2). An abstract noun (evil or what is evil) is created by prefixing the definite article to the ms Geminate adjective רַע (you did evil).

1 Samuel 15:20

אֲשֶׁר Though rare by comparison with other uses, אֲשֶׁר may introduce direct speech. In such cases, אֲשֶׁר does not need to be translated. (And Saul said to Samuel, "I have obeyed Yahweh.")

וָאֵלֵךְ בַּדֶּרֶךְ The Waw Consecutive and the א preformative identify this form as Imperfect 1cs. The Tsere preformative vowel and the Tsere stem vowel are diagnostic of the Qal Imperfect I-י (Type 1) weak verb class. In this case, the root is the common verb הָלַךְ, which inflects just like the I-י verb (I have gone on the mission).

שְׁלָחַנִי Note that the spelling of this Qal Perfect 3ms has changed from שָׁלַח to שְׁלָח with the addition of the 1cs pronominal suffix. With the accent on the penultima (שְׁלָחַ֫נִי), the change in the first syllable is the result of propretonic reduction; the pretonic syllable has been lengthened from Pathach to Qamets (19.3.1). The clause אֲשֶׁר־שְׁלָחַנִי יְהוָה may be translated, "on which Yahweh sent me."

וָאָבִיא Although the Qamets preformative vowel on this Hiphil Imperfect 1cs of בּוֹא also appears in the Qal stem, Hireq Yod stem vowel identifies the form as Hiphil. The stem vowel in the Qal would be Holem Waw. The verb is prefixed with the Waw Consecutive (I have brought).

אֶת־אֲגַג מֶלֶךְ עֲמָלֵק This definite direct object of the preceding verb is composed of the proper name אֲגַג followed by the appositional construct chain מֶלֶךְ עֲמָלֵק (Agag, king of the Amalekites).

הֶחֱרַמְתִּי Two other Hiphil Perfects of חָרַם have appeared in this reading (הֶחֱרַמְנוּ in verse 15 and וְהַחֲרַמְתָּה in verse 18). This is the Hiphil Perfect 1cs of חָרַם. With these three forms, note the vowel pattern variation between Seghol or Pathach under the ה prefix and the corresponding Hateph Seghol or Hateph Pathach beneath the guttural in first root position. With its direct object (וְאֶת־עֲמָלֵק) in initial position, the clause translates, "I have completely destroyed the Amalekites."

1 Samuel 15:21

מֵהַשָּׁלָל This form is composed of the preposition מִן, the definite article, and the noun שָׁלָל. Translate the preposition מִן with its partitive (6.6.3) nuance (*some* of the plunder).

רֵאשִׁית הַחֵרֶם This is a definite construct chain consisting of the construct noun רֵאשִׁית and the absolute noun הַחֵרֶם (the best of what was devoted to the ban).

לִזְבֹּחַ With the prefixed preposition לְ (spelled with Hireq according to the Rule of Shewa [4.11.1]) and the Shewa-Holem vowel pattern, the Qal Infinitive Construct is easy to identify. When prefixed with the preposition לְ, the Infinitive Construct often denotes purpose or intention (20.12.1). This Qal Infinitive Construct of זָבַח with the preposition לְ translates as "[in order] to sacrifice."

1 Samuel 15:22

הַחֵפֶץ This is the noun חֵפֶץ (joy, pleasure, delight) with the interrogative particle (8.10). When prefixed to a guttural consonant, the interrogative is spelled הַ (with Pathach). Though the particle on this noun could be confused with the definite article, context requires that it be identified as the interrogative.

בְּעֹלוֹת Here, the preposition בְּ is prefixed to the plural of עֹלָה, "in burnt offerings" or "with burnt offerings."

וּזְבָחִים The conjunction וְ is prefixed to the mp of זֶבַח (sacrifice). Given that זְבָחִים (like preceding עֹלוֹת) is functioning as an object, it would be expected that the governing preposition בְּ on עֹלוֹת would be repeated on זְבָחִים. Normally, the preposition appears on both nouns in this type of construction. It is not uncommon, however, for the governing preposition not to be repeated on the second noun (and [with] sacrifices).

כִּשְׁמֹעַ בְּקוֹל יְהוָה This is the preposition כְּ prefixed to the Qal Infinitive Construct of שָׁמַע. The verb שָׁמַע followed by בְּקוֹל (the noun קוֹל with preposition בְּ) should be translated as "to obey" or "to obey the voice of." This whole construction is translated as "as in obeying the voice of Yahweh."

הַחֵפֶץ ... יְהוָה Literally, this interrogative construction translates, "is there to Yahweh delight in burnt offerings and [in] sacrifices as [in] obeying the voice of Yahweh." Idiomatically, it may be translated, "does Yahweh take as much delight in burnt offerings and sacrifices as he does in obeying the voice of Yahweh?"

שְׁמֹעַ מִזֶּבַח טוֹב The Qal Infinitive Construct of שָׁמַע is being used as a verbal noun (see Joüon-Muraoka, 124a-b; 124m-n for comment on the use of the Infinitive Construct as the subject of a nominal clause). The preposition מִן on זֶ֫בַח and the adjective טוֹב are being used to denote the quality of comparison between the Infinitive שְׁמֹעַ and the noun זֶ֫בַח to which the preposition has been prefixed (to obey *is better than* sacrifice).

לְהַקְשִׁיב מֵחֵלֶב אֵילִים The comparative use of מִן in the preceding clause is carried forward to this construction (and to give heed *is better than* the fat of rams). הַקְשִׁיב is easily identified as the Hiphil Infinitive Construct of קָשַׁב (הַ prefix and Hireq Yod stem vowel) with the preposition לְ. The preposition מִן is prefixed to the construct noun חֵ֫לֶב. The absolute noun in this construct chain is the plural of אַ֫יִל.

1 Samuel 15:23

חַטַּאת־קֶסֶם מֶרִי The construct chain חַטַּאת־קֶסֶם (sin of divination) and the ms noun מְרִי (rebellion) form a verbless clause (rebellion *is* [as] the sin of divination).

וְאָוֶן וּתְרָפִים הַפְצַר The nouns אָוֶן (iniquity) and תְּרָפִים (idolatry) form a verbless clause with הַפְצַר. The form הַפְצַר is the Hiphil Infinitive Absolute of the rare verb פָּצַר (to urge, coerce). The construction may be translated, "and arrogance is as iniquity and idolatry."

יַעַן מָאַסְתָּ אֶת־דְּבַר יְהוָה The particle יַ֫עַן is frequently used as a causal conjunction (because). Followed by the Qal Perfect 2ms of מָאַס and its direct object (אֶת־דְּבַר יְהוָה), the clause is translated as "because you have rejected the word of Yahweh."

וַיִּמְאָסְךָ מִמֶּלֶךְ In this Qal Imperfect 3ms of מָאַס with Waw Consecutive, note that the original Pathach stem vowel of the II-Guttural verb has lengthened to Qamets before the 2ms pronominal suffix (19.7.2). The final clause of this verse translates as "[and] he has rejected you from [being] king."

This second half of verse 23 clearly illustrates the expression of logical succession in the use of Waw Consecutive on the Imperfect. Primarily, of course, the Imperfect with Waw Consecutive is used to describe actions or situations that are temporally related, that is, in terms of chronological succession, but the nature of the succession may also be logical (because you have rejected the word of Yahweh, he has rejected you as king).

1 Samuel 15:24

חָטָאתִי This form is easily identified as the Qal Perfect 1cs of חָטָא. Note the lengthening of the stem vowel from Pathach to Qamets and the elimination of the expected Daghesh Lene in the sufformative consonant because of the quiescent א (14.4-5).

אֶת־פִּי־יְהוָה As the direct object of עָבַרְתִּי which precedes immediately, this construct chain is composed of פִּי (the construct form of פֶּה) and the divine name. In construct with יְהוָה, the noun פֶּה is often translated as "command." With כִּי־עָבַרְתִּי, the entire construction may be rendered, "for I have transgressed the command of Yahweh."

כִּי יָרֵאתִי אֶת־הָעָם The conjunction כִּי precedes the Qal Perfect 1cs of יָרֵא which is both stative and III-א (14.18). The Tsere stem vowel is explained by its status as a stative verb. The absence of the Daghesh Lene in the ת of the Perfect sufformative is the result of the quiescent א in third root position (because I feared the people).

וָאֶשְׁמַע בְּקוֹלָם This is the same construction as in verse 22 with the verb שָׁמַע. Here, the Qal Imperfect 1cs of שָׁמַע with Waw Consecutive is followed by the noun קוֹל with the preposition בְּ and a 3mp pronominal suffix (I obeyed their voice).

2 Samuel 7:1-9

David's Desire to Build the Temple

1 וַיְהִי כִּי־יָשַׁב הַמֶּלֶךְ בְּבֵיתוֹ וַיהוָה הֵנִיחַ־לוֹ מִסָּבִיב מִכָּל־אֹיְבָיו

2 וַיֹּאמֶר הַמֶּלֶךְ אֶל־נָתָן[1] הַנָּבִיא רְאֵה נָא אָנֹכִי יוֹשֵׁב בְּבֵית

אֲרָזִים וַאֲרוֹן הָאֱלֹהִים יֹשֵׁב בְּתוֹךְ הַיְרִיעָה 3 וַיֹּאמֶר נָתָן

אֶל־הַמֶּלֶךְ כֹּל אֲשֶׁר בִּלְבָבְךָ לֵךְ עֲשֵׂה כִּי יְהוָה עִמָּךְ 4 וַיְהִי

בַּלַּיְלָה הַהוּא וַיְהִי דְּבַר־יְהוָה אֶל־נָתָן לֵאמֹר 5 לֵךְ וְאָמַרְתָּ

אֶל־עַבְדִּי אֶל־דָּוִד כֹּה אָמַר יְהוָה הַאַתָּה תִּבְנֶה־לִּי בַיִת לְשִׁבְתִּי

6 כִּי לֹא יָשַׁבְתִּי בְּבַיִת לְמִיּוֹם הַעֲלֹתִי אֶת־בְּנֵי יִשְׂרָאֵל מִמִּצְרַיִם

וְעַד הַיּוֹם הַזֶּה וָאֶהְיֶה מִתְהַלֵּךְ בְּאֹהֶל וּבְמִשְׁכָּן 7 בְּכֹל

אֲשֶׁר־הִתְהַלַּכְתִּי בְּכָל־בְּנֵי יִשְׂרָאֵל הֲדָבָר דִּבַּרְתִּי אֶת־אַחַד

שִׁבְטֵי יִשְׂרָאֵל אֲשֶׁר צִוִּיתִי לִרְעוֹת אֶת־עַמִּי אֶת־יִשְׂרָאֵל לֵאמֹר

---

1. נָתָן Nathan (42).

לָמָּה לֹא־בְנִיתֶם לִי בֵּית אֲרָזִים 8 וְעַתָּה כֹּה־תֹאמַר לְעַבְדִּי לְדָוִד

כֹּה אָמַר יְהוָה צְבָאוֹת אֲנִי לְקַחְתִּיךָ מִן־הַנָּוֶה[2] מֵאַחַר הַצֹּאן

לִהְיוֹת נָגִיד[3] עַל־עַמִּי עַל־יִשְׂרָאֵל 9 וָאֶהְיֶה עִמְּךָ בְּכֹל אֲשֶׁר

הָלַכְתָּ וָאַכְרִתָה אֶת־כָּל־אֹיְבֶיךָ מִפָּנֶיךָ וְעָשִׂתִי לְךָ שֵׁם גָּדוֹל

כְּשֵׁם הַגְּדֹלִים אֲשֶׁר בָּאָרֶץ

Parse the following verbs from 2 Samuel 7:1-9.

2 Samuel 7:1

יָשַׁב ______________________________

הֵנִיחַ ______________________________

אֹיְבָיו ______________________________

2 Samuel 7:2

רְאֵה ______________________________

יוֹשֵׁב ______________________________

יֹשֵׁב ______________________________

2 Samuel 7:3

לֵךְ ______________________________

---

2. נָוֶה (ms) pasture, dwelling (32).
3. נָגִיד leader, ruler, prince (44).

עֲשֵׂה ______________________________

2 Samuel 7:5

לֵךְ ______________________________

וְאָמַרְתָּ ______________________________

אָמַר ______________________________

תִּבְנֶה ______________________________

לְשִׁבְתִּי ______________________________

2 Samuel 7:6

יָשַׁבְתִּי ______________________________

הַעֲלֹתִי ______________________________

וָאֶהְיֶה ______________________________

מִתְהַלֵּךְ ______________________________

2 Samuel 7:7

הִתְהַלַּכְתִּי ______________________________

דִּבַּרְתִּי ______________________________

צִוִּיתִי ______________________________

לִרְעוֹת ______________________________

בְנִיתֶם ______________________________

2 Samuel 7:8

תֹאמַר ______________________________

לְקַחְתִּיךָ ______________________________

לִהְיוֹת ______________________________

2 Samuel 7:9

הָלַכְתָּ ________________

וָאַכְרִתָה ________________

אֹיְבֶיךָ ________________

וְעָשִׂתִי ________________

Grammatical Commentary: 2 Samuel 7:1-9

2 Samuel 7:1

וַיְהִי כִּי־יָשַׁב הַמֶּלֶךְ The narrative is introduced with the temporal modifier וַיְהִי (Qal Imperfect 3ms of הָיָה with Waw Consecutive) followed by the conjunction כִּי which, in this context, should be translated with its temporal usage (when the king dwelt).

בְּבֵיתוֹ This is the noun בַּיִת with preposition בְּ and 3ms pronominal suffix (in his house).

וַיהוָה הֵנִיחַ־לוֹ The stem of the verb הֵנִיחַ is identified by the הֵ prefix and Hireq Yod stem vowel, a spelling pattern that distinguishes (in the absence of a sufformative) the 3ms Perfect of a Hiphil Biconsonantal (27.14; 27.15.2). The verbal root is נוּחַ. This verb is preceded by its subject and followed by its indirect object (and Yahweh had given [to] him rest).

מִסָּבִיב In this form, the preposition מִן is prefixed to סָבִיב ("from all sides" or "all around").

מִכָּל־אֹיְבָיו This is the preposition מִן prefixed to כֹּל and joined by Maqqef to the Qal active Participle mp of אֹיֵב with a 3ms (Type 2) pronominal suffix. The Participle is used substantively (from all his enemies).

2 Samuel 7:2

רְאֵה נָא The ה ֵ ending is distinctive of the Imperative 2ms of III-ה verbs in the Qal and derived stems. רְאֵה is the Qal Imperative 2ms of רָאָה (18.5). Though the particle נָא may mark any of the volitional conjugations (18.10), it follows an Imperative verb approximately 200 times in the Hebrew Bible. It may be preferable, in many instances, not to translate this particle.

אָנֹכִי יוֹשֵׁב The 1cs personal pronoun precedes the Qal active Participle ms of יָשַׁב. The Participle is spelled with Holem Waw rather than the more common spelling with Holem as in יֹשֵׁב toward the end of the verse ("I dwell" or "I am dwelling").

בְּבֵית אֲרָזִים The preposition בְּ is prefixed to an indefinite construct chain which functions as the object of the preposition. The absolute noun in this construct chain is the mp form of אֶ֫רֶז. This noun designates a kind of tree and its wood, traditionally cedar, though its identification is uncertain (in a house of cedar).

וַאֲרוֹן הָאֱלֹהִים Here, a disjunctive Waw is prefixed to the construct noun אֲרוֹן (but the ark of God). In this usage, the Waw may be further categorized as contrastive (24.17.3; Arnold-Choi, 4.3.3).

יֹשֵׁב בְּתוֹךְ הַיְרִיעָה The Qal active Participle ms of יָשַׁב precedes a prepositional phrase with the definite noun יְרִיעָה ("dwells in the tent" or "is dwelling in the tent"). The Daghesh Forte of the definite article is normally given up in syllables beginning with יְ (5.5).

2 Samuel 7:3

כֹּל אֲשֶׁר בִּלְבָבְךָ Preceded by the noun כֹּל and the relative pronoun אֲשֶׁר, בִּלְבָבְךָ is composed of the noun לֵבָב prefixed with the preposition בְּ and a 2ms pronominal suffix (all that is in your heart).

לֵךְ עֲשֵׂה These are two contiguous Qal Imperative verbs: לֵךְ is from הָלַךְ and עֲשֵׂה is from עָשָׂה (18.6). Both forms are ms.

כִּי יְהוָה עִמָּךְ Translate the conjunction כִּי with its causal value as "*because* Yahweh is with you" or "*for* Yahweh is with you." Note the pausal spelling (36.3) of the 2ms pronominal suffix (ָךְ instead of ְךָ). In *BHS,* this form appears with Silluq under the מ (עִמָּֽךְ).

2 Samuel 7:4

וַיְהִי בַּלַּיְלָה הַהוּא At the beginning of this verse, וַיְהִי is functioning as a temporal modifier. It is followed by the definite noun לַ֫יְלָה prefixed with the preposition בְּ which, in turn, is followed by the demonstrative adjective הַהוּא. This construction translates as "and it came to pass in that night" or simply, "in that night."

וַיְהִי דְּבַר־יְהוָה אֶל־נָתָן Here, וַיְהִי is functioning as the verb of its clause and not as a temporal modifier (the word of Yahweh came [was] to Nathan).

לֵאמֹר This is the Qal Infinitive Construct of אָמַר prefixed with the preposition לְ. This form introduces direct quotations and is often reflected in English translation with punctuation (comma and quotation marks).

2 Samuel 7:5

לֵךְ וְאָמַרְתָּ Here, the Qal Imperative 2ms of הָלַךְ is followed by the Qal Perfect 2ms of אָמַר with Waw Consecutive. This is another example of the Imperative followed by a Perfect with Waw Consecutive, in which the Perfect carries the full force of the preceding Imperative (the two forms are related in terms of consecution of action). The construction translates, "go and say" (17.6.3; 23.6.3; Waltke-O'Connor, 32.2.2).

הַאַתָּה תִבְנֶה־לִּי בַיִת The form הַאַתָּה is the 2ms personal pronoun with the interrogative הֲ (spelled with Pathach because it is prefixed to a guttural consonant). The ה ֶ ending on תִבְנֶה signals an Imperfect in the III-ה class of weak verbs (Qal and derived stems). This spelling can only be that of the Qal stem. The verb is joined by Maqqef to the preposition לְ with 1cs suffix and conjunctive Daghesh in the לּ. The presence of אַתָּה highlights the subject of the verb, "will *you* build for me a house?"

לְשִׁבְתִּי This is a difficult form to identify. It is the Qal Infinitive Construct of יָשַׁב with the preposition לְ and a 1cs pronominal suffix. In the formation of the Infinitive Construct, both I-י (20.6) and I-נ (20.5) verbs may drop the first root consonant and add ת to the end of the form (יָשַׁב becomes שֶׁבֶת). With the addition of the pronominal suffix, the two Seghol vowels become Hireq in a closed syllable (for my dwelling).

2 Samuel 7:6

כִּי לֹא יָשַׁבְתִּי בְּבַיִת Following the interrogative clause in the preceding verse (beginning with הַאַתָּה), the conjunction כִּי introduces a subordinate clause of response and definition (for I have not dwelt in a house).

לְמִיּוֹם This is the noun יוֹם prefixed with the two prepositions לְ and מִן ("since the day" or "from the day").

הַעֲלֹתִי At first glance, it might be tempting to identify this form as a Hiphil Perfect of עָלָה, but the stem vowel will not allow for that identification. With the removal of the 1cs suffix, הַעֲלֹת is the

Hiphil Infinitive Construct of עָלָה with defectively written Holem Waw (הַעֲלוֹת). As a I-Guttural weak verb, the ה prefix takes Pathach with Hateph Pathach under the guttural consonant in first root position (27.2). As a III-ה Infinitive Construct, it takes the וֹת ending in all verbal stems (27.8). Followed by the direct object (אֶת־בְּנֵי יִשְׂרָאֵל) and a prepositional phrase (מִמִּצְרַיִם), this construction translates as "(since the day) I brought up the children of Israel from Egypt."

וָאֶהְיֶה מִתְהַלֵּךְ The Qal Imperfect 1cs of הָיָה with Waw Consecutive complements the Hithpael Participle ms of הָלַךְ (but I have been wandering). Note that with the prefixing of the Waw Consecutive to this III-ה Imperfect form, the ֶה ending is not dropped as might be expected. In fact, with the Imperfect 1cs of III-ה verbs with Waw Consecutive, the appearance of the final vowel letter is more common (60 times) than its absence (51 times). This Hithpael Participle (though I-Guttural) preserves all of the diagnostic points of spelling of the strong verb (34.10-11).

2 Samuel 7:7

בְּכֹל אֲשֶׁר־הִתְהַלַּכְתִּי As with מִתְהַלֵּךְ in the preceding verse, the Hithpael Perfect 1cs of this I-Guttural verb inflects just like a strong verb (34.3-4). Preceded by כֹּל with the preposition בְּ and the relative pronoun אֲשֶׁר, the beginning of this verse translates as "in all (places) where I have wandered."

הֲדָבָר דִּבַּרְתִּי Preceding the Piel Perfect 1cs of דָּבַר is the noun דָּבָר prefixed with the interrogative particle (a word did I speak?).

אֶת־אַחַד שִׁבְטֵי יִשְׂרָאֵל The preposition אֵת (אֶת־) is prefixed to the cardinal number (ms construct) אַחַד (11.2). On the use of אֶת־ in this context, see Waltke-O'Connor, 10.3.1b. שִׁבְטֵי is the mp construct of שֵׁבֶט. The absolute noun in this definite construct chain is the proper name יִשְׂרָאֵל (with one of the tribes of Israel).

צִוִּיתִי The Hireq under the first root consonant and the Daghesh Forte in the second root consonant (וּ) identify this verb as Piel Perfect. The sufformative is 1cs and the verbal root is identified by the stem vowel. The Hireq Yod stem vowel is present in III-ה Perfects of the Qal, Piel, Hiphil and Hithpael (I commanded).

לִרְעוֹת אֶת־עַמִּי The spelling of לִרְעוֹת with the preposition לְ and the וֹת ending suggests a III-ה Infinitive Construct of the Qal stem. The verbal root is רָעָה. The direct object is the Geminate noun עַם with a 1cs pronominal suffix (to shepherd my people). Note the Daghesh Forte in the מ of עַמִּי which represents the lost Geminate consonant (4.8.4). It reappears, so to speak, when the noun is pluralized or receives a pronominal suffix (9.15).

לֵאמֹר לָמָּה לֹא־בְנִיתֶם לִי בֵּית אֲרָזִים It has been observed a number of times that לֵאמֹר, in most contexts, is best reflected in English translation with punctuation that introduces direct quotations. Here, however, the context warrants the translation value "saying." The negated verb לֹא־בְנִיתֶם is the Qal Perfect 2mp of בָּנָה (saying, "Why have you not built for me a house of cedar?").

2 Samuel 7:8

כֹּה־תֹאמַר לְעַבְדִּי The adverb כֹּה is joined by Maqqef to the Qal Imperfect 2ms of אָמַר. The vowel pattern of this I-א Imperfect verb (Holem preformative vowel and Pathach stem vowel) is attested with only six verbs, אָמַר being the most frequent (16.3.3). לְעַבְדִּי is the Segholate noun עֶבֶד with the preposition לְ and a 1cs pronominal suffix (thus you will say to my servant).

אֲנִי לְקַחְתִּיךָ The 1cs personal pronoun precedes the Qal Perfect 1cs of לָקַח with a 2ms pronominal suffix (I took you).

לִהְיוֹת נָגִיד As with לִרְעוֹת in verse 7, the prefixed preposition לְ and the וֹת ending are distinctive of the III-ה Infinitive Construct (to be a prince).

2 Samuel 7:9

וָאֶהְיֶה עִמְּךָ This is another example of the Qal Imperfect 1cs of הָיָה with Waw Consecutive in which the final ה vowel letter is retained when prefixed with the Waw Consecutive. See the comments with וָאֶהְיֶה מִתְהַלֵּךְ above in verse 6. With the Geminate preposition עִם (with the 2ms pronominal suffix), translate this clause, "and I have been with you."

בְּכֹל אֲשֶׁר הָלַכְתָּ Translate this Qal Perfect 2ms of הָלַךְ metaphorically (in all that you *undertook*).

וָאַכְרִתָה With a Pathach preformative vowel and a defectively written Hireq Yod stem vowel, this 1cs Imperfect with Waw Consecutive is Hiphil (and I have cut off). This verb also has the Paragogic ה that may be related to the identical suffix added to the Imperative. Note that long 1cs III-ה forms (as וָאֶהְיֶה above) and other 1cs lengthened forms (as וָאַכְרִתָה here), both with Waw Consecutive, frequently appear together (see, for example, Judg 12:3; 2 Sam 22:24; Prov 8:30; Dan 8:2).

אֶת־כָּל־אֹיְבֶיךָ This is the direct object of the preceding verb. It consists of the definite direct object marker אֵת joined by Maqqef to the noun כֹּל which, in turn, is joined by Maqqef to the Qal active Participle mp אֹיְבִים with a 2ms pronominal suffix (all of your enemies).

מִפָּנֶיךָ This is the noun פָּנִים (lexical form פָּנֶה) with the preposition מִן and a 2ms pronominal suffix (from before you).

וְעָשִׂתִי In this Qal Perfect 1cs of עָשָׂה with Waw Consecutive, the Hireq Yod stem vowel which identifies the verbal root as III-ה is written defectively as Hireq (and I will make).

כְּשֵׁם הַגְּדֹלִים The preposition כְּ is prefixed to the ms construct noun שֵׁם. The absolute noun in this definite construct chain is the mp adjective גָּדוֹל used substantively, "like the name of the great ones." The use of the definite adjective creates a construction that may also be understood as a superlative (like the name of the greatest ones). For a study of the superlative degree with specific reference to this text, see Waltke-O'Connor, 14.5; Joüon-Muraoka, 141j.

Translation 19

1 Kings 8:22-26

Solomon's Prayer

22 וַיַּעֲמֹד שְׁלֹמֹה לִפְנֵי מִזְבַּח יְהוָה נֶגֶד כָּל־קְהַל יִשְׂרָאֵל וַיִּפְרֹשׂ
כַּפָּיו הַשָּׁמָיִם 23 וַיֹּאמַר יְהוָה אֱלֹהֵי יִשְׂרָאֵל אֵין־כָּמוֹךָ אֱלֹהִים
בַּשָּׁמַיִם מִמַּעַל וְעַל־הָאָרֶץ מִתָּחַת שֹׁמֵר הַבְּרִית וְהַחֶסֶד
לַעֲבָדֶיךָ הַהֹלְכִים לְפָנֶיךָ בְּכָל־לִבָּם 24 אֲשֶׁר שָׁמַרְתָּ לְעַבְדְּךָ דָּוִד
אָבִי אֵת אֲשֶׁר־דִּבַּרְתָּ לוֹ וַתְּדַבֵּר בְּפִיךָ וּבְיָדְךָ מִלֵּאתָ כַּיּוֹם הַזֶּה
25 וְעַתָּה יְהוָה אֱלֹהֵי יִשְׂרָאֵל שְׁמֹר לְעַבְדְּךָ דָוִד אָבִי אֵת אֲשֶׁר
דִּבַּרְתָּ לּוֹ לֵאמֹר לֹא־יִכָּרֵת לְךָ אִישׁ מִלְּפָנַי יֹשֵׁב עַל־כִּסֵּא
יִשְׂרָאֵל רַק אִם־יִשְׁמְרוּ בָנֶיךָ אֶת־דַּרְכָּם לָלֶכֶת לְפָנַי כַּאֲשֶׁר
הָלַכְתָּ לְפָנָי 26 וְעַתָּה אֱלֹהֵי יִשְׂרָאֵל יֵאָמֶן נָא דְבָרֶיךָ [דְּבָרְךָ]
אֲשֶׁר דִּבַּרְתָּ לְעַבְדְּךָ דָּוִד אָבִי

Parse the following verbs from 1 Kings 8:22-26.

1 Kings 8:22

וַיַּעֲמֹד ______________________

וַיִּפְרֹשׂ ______________________

1 Kings 8:23

שֹׁמֵר ______________________

הַהֹלְכִים ______________________

1 Kings 8:24

שָׁמַרְתָּ ______________________

דִּבַּרְתָּ ______________________

וַתְּדַבֵּר ______________________

מִלֵּאתָ ______________________

1 Kings 8:25

שְׁמֹר ______________________

יִכָּרֵת ______________________

יֹשֵׁב ______________________

יִשְׁמְרוּ ______________________

לָלֶכֶת ______________________

הָלַכְתָּ ______________________

1 Kings 8:26

יֵאָמֶן ______________________

Grammatical Commentary: 1 Kings 8:22-26

1 Kings 8:22

וַיַּעֲמֹד שְׁלֹמֹה In the absence of a sufformative, the Waw Consecutive and the preformative identify this verb as Imperfect 3ms. Apart from the Holem stem vowel, the spelling of this I-Guttural verb could be identified as either Qal or Hiphil (16.2; 16.3.2; 27.2). The Holem identifies the Imperfect as Qal (then Solomon stood).

נֶגֶד כָּל־קְהַל יִשְׂרָאֵל In this construction, the preposition נֶגֶד (before, in the presence of) precedes the construct chain כָּל־קְהַל יִשְׂרָאֵל. The entire construct chain is definite because the absolute noun is the proper name יִשְׂרָאֵל (in the presence of the whole assembly of Israel).

וַיִּפְרֹשׂ כַּפָּיו The verb פָּרַשׂ often appears with כַּפַּיִם (dual of the Geminate noun כַּף) with the meaning "to spread out the hands (in prayer)." Here the dual form has a 3ms (Type 2) pronominal suffix (and he spread out his hands).

1 Kings 8:23

אֵין־כָּמוֹךָ אֱלֹהִים Hebrew may express the non-existence or absence of someone or something by using the particle אַיִן (construct spelling אֵין), which translates either "(there) is not" or "(there) are not." By contrast, the existence of someone or something may be expressed by using the particle יֵשׁ (21.9). Here, the particle אֵין is joined by Maqqef to the preposition כְּ with a 2ms pronominal suffix. With this inseparable preposition, any of those forms with a singular suffix and also the one with a 1cp suffix exhibit a longer, alternate spelling of the preposition (כְּמוֹ) as in כָּמוֹךָ (9.12). This important declaration is translated as "there is no God like you."

בַּשָּׁמַיִם מִמַּעַל This construction is composed of the preposition בְּ prefixed to the definite noun שָׁמַיִם and followed by מַעַל with the preposition מִן (in heaven above). Commonly, the preposition מִן is compounded with other prepositions as in מִמַּעַל and מִתָּחַת (מִן prefixed to תַּחַת) in the next clause. For a brief study of compound and complex prepositions, see Waltke-O'Connor, 11.3.

וְעַל־הָאָרֶץ מִתָּחַת The form מִתָּחַת is the preposition מִן prefixed to the preposition תַּחַת (or on [the] earth below).

שֹׁמֵר הַבְּרִית וְהַחֶסֶד The definite nouns הַבְּרִית and הַחֶסֶד are direct objects of the Qal active Participle ms of שָׁמַר (keeping [the] covenant and [showing] steadfast love).

לַעֲבָדֶיךָ This is the mp noun עֲבָדִים (lexical form עֶבֶד) with the preposition לְ and a 2ms pronominal suffix (to your servants).

הַהֹלְכִים לְפָנֶיךָ This Qal active Participle mp of הָלַךְ is in an attributive relationship with עֲבָדִים (22.5.1), agreeing in gender, number, and definiteness (who walk before you).

בְּכָל־לִבָּם The preposition בְּ is prefixed to כֹּל and joined by Maqqef to the noun לֵב with a 3mp pronominal suffix (with all their heart). The noun לֵב is a Geminate noun, that is, the ב was originally written twice (cf. לֵבָב). The term "Geminate" comes from the Latin *gemini*, meaning "twins." Over the years, however, the two identical consonants came to be written only once. When Geminate nouns are pluralized or receive a pronominal suffix, a Daghesh Forte appears in the Geminate consonant, representing its lost "twin" (4.8.4).

1 Kings 8:24

אֲשֶׁר שָׁמַרְתָּ לְעַבְדְּךָ דָּוִד The antecedent of the relative pronoun אֲשֶׁר is יְהוָה (who has kept to [with] your servant David). The form לְעַבְדְּךָ is the noun עֶבֶד with the preposition לְ and a 2ms pronominal suffix (cf. לַעֲבָדֶיךָ in the preceding verse).

אֵת אֲשֶׁר־דִּבַּרְתָּ לוֹ The definte direct object marker אֵת marks the relative clause beginning with אֲשֶׁר as the direct object of שָׁמַרְתָּ. The relative pronoun אֲשֶׁר precedes the Piel Perfect 2ms of דָּבַר (what you spoke [promised] to him).

וַתְּדַבֵּר בְּפִיךָ All of the diagnostic points of spelling are present to identify this Piel Imperfect 2ms of דָּבַר with Waw Consecutive (Shewa preformative vowel, Pathach under the first root consonant, and Daghesh Forte in the second root consonant). The form בְּפִיךָ is the noun פֶּה with the preposition בְּ and a 2ms pronominal suffix (you spoke with your mouth).

וּבְיָדְךָ This form consists of the conjunction וְ (spelled as Shureq before Vocal Shewa), the preposition בְּ, and the fs noun יָד with a 2ms pronominal suffix (and with your hand).

מִלֵּאתָ The Hireq under the first root consonant and the Daghesh Forte in the second root consonant identify this form as Piel Perfect. The sufformative is 2ms (spelled without the Daghesh Lene because of the quiescent א). Idiomatically, the verb translates as "you fulfilled [it]."

1 Kings 8:25

שְׁמֹר לְעַבְדְּךָ דָוִד The vowel pattern of שְׁמֹר could be identified as either Qal Imperative ms or Qal Infinitive Construct. Context requires its identification as an Imperative (*keep* to [with] your servant David).

לֹא־יִכָּרֵת לְךָ The Hireq preformative vowel, Daghesh Forte in the first root consonant (assimilated נ of the Niphal stem), and Qamets under the first root consonant identify this verb as a Niphal Imperfect (24.6-7). Literally, the negated verb followed by לְךָ translates as "it (there) shall never be cut off to you." Idiomatically, it translates as "it (there) shall never fail you."

אִישׁ מִלְּפָנַי The form מִלְּפָנַי is the noun פָּנִים (mp of פָּנֶה) with the prepositions מִן and לְ together with a 1cs pronominal suffix (a man [from] before me).

יֹשֵׁב עַל־כִּסֵּא יִשְׂרָאֵל Context allows for the translation of this Qal active Participle as an Infinitive (*to sit* upon the throne of Israel). The phrase כִּסֵּא יִשְׂרָאֵל is a definite construct chain.

רַק אִם־יִשְׁמְרוּ בָנֶיךָ The adverb רַק is followed by the conditional particle אִם (*HALOT* 1:60; GKC 151e) which is joined by Maqqef to an Imperfect verb followed by its subject בָנֶיךָ (if only your sons observe).

אֶת־דַּרְכָּם This is the noun דֶּרֶךְ with a 3mp pronominal suffix which functions as the direct object of יִשְׁמְרוּ ([if only your sons observe] their way).

לָלֶכֶת לְפָנַי In the Qal Infinitive Construct, most I-י verbs drop the first root consonant and add a final ת. The form לֶכֶת is the Qal Infinitive Construct of הָלַךְ (which behaves like a I-י verb [20.6]) prefixed with the preposition לְ. Followed by לְפָנַי, this construction translates as "to walk before me" or "by walking before me."

1 Kings 8:26

וְעַתָּה אֱלֹהֵי יִשְׂרָאֵל Following the adverb עַתָּה with the conjunction וְ, the construct chain אֱלֹהֵי יִשְׂרָאֵל is a vocative (and now, O God of Israel).

יֵאָמֶן נָא דְּבָרֶיךָ In the verb יֵאָמֶן, the spelling with Tsere beneath the preformative and Qamets under the guttural in first root position signals the Niphal stem (25.6-7). Since the guttural cannot assimilate the נ of the Niphal stem, the preformative vowel is lengthened from Hireq to Tsere (compensatory lengthening). The נָא particle suggests the volitional nuance (*may* or *let* your word be confirmed).

Translation 20

2 Kings 17:34-40

You Shall Fear Yahweh

34 עַד הַיּוֹם הַזֶּה הֵם עֹשִׂים כַּמִּשְׁפָּטִים הָרִאשֹׁנִים אֵינָם יְרֵאִים
אֶת־יְהוָה וְאֵינָם עֹשִׂים כְּחֻקֹּתָם וּכְמִשְׁפָּטָם וְכַתּוֹרָה וְכַמִּצְוָה
אֲשֶׁר צִוָּה יְהוָה אֶת־בְּנֵי יַעֲקֹב אֲשֶׁר־שָׂם שְׁמוֹ יִשְׂרָאֵל 35 וַיִּכְרֹת
יְהוָה אִתָּם בְּרִית וַיְצַוֵּם לֵאמֹר לֹא תִירְאוּ אֱלֹהִים אֲחֵרִים
וְלֹא־תִשְׁתַּחֲווּ לָהֶם וְלֹא תַעַבְדוּם וְלֹא תִזְבְּחוּ לָהֶם
36 כִּי אִם־אֶת־יְהוָה אֲשֶׁר הֶעֱלָה אֶתְכֶם מֵאֶרֶץ מִצְרַיִם בְּכֹחַ
גָּדוֹל וּבִזְרוֹעַ נְטוּיָה אֹתוֹ תִירָאוּ וְלוֹ תִשְׁתַּחֲווּ וְלוֹ תִזְבָּחוּ
37 וְאֶת־הַחֻקִּים וְאֶת־הַמִּשְׁפָּטִים וְהַתּוֹרָה וְהַמִּצְוָה אֲשֶׁר כָּתַב
לָכֶם תִּשְׁמְרוּן לַעֲשׂוֹת כָּל־הַיָּמִים וְלֹא תִירְאוּ אֱלֹהִים אֲחֵרִים
38 וְהַבְּרִית אֲשֶׁר־כָּרַתִּי אִתְּכֶם לֹא תִשְׁכָּחוּ וְלֹא תִירְאוּ אֱלֹהִים
אֲחֵרִים 39 כִּי אִם־אֶת־יְהוָה אֱלֹהֵיכֶם תִּירָאוּ וְהוּא יַצִּיל אֶתְכֶם

מִיַּד כָּל־אֹיְבֵיכֶם 40 וְלֹא שָׁמֵעוּ כִּי אִם־כְּמִשְׁפָּטָם הָרִאשׁוֹן הֵם
עֹשִׂים

Parse the following verbs from 2 Kings 17:34-40.

2 Kings 17:34

עֹשִׂים ______________________________

צִוָּה ______________________________

שָׂם ______________________________

2 Kings 17:35

וַיִּכְרֹת ______________________________

וַיְצַוֵּם ______________________________

תִירְאוּ ______________________________

תִשְׁתַּחֲווּ ______________________________

תַעַבְדוּם ______________________________

תִזְבְּחוּ ______________________________

2 Kings 17:36

הֶעֱלָה ______________________________

נְטוּיָה ______________________________

תִירָאוּ ______________________________

2 Kings 17:37

כָּתַב ______________________________

תִּשְׁמְרוּן ______________________

לַעֲשׂוֹת ______________________

2 Kings 17:38

כָּרַתִּי ______________________

תִשְׁכָּחוּ ______________________

2 Kings 17:39

יַצִּיל ______________________

אֹיְבֵיכֶם ______________________

2 Kings 17:40

שָׁמֵעוּ ______________________

Grammatical Commentary: 2 Kings 17:34-40

2 Kings 17:34

עַד הַיּוֹם הַזֶּה Here, the preposition עַד precedes the definite noun יוֹם with the demonstrative adjective (to this day).

הֵם עֹשִׂים The 3mp independent personal pronoun הֵם precedes the Qal active Participle mp of עָשָׂה ("they do" or "they are doing"). The third consonant of the verbal root is lost in all forms of the Qal Participle (cf. עֹשִׂים and עֹשׂוֹת). In the singular forms (עֹשֶׂה and עֹשָׂה), the presence of the vowel letter ה helps with the identification of the verbal root (22.4.4).

כַּמִּשְׁפָּטִים הָרִאשֹׁנִים In the first form, the preposition כְּ is prefixed to the definite plural noun מִשְׁפָּטִים. The noun מִשְׁפָּט has a semantic range dealing with the areas of legal decision, arbitration, ordinance, specification, or claim, but it can also mean mode of life, custom, or habit, as it is used here (according to the customs). The adjective רִאשׁוֹן (former, preceding, first) agrees with the noun in gender, number, and definiteness (attributive usage).

אֵינָם יְרֵאִים אֶת־יְהוָה The form אֵינָם is the negative particle אַיִן with a 3mp pronominal suffix (21.9). With this particle, Hebrew can express the non-existence or absence of someone or something. It is usually translated as either "(there) is not" or "(there) are not." Followed by the mp adjective יְרֵאִים the construction is translated as "they do not fear Yahweh."

וְאֵינָם עֹשִׂים This is the same use of אַ֫יִן as in אֵינָם יְרֵאִים above. Here, however, it is followed by the Qal active Participle mp of עָשָׂה. The construction is translated as "and they do not do."

כְּחֻקֹּתָם This form consists of the preposition כְּ prefixed to the fp noun חֻקֹּת (lexical form חֻקָּה) with a 3mp pronominal suffix (according to their statutes).

וּכְמִשְׁפָּטָם Here, the conjunction וְ (spelled as Shureq before Vocal Shewa) and the preposition כְּ are prefixed to the noun מִשְׁפָּט with a 3mp pronominal suffix (and according to their ordinances).

וְכַתּוֹרָה וְכַמִּצְוָה Both nouns, תּוֹרָה and מִצְוָה, are prefixed with the conjunction וְ, the preposition כְּ, and the definite article (and according to the law and according to the commandment).

אֲשֶׁר צִוָּה יְהוָה With regard to the spelling of צִוָּה, the Hireq under the first root consonant and the Daghesh Forte in the second root consonant are diagnostic of the Piel Perfect (31.4). This form is the Piel Perfect 3ms of צָוָה (which Yahweh commanded). The ה ָ marks the 3ms Perfect of a III-ה verb in the Qal and derived stems.

אֲשֶׁר־שָׂם שְׁמוֹ יִשְׂרָאֵל The relative pronoun precedes the Qal Perfect 3ms of שִׂים (14.12). The form שְׁמוֹ is the noun שֵׁם with a 3ms pronominal suffix (idiomatically, "whom he named Israel").

2 Kings 17:35

וַיִּכְרֹת יְהוָה אִתָּם בְּרִית The verb כָּרַת (to cut) with the object בְּרִית (covenant) is a figure of speech for the act of making a covenant, "Yahweh *cut* a covenant with them." Idiomatically, the construction is often translated as "Yahweh *made* a covenant with them."

וַיְצַוֵּם The three diagnostics of a Piel Imperfect are a Shewa preformative vowel, Pathach under the first root consonant, and a Daghesh Forte in the second root consonant (30.5-6; 31.4). Though the root of this verb is III-ה, each of these diagnostics is present in this Imperfect 3ms with Waw Consecutive. The verb also appears with a 3mp pronominal suffix (and he commanded them). For the loss of the Daghesh Forte in the Imperfect preformative, see 30.15.

לֹא תִירְאוּ The ת preformative and Shureq sufformative identify the verb as a 2mp Imperfect. The Hireq Yod preformative vowel identifies both the stem (Qal) and verbal root (I-י). יָרֵא is a stative verb that inflects according to the pattern of I-י (Type 2) verbs (16.6-7). Every form of the paradigm has a Hireq Yod preformative vowel (you shall not fear).

אֱלֹהִים אֲחֵרִים The noun אֱלֹהִים may refer to God or gods. Followed by the plural adjective אֲחֵרִים (lexical form אַחֵר), it refers to the latter in this context (other gods).

וְלֹא־תִשְׁתַּחֲווּ The verb חָוָה (to bow down, worship) appears 173 times in the Hebrew Bible and it occurs only in a stem called the Hishtaphel (34.16). The forms of חָוָה are easy to identify because of the distinctive prefixes and preformatives of the Hishtaphel stem (תִּשְׁתּ on the 2mp Imperfect). As a III-ה verb, it will exhibit the distinctive endings of this weak verb class, inflecting quite regularly. The parsing for תִשְׁתַּחֲווּ is Hishtaphel Imperfect 2mp of חָוָה (and you shall not bow down).

וְלֹא תַעַבְדוּם This Qal Imperfect 2mp of עָבַד inflects according to the pattern of a I-Guttural (Type 2) verb (16.2-3) with a Pathach preformative vowel and a Pathach (in a closed syllable) under the first consonant of the verbal root. Those Imperfect forms that have a sufformative consisting of a vowel (2fs, 3mp, 2mp) exhibit this pattern (16.3.2). The negated verb with 3mp object suffix translates as "and you shall not serve them."

וְלֹא תִזְבְּחוּ לָהֶם This is another in this series of negated 2mp Imperfect verbs. Followed by לָהֶם (the preposition לְ with a 3mp pronominal suffix), this construction translates as "and you shall not sacrifice to them."

2 Kings 17:36

כִּי אִם־אֶת־יְהוָה After the series of four negated Imperfect verbs in verse 35, each declaring Yahweh's prohibitions with respect to other gods, כִּי אִם (but rather) introduces the true object of the verbal actions expressed in the series of verbs (but rather Yahweh). The divine name is marked by אֶת־ as the definite direct object of another series of 2mp Imperfect verbs later in verse 36.

אֲשֶׁר הֶעֱלָה אֶתְכֶם The relative pronoun אֲשֶׁר is followed by the Hiphil Perfect 3ms of עָלָה. As a I-Guttural verb, the ה prefix of the Hiphil has Seghol followed by the guttural with Hateph Seghol (27.2-3). As a III-ה verb, this Perfect 3ms form ends in ָה (27.8-9). The form אֶתְכֶם is the definite direct object marker with 2mp suffix. This relative clause is modifying יְהוָה.

בְּכֹחַ גָּדוֹל The first form is the noun כֹּחַ (strength, power) prefixed with the preposition בְּ and followed by the ms adjective גָּדוֹל in the attributive usage (with great power).

וּבִזְרוֹעַ נְטוּיָה The noun זְרוֹעַ is prefixed with the conjunction וְ (spelled as Shureq before ב, מ, פ, and Vocal Shewa) and with the preposition בְּ. The form נְטוּיָה is the Qal passive Participle fs of נָטָה (and with an outstretched arm). The form of the passive Participle is quite unusual at first glance. In every form of the paradigm, the consonant י stands in the place of the third root consonant, reminiscent of the fact that III-ה verbs were originally III-י (14.7.4; 22.8.4). You should think of this י as indicative of the III-ה class of weak verbs.

אֹתוֹ תִירָאוּ The direct object (definite direct object marker אֵת with 3ms pronominal suffix, referring to יְהוָה) is followed by the Qal Imperfect 2mp of יָרֵא (him you shall fear). The verb תִירָאוּ exhibits the pausal spelling (compare with the non-pausal spelling תִירְאוּ in verse 35), appearing in *BHS* with Athnach (תִירָ֑אוּ).

וְלוֹ תִשְׁתַּחֲווּ Compare this same verb in verse 35 but here preceded by וְלוֹ not וְלֹא as there (and *to him* you shall bow down).

וְלוֹ תִזְבָּחוּ This verb is the same form as תִזְבְּחוּ in verse 35, but here it appears with the pausal spelling (appearing in *BHS* with Silluq, תִזְבָּֽחוּ) and preceded by וְלוֹ not וְלֹא (and *to him* you shall sacrifice).

2 Kings 17:37

וְאֶת־הַחֻקִּים The conjunction וְ and the definite direct object marker אֵת are joined by Maqqef to the definite noun חֻקִּים (mp of חֹק). This is the first in a succession of four nouns, each of which functions as a direct object of the verb תִּשְׁמְרוּן. Though in a different context and grammatical construction and with slight variations in spelling, these are the same nouns that appear in verse 34.

תִּשְׁמְרוּן לַעֲשׂוֹת The preformative and sufformative identify תִּשְׁמְרוּן as the Qal Imperfect 2mp of שָׁמַר. Note the Paragogic נ at the end of this form (see comment on Exodus 3:12). This Imperfect verb complements the Qal Infinitive Construct of עָשָׂה (עֲשׂוֹת with the preposition לְ) which follows. The וֹת ending of the Infinitive

Construct is diagnostic of the III-ה weak verb class. This construction translates as "you will be careful to do."

כָּל־הַיָּמִים This is a definite construct chain with כֹּל in construct with the definite absolute noun יָמִים which is the plural of יוֹם (literally, "all of the days"). With כָּל־הַיָּמִים, the preceding construction may be translated, "you will always be careful to do (them)."

וְלֹא תִירְאוּ אֱלֹהִים אֲחֵרִים This is precisely the same construction as in verse 35. It will appear again in verse 38.

2 Kings 17:38

כָּרַתִּי This verb is the Qal Perfect 1cs of כָּרַת. When a verbal root ending in ת receives a sufformative beginning with ת, as in this form, the third consonant of verbal root assimilates into the sufformative consonant and is represented by a Daghesh Forte: כָּרַתְתִּי becomes כָּרַתִּי (13.8). This assimilation occurs in the five forms of the Perfect paradigm that have a sufformative beginning with ת. The relative clause אֲשֶׁר־כָּרַתִּי אִתְּכֶם translates as "that I made (cut) with you."

תִשְׁכָּחוּ The preformative and sufformative identify this verb as Qal Imperfect 2mp of שָׁכַח (you will not forget). Note the pausal spelling (36.3) of the stem vowel with Qamets, תִּשְׁכָּחוּ (appearing in *BHS* with Athnach under the כ, תִּשְׁכָּ֑חוּ) instead of the non-pausal form תִּשְׁכְּחוּ.

2 Kings 17:39

כִּי אִם־אֶת־יְהוָה אֱלֹהֵיכֶם Compare the similar construction in verse 36 (but rather Yahweh your God).

תִּירָאוּ This is the fifth occurrence in this text of the Qal Imperfect 2mp of יָרֵא (to fear), two of which exhibit pausal spelling (36.3) of the stem vowel (you will fear).

וְהוּא יַצִּיל אֶתְכֶם Preceded by the 3ms personal pronoun, the verb יַצִּיל is the Hiphil Imperfect 3ms of נָצַל. The form is identified as a Hiphil by the Pathach preformative vowel and the Hireq Yod stem vowel. The key to identifying the verbal root is the Daghesh Forte in the צ (the second root consonant). This Daghesh Forte represents the assimilated נ, the first consonant of the verbal root (27.10-11). The form אֶתְכֶם is the direct object of יַצִּיל (and he will deliver you).

מִ‍יַּ‍ד כָּל־אֹיְבֵיכֶם In the first form, the preposition מִן is prefixed to the noun יַד (the construct of יָד). The noun כֹּל (construct כָּל־ with Qamets Hatuf) is joined by Maqqef to the Qal active Participle mp (אֹיְבִים) with a 2mp pronominal suffix. This Participle is being used substantively as the absolute noun in the construct chain (from the hand of all your enemies).

2 Kings 17:40

וְלֹא שָׁמֵעוּ Here, a disjunctive Waw (24.17) is prefixed to the negative particle. The verb is the Qal Perfect 3cp of שָׁמַע with pausal spelling (שָׁמֵֽעוּ), appearing in *BHS* with Athnach (but they did not listen).

כִּי אִם־ כְּמִשְׁפָּטָם הָרִאשׁוֹן For a third time in this reading, כִּי אִם introduces a contrastive statement (but rather). Similar to the construction in verse 34, the singular noun מִשְׁפָּט (with the preposition כְּ and a 3mp pronominal suffix) is followed by the modifying adjective רִאשׁוֹן (but rather according to their former way of life).

הֵם עֹשִׂים The 3mp personal pronoun precedes the Qal active Participle mp of עָשָׂה (they did). The Qal Participle is easily recognized by the Holem with the first root consonant (22.4.4).

Isaiah 43:1-6

You are Precious in My Eyes

1 וְעַתָּה כֹּה־אָמַר יְהוָה בֹּרַאֲךָ[1] יַעֲקֹב וְיֹצֶרְךָ יִשְׂרָאֵל

אַל־תִּירָא כִּי גְאַלְתִּיךָ קָרָאתִי בְשִׁמְךָ לִי־אָתָּה

2 כִּי־תַעֲבֹר בַּמַּיִם אִתְּךָ־אָנִי וּבַנְּהָרוֹת לֹא יִשְׁטְפוּךָ[2]

כִּי־תֵלֵךְ בְּמוֹ[3]־אֵשׁ לֹא תִכָּוֶה[4] וְלֶהָבָה[5] לֹא תִבְעַר־בָּךְ

3 כִּי אֲנִי יְהוָה אֱלֹהֶיךָ קְדוֹשׁ יִשְׂרָאֵל מוֹשִׁיעֶךָ

נָתַתִּי כָפְרְךָ[6] מִצְרַיִם כּוּשׁ[7] וּסְבָא[8] תַּחְתֶּיךָ

---

1. בָּרָא (Q) to create (only with God as subject); (Ni) be created (48).
2. שָׁטַף (Q) to flood (over), overflow, rinse, wash (away) (31).
3. בְּמוֹ (prep) in, at, with, by, against; alternate (poetic) form of prep בְּ (10).
4. כָּוָה (Q) to burn, scorch; (Ni) be burned, be scorched (2).
5. לֶהָבָה flame (19).
6. כֹּפֶר ransom, bribe (13).
7. כּוּשׁ Cush, Ethiopia (29).
8. סְבָא Seba (4).

4 מֵאֲשֶׁר יָקַרְתָּ[9] בְעֵינַי נִכְבַּדְתָּ וַאֲנִי אֲהַבְתִּיךָ

וְאֶתֵּן אָדָם תַּחְתֶּיךָ וּלְאֻמִּים[10] תַּחַת נַפְשֶׁךָ

5 אַל־תִּירָא כִּי אִתְּךָ־אָנִי

מִמִּזְרָח אָבִיא זַרְעֶךָ וּמִמַּעֲרָב[11] אֲקַבְּצֶךָּ

6 אֹמַר לַצָּפוֹן תֵּנִי וּלְתֵימָן[12] אַל־תִּכְלָאִי[13]

הָבִיאִי בָנַי מֵרָחוֹק וּבְנוֹתַי מִקְצֵה הָאָרֶץ

Parse the following verbs from Isaiah 43:1-6.

Isaiah 43:1

אָמַר ____________________

בֹּרַאֲךָ ____________________

וְיֹצֶרְךָ ____________________

תִּירָא ____________________

---

9. יָקַר (Q) to be difficult, precious, prized, highly valued, esteemed (11).
10. לְאֹם people, nation; (mp) לְאֻמִּים (31).
11. מַעֲרָב west, sunset (14).
12. תֵּימָן (fs) south; (with directional ה) תֵּימָ֫נָה "southward" (24).
13. כָּלָא (Q) to shut up, restrain, withhold, keep back (17).

גְאַלְתִּיךָ

קָרָאתִי

Isaiah 43:2

תַעֲבֹר

יִשְׁטְפוּךָ

תֵלֵךְ

תִכָּוֶה

תִבְעַר

Isaiah 43:3

מוֹשִׁיעֶךָ

נָתַתִּי

Isaiah 43:4

יָקַרְתָּ

נִכְבַּדְתָּ

אֲהַבְתִּיךָ

וְאֶתֵּן

Isaiah 43:5

תִּירָא

אָבִיא

אֲקַבְּצֶךָּ

Isaiah 43:6

אֹמַר

תֵּנִי

תִּכְלָאִי ______________________________

הָבִיאִי ______________________________

Grammatical Commentary: Isaiah 43:1-6

Isaiah 43:1

כֹּה־אָמַר יְהוָה This introductory formula appears 293 times in the Hebrew Bible. It introduces the word of Yahweh delivered by a prophet. More than half of the total occurrences of this construction appear in Jeremiah (153 times). While the King James translation, "thus saith Yahweh," is classic, modern translations include "thus says Yahweh" (ESV) and "this is what Yahweh says" (NIV).

בֹּרַאֲךָ The Holem following the first root letter identifies this form as a Qal active Participle of בָּרָא (with a 2ms pronominal suffix). The use of a Type 1 pronominal suffix and the lack of an inflectional ending mark this form as masculine singular. This Participle stands in apposition to יְהוָה and may be translated with an English relative clause, "who created you."

יַעֲקֹב The use of this proper name is vocative. The vocative is the case of direct address and is normally used when addressing someone or something.

וְיֹצֶרְךָ יִשְׂרָאֵל This expression is parallel to בֹּרַאֲךָ יַעֲקֹב in both form and function. The Qal active Participle ms of יָצַר with a 2ms pronominal suffix is followed by the vocative יִשְׂרָאֵל (and who formed you, O Israel).

אַל־תִּירָא The use of the negative particle אַל followed by the Imperfect is used for immediate and specific prohibitions. The verbal form תִּירָא (Qal Imperfect 2ms) follows the I-י (Type 2) pattern of inflection (16.6; 16.7.3).

קָרָאתִי The changes in the vocalization of this form are occasioned by the א in third root position. In this Qal Perfect 1cs form, the א is quiescent or silent (14.4-5). The quiescent א causes the lengthening of the stem vowel (Pathach to Qamets) and the loss of Daghesh Lene in the ת of the sufformative (תִּי to תִי).

בְשִׁמְךָ This prepositional phrase begins with the preposition בְּ, which is followed by its object, שֵׁם (name), with a 2ms pronominal suffix. When the verb קָרָא (to call) is followed by the preposition בְּ, the nuance "to name," "appoint," or "summon" is often present. In this case, the expression קָרָאתִי בְשִׁמְךָ may be translated as either "I have summoned you by name" (NIV) or "I have called you by name" (ESV).

לִי־אָתָּה The preposition לְ with a 1cs pronominal suffix is followed by the 2ms independent personal pronoun. The use of the preposition לְ in a verbless clause of this type is one of the ways in which Hebrew can express possession, "you belong to me" or "you are mine."

Isaiah 43:2

כִּי־תַעֲבֹר The particle כִּי is followed by the Qal Imperfect 2ms of עָבַר. The spelling of the Imperfect verb with a Pathach preformative vowel and Hateph Pathach under the first root letter is occasioned by the guttural consonant in first root position (16.2; 16.3.2). The subject of this verb is יַעֲקֹב and יִשְׂרָאֵל from verse 1. The use of כִּי in this context is temporal and best translated as "when" (Waltke-O'Connor, 38.7).

אִתְּךָ־אָנִי This is a verbless clause of classification (23.8.2) with the predicate אִתְּךָ followed by the subject אָנִי (I *am* with you).

כִּי־תֵלֵךְ This expression is parallel to כִּי־תַעֲבֹר above with כִּי used temporally and translated, "when." With the verb תֵּלֵךְ, the Tsere preformative vowel and the Tsere stem vowel are diagnostic of the I-י (Type 1) weak verb class in the Qal Imperfect (16.6-7). In this case, however, the verbal root is הָלַךְ, which inflects just like I-י verbs of this type (16.7.2).

בְּמוֹ This is the rare long form of the inseparable preposition בְּ. It appears only 10 times in the Hebrew Bible. You may recall the more common long form of the preposition כְּ as כְּמוֹ, appearing 110 times in the Hebrew Bible (9.12-13). The preposition לְ also has the long form לְמוֹ, though it appears only four times in the Hebrew Bible (Job 27:14; 29:21; 38:40; 40:4). In general, long forms appear in poetic texts, especially Isaiah, Psalms, and Job.

תִּכָּוֶה The Hireq preformative vowel and the Qamets under the first root letter with Daghesh Forte identify this form as Niphal Imperfect. The Daghesh Forte in the first root letter represents the assimilated נ of the Niphal stem and the הֶ ending is characteristic of III-ה verbal roots in the Imperfect and Participle (ms).

תִּבְעַר The Pathach stem vowel in this Qal Imperfect 3fs form is occasioned by the guttural consonant in second root position (16.4-5). Guttural consonants prefer a-type vowels.

בָּךְ This is the inseparable preposition בְּ with a 2ms pronominal suffix, the antecedent of which is still יַעֲקֹב and יִשְׂרָאֵל from verse 1. The spelling of this construction (normally בְּךָ) is pausal (36.3). In *BHS*, this form appears with Silluq under the ב (בָֽךְ).

Isaiah 43:3

אֲנִי יְהוָה This is a verbless clause of identification (23.8.2) translated, "I am Yahweh." The proper name יְהוָה is followed by three appositional expressions: אֱלֹהֶיךָ (your God); קְדוֹשׁ יִשְׂרָאֵל (the Holy One of Israel); and מוֹשִׁיעֶךָ (your Savior).

מוֹשִׁיעֶךָ The מ prefix identifies this form as a Participle and the Hireq Yod stem vowel is diagnostic of the Hiphil Stem. The Holem Waw following the מ prefix is diagnostic of the I-י weak verb class (Hiphil Participle ms of יָשַׁע with a 2ms pronominal suffix). Remember that most I-י verbs were originally I-ו and this Waw reappears in the Niphal, Hiphil, and Hophal stems as either consonantal Waw, Holem Waw, or Shureq.

נָתַתִּי The second half of this verse is governed by the verb נָתַתִּי. There are three proper names that function as direct objects of this verb: מִצְרַיִם (Egypt); כּוּשׁ (Cush, Ethiopia); and סְבָא (Seba; see Gen 10:7). There are also two adverbial expressions: כָפְרְךָ (as your ransom) and תַּחְתֶּיךָ (in exchange for you). The accents in the Hebrew text suggest that the second half of this verse is to be translated, "I have given Egypt as your ransom, [and I have given] Cush and Seba in exchange for you."

Isaiah 43:4

מֵאֲשֶׁר This expression is a combination of the preposition מִן and the relative pronoun אֲשֶׁר. The Tsere under the מ is the result of compensatory lengthening. The נ of the preposition could not assimilate into the guttural א and so the Hireq lengthened to Tsere according to the rules for compensatory lengthening. The compound מֵאֲשֶׁר is rare, appearing only 17 times in the Hebrew Bible. In this context, the translation "because" is best (Waltke-O'Connor, 38.4).

נִכְבַּדְתָּ The נ prefixed to this verb is not the Imperfect 1cp preformative (as in נִקְטֹל). The Perfect 2ms sufformative (תָּ) precludes this identification. Given that the sufformative identifies this verbal form as Perfect 2ms, the נ prefix must be the נ of the Niphal stem (Niphal Perfect 2ms of כָּבֵד). The Pathach stem vowel is also diagnostic of the Niphal stem.

וְאֶתֵּן This is the Qal Imperfect 1cs of נָתַן with the conjunction וְ. The נ in first root position assimilated and is now represented by the Daghesh Forte in the second root letter (16.8; 16.19.4). The Tsere stem vowel occurs with certain high frequency Qal Imperfect weak verbs. See, for example, יָצָא and נָתַן in 16.14.

תַּחְתֶּיךָ Translate the preposition תַּ֫חַת (two times in this verse) as "in exchange for," as suggested above in verse 3.

Isaiah 43:5

אַל־תִּירָא See verse 1 above.

כִּי אִתְּךָ־אָנִי The particle כִּי introduces the verbless clause אִתְּךָ־אָנִי (see verse 2 above), which provides the basis for the command not to fear. In this case, the promise of the divine presence provides the reason or motive supporting the prohibition.

מִמִּזְרָח The second half of this verse, beginning with מִמִּזְרָח, contains two statements with the following sentence typology: prepositional phrase, verb, direct object.

אָבִיא The א preformative consonant identifies this form as Imperfect 1cs and the Qamets preformative vowel is characteristic of the Biconsonantal weak verb class (also Hollow or II-ו/י). Because the verbal root is בּוֹא, the Hireq Yod stem vowel is diagnostic of the Hiphil Stem (27.14-15). The sum of these diagnostic features identifies this form as the Hiphil Imperfect 1cs of בּוֹא. In the Hiphil stem, the verbal root בּוֹא is translated, "to bring."

אֲקַבְּצֶךָ Once again, the א preformative consonant identifies this form as Imperfect 1cs. The Hateph Pathach preformative vowel, Pathach under the first root letter, and Daghesh Forte in the second root letter are diagnostic features of the Piel stem. The Hateph Pathach preformative vowel is occasioned by the guttural preformative consonant. The Vocal Shewa of the Piel and Pual preformative changes to Hateph Pathach in the 1cs because gutturals cannot take

Vocal Shewa (30.6.1). The 2ms pronominal suffix ךָּ ֶ appearing with this verb is an example of the alternate Nun-suffixes that may appear with the Imperfect conjugation (19.6).

Isaiah 43:6

אֹמַר This is the Qal Imperfect 1cs of אָמַר. You would expect the א to be written twice, once for the Imperfect preformative and once for the first consonant of the verbal root. In this case, however, it is written only once (16.3.3). This verb is followed by two indirect objects marked by the preposition לְ (לַצָּפוֹן and וּלְתֵימָן).

תֵּנִי This is the Qal Imperative 2fs of נָתַן (18.6). The Hireq Yod sufformative is diagnostic for both the Imperfect and Imperative 2fs. The three feminine verbal forms in this verse are occasioned by the compass points צָפוֹן (north) and תֵּימָן (south), both of which are feminine.

תִּכְלָאִי The תִּ preformative and the Hireq Yod sufformative identify this form as the Qal Imperfect 2fs of כָּלָא. The expected stem vowel for this form is Vocal Shewa under the second root consonant, as in תִּכְלְאִי. The spelling with Qamets is the pausal spelling (36.3.4), appearing with Athnach under the ל in *BHS* (תִּכְלָ֑אִי).

הָבִיאִי This is the third 2fs verbal form in this verse. The הָ prefix and the Hireq Yod stem vowel mark this form as Hiphil (Biconsonantal), and the Hireq Yod sufformative is diagnostic of the Imperative 2fs (accented on the penultima). This form is not to be confused with the Hiphil Infinitive Construct (הָבִיא) with a 1cs suffix. In this latter case, the accent would fall on the ultima with the addition of the pronominal suffix, and the preformative vowel would reduce to Hateph Pathach (הֲבִיאִי).

מִקְצֵה הָאָרֶץ This is a definite construct chain (from the end of the earth). The construct noun is prefixed with the preposition מִן. Normally, the נ of the preposition assimilates and is represented by Daghesh Forte in the following consonant. In this case, however, the Daghesh Forte does not appear in the ק with Shewa (see 5.5 and 30.15). Finally, recall that nouns ending in ה ֶ (as in קָצֶה) have a singular construct form ending in ה ֵ (as in קְצֵה). See 10.3.2d.

Jeremiah 31:31-34

A New Covenant

31 הִנֵּה יָמִים בָּאִים נְאֻם־יְהוָה וְכָרַתִּי אֶת־בֵּית יִשְׂרָאֵל וְאֶת־בֵּית
יְהוּדָה בְּרִית חֲדָשָׁה 32 לֹא כַבְּרִית אֲשֶׁר כָּרַתִּי אֶת־אֲבוֹתָם
בְּיוֹם הֶחֱזִיקִי בְיָדָם לְהוֹצִיאָם מֵאֶרֶץ מִצְרָיִם אֲשֶׁר־הֵמָּה הֵפֵרוּ[1]
אֶת־בְּרִיתִי וְאָנֹכִי בָּעַלְתִּי[2] בָם נְאֻם־יְהוָה 33 כִּי זֹאת הַבְּרִית
אֲשֶׁר אֶכְרֹת אֶת־בֵּית יִשְׂרָאֵל אַחֲרֵי הַיָּמִים הָהֵם נְאֻם־יְהוָה
נָתַתִּי אֶת־תּוֹרָתִי בְּקִרְבָּם וְעַל־לִבָּם אֶכְתֲּבֶנָּה וְהָיִיתִי לָהֶם
לֵאלֹהִים וְהֵמָּה יִהְיוּ־לִי לְעָם 34 וְלֹא יְלַמְּדוּ עוֹד אִישׁ אֶת־רֵעֵהוּ
וְאִישׁ אֶת־אָחִיו לֵאמֹר דְּעוּ אֶת־יְהוָה כִּי־כוּלָּם יֵדְעוּ אוֹתִי
לְמִקְטַנָּם וְעַד־גְּדוֹלָם נְאֻם־יְהוָה כִּי אֶסְלַח[3] לַעֲוֹנָם וּלְחַטָּאתָם
לֹא אֶזְכָּר־עוֹד

---

1. פָּרַר (Hi) to break (out), destroy, put an end to, frustrate, make ineffectual (47).
2. בָּעַל (Q) to rule over, be lord (husband), marry, own (16).
3. סָלַח (Q) to pardon, forgive; (Ni) be forgiven (47).

Parse the following verbs from Jeremiah 31:31-34.

Jeremiah 31:31

בָּאִים ______________________________

וְכָרַתִּי ______________________________

Jeremiah 31:32

כָּרַתִּי ______________________________

הֶחֱזִיקִי ______________________________

לְהוֹצִיאָם ______________________________

הֵפֵרוּ ______________________________

בָּעַלְתִּי ______________________________

Jeremiah 31:33

אֶכְרֹת ______________________________

נָתַתִּי ______________________________

אֶכְתֲּבֶנָּה ______________________________

וְהָיִיתִי ______________________________

יִהְיוּ ______________________________

Jeremiah 31:34

יְלַמְּדוּ ______________________________

לֵאמֹר ______________________________

דְּעוּ ______________________________

יֵדְעוּ ______________________________

אֶסְלַח ______________________________

אֶזְכָּר ______________________________

Grammatical Commentary: Jeremiah 31:31-34

Jeremiah 31:31

יָמִים בָּאִים The mp noun יָמִים (lexical form יוֹם) is followed by the Qal active Participle mp of בּוֹא (days are coming). In the Qal stem, the Participle of the Biconsonantal weak verb is the only one without the diagnostic Holem vowel associated with the first root letter (22.4.5).

נְאֻם־יְהוָה The noun נְאֻם is joined by Maqqef to the divine name (literally, utterance of Yahweh). This is a common prophetic formula, occurring 268 times in the Hebrew Bible. It is interesting to note that of these occurrences, almost two-thirds (168 or 62.7 percent) appear in the book of Jeremiah. This expression appears four times in Jer 31:31-34 and is commonly translated, "declares Yahweh" (NIV, ESV, NASB) or "says Yahweh" (RSV, KJV [saith]).

וְכָרַתִּי The Perfect sufformative תִּי and the Qamets-Pathach vowel pattern identify this verb as Qal Perfect 1cs. The verbal root is כָּרַת. When a verbal root ending in ת receives a sufformative beginning with ת, as in this form, the third consonant of the verbal root assimilates into the sufformative consonant and is represented as a Daghesh Forte. In other words, כָּרַתְתִּי becomes כָּרַתִּי (13.8). This assimilation occurs in the five forms of the Perfect paradigm that have a sufformative beginning with ת. Prefixed with the Waw Consecutive, this construction may be translated, "when I will make [cut]."

אֶת־בֵּית יִשְׂרָאֵל וְאֶת־בֵּית יְהוּדָה The verb וְכָרַתִּי is followed by two prepositional phrases, each beginning with אֶת (with) joined by Maqqef to its object. Though the definite direct object marker אֵת is identical in spelling with the preposition אֵת (without pronominal suffixes), the context of this clause requires their identification as prepositions.

בְּרִית חֲדָשָׁה The fs noun בְּרִית followed by the fs adjective חֲדָשָׁה (lexical form חָדָשׁ) functions as the (indefinite) object of the verb וְכָרַתִּי. The noun and adjective agree in gender, number, and (in)definiteness and, in this context, the adjective is translated attributively, "a new covenant."

לֹא כַבְּרִית The negative particle לֹא is followed by a prepositional phrase with the preposition כְּ prefixed to the definite article and the fs noun בְּרִית (not like the covenant).

אֲשֶׁר כָּרַתִּי The relative pronoun אֲשֶׁר is followed by the Qal Perfect 1cs of כָּרַת. In the preceding verse, this same verb is prefixed with the Waw Consecutive and translated with the English future tense (when I will make [cut]). In this verse, the Perfect verb is not prefixed with the Waw Consecutive and so it is translated with the English past tense (which I made [cut]).

אֶת־אֲבוֹתָם The preposition אֶת־ is joined by Maqqef to its object. The form אֲבוֹתָם is the (irregular) mp of אָב (father) with a 3mp pronominal suffix (with their fathers).

בְּיוֹם הֶחֱזִיקִי בְיָדָם The preposition בְּ is prefixed to the ms construct noun יוֹם followed by an Infinitive Construct and another prepositional phrase. With regard to the verb הֶחֱזִיקִי, the ה prefix and the Hireq Yod stem vowel identify the Hiphil stem. The Seghol and Hateph Seghol vowels are the result of the guttural in first root position. Normally, one would expect Pathach and Hateph Pathach (27.2-3) with a I-Guttural Hiphil Infinitive Construct. In only this one case, however, the Seghol vowels are used. The 1cs pronominal suffix functions as the subject of the verbal action and its object, marked by the preposition בְּ, is the noun יָד with a 3mp pronominal suffix (on the day I took their hand).

לְהוֹצִיאָם The ה prefix and the Hireq Yod stem vowel identify the Hiphil Stem. The Holem Waw following the Hiphil prefix is diagnostic of the I-י weak verb class (יָצָא). The prefixed preposition לְ helps to identify the Infinitive Construct conjugation. With the 3mp pronominal suffix functioning as the object of the verbal action, this construction translates as "[in order] to bring them out."

אֲשֶׁר־הֵמָּה הֵפֵרוּ אֶת־בְּרִיתִי The verb הֵפֵרוּ, identified by the ה prefix and Perfect sufformative, is Hiphil Perfect 3cp. The verbal root is פָּרַר. The Daghesh Forte expected in the remaining Geminate consonant is not permitted in the semi-guttural ר. The verb is preceded by the relative pronoun and the 3mp personal pronoun and it is followed by its object אֶת־בְּרִיתִי. Translate this clause, "because they themselves broke my covenant." In this context, the relative pronoun אֲשֶׁר is used as a conjunction expressing reason and translated, "because" (*HALOT* 1:99).

וְאָנֹכִי בָּעַלְתִּי בָם The conjunction וְ prefixed to the 1cs personal pronoun is followed by the Qal Perfect 1cs of בָּעַל. The conjunction וְ (see 24.17) may be translated concessively, "*though* I was a husband to them."

Jeremiah 31:33

כִּי זֹאת הַבְּרִית Following a negative construction (לֹא כַבְּרִית in verse 32), the particle כִּי may be used as a contrastive conjunction and translated, "but." In this context, כִּי introduces a verbless clause beginning with the fs demonstrative pronoun זֹאת followed by the predicate nominative הַבְּרִית (but this *is* the covenant).

אַחֲרֵי הַיָּמִים הָהֵם The preposition אַחֲרֵי is followed by the definite mp noun יָמִים (lexical form יוֹם), which is modified by the mp demonstrative adjective הֵם (after those days). The noun and demonstrative adjective agree in gender, number, and definiteness.

נָתַתִּי אֶת־תּוֹרָתִי The sufformative תִּי is easy to identify in this Qal Perfect 1cs form. The verbal root is נָתַן. The נ in third root position has assimilated into the ת of the Perfect sufformative and is represented by the Daghesh Forte (similar to וְכָרַתִּי in verse 31 above). The definite direct object is תּוֹרָה with a 1cs pronominal suffix (I [will] place my law). Remember that feminine singular nouns ending in ָה, like תּוֹרָה, replace the ה with ת before the addition of a pronominal suffix (9.7.1).

בְּקִרְבָּם This is a prepositional phrase consisting of the preposition בְּ prefixed to the ms noun קֶרֶב with a 3mp pronominal suffix (in their midst).

וְעַל־לִבָּם The object of this prepositional phrase is the ms Geminate noun לֵב with a 3mp pronominal suffix (and upon their heart). With the addition of the pronominal suffix, the original Geminate consonant of לֵב reappears as a Daghesh Forte (4.8.4).

אֶכְתֲּבֶנָּה The 1cs preformative and verbal root are easy to identify in this Qal Imperfect 1cs of כָּתַב (I will write it). The pronominal suffix ֶנָּה is 3fs and belongs to the class of pronominal suffixes known as Nun-suffixes (19.6). The antecedent of the 3fs suffix is תּוֹרָה.

וְהָיִיתִי לָהֶם לֵאלֹהִים The Qal Perfect 1cs of הָיָה is prefixed with Waw Consecutive and followed by two prepositional phrases. The preposition לְ with a 3mp pronominal suffix (לָהֶם) is used to express possession. The preposition לְ with אֱלֹהִים marks the predicate nominative of the verb (I will be their God).

וְהֵמָּה יִהְיוּ־לִי לְעָם Similar in construction to the preceding clause, the first prepositional phrase (לִי) expresses possession and the second (לְעָם) marks the predicate nominative of the verb. With regard to the verb, the preformative and sufformative combination identify the form as Qal Imperfect 3mp. The verbal root is הָיָה (and they will be my people). This clause, together with the preceding clause, constitutes one variation of the so-called covenant formula that appears throughout the Hebrew Bible. For other occurrences, see Gen 17:8; Exod 6:7; Jer 24:7; 31:33; 32:38; Ezek 11:20; 37:23, 27; Zech 8:8).

Jeremiah 31:34

וְלֹא יְלַמְּדוּ עוֹד אִישׁ The conjunction וְ is prefixed to the negative particle לֹא followed by a verb, an adverb (עוֹד), and the verbal subject (אִישׁ). The preformative and sufformative combination of the verb יְלַמְּדוּ identify it as Imperfect 3mp. The Shewa preformative vowel, Pathach under the first root consonant, and Daghesh Forte in the second root consonant identify the Piel stem. In the Piel stem, the verbal root לָמַד translates, "to teach." In this context, note how the plural verb takes the singular subject אִישׁ. When the ms noun אִישׁ appears as the subject of a plural verb, it is to be translated distributively as "each" or "anyone" (and no longer will anyone teach).

אֶת־רֵעֵהוּ וְאִישׁ אֶת־אָחִיו Both direct objects of the verb יְלַמְּדוּ are marked with אֶת־, the definite direct object marker. The first object is the ms noun רֵעַ with a 3ms pronominal suffix (ֵ הוּ). The second object is the ms noun אָח with a 3ms pronominal suffix (ו) preceded by a restatement of the verbal subject אִישׁ ("his friend" or "his brother"). With regard to the noun אָח, remember that certain singular monosyllabic nouns will add Hireq Yod before pronominal suffixes (9.9) or in the construct state (10.3.2e).

דְּעוּ This form is Qal Imperative 2mp. With only two root letters remaining, the verbal root could be I-נ, I-י, III-ה, or Geminate. In this case, the verbal root is the I-י verb יָדַע (know!).

כּוּלָּם In the singular absolute state, the noun כֹּל is spelled with Holem. In the construct state, it is spelled כָּל with Qamets Hatuf. With a pronominal suffix, it is normally spelled כֻּל with Qibbuts and

Daghesh Forte. In this one instance only, the expected Qibbuts is spelled with Shureq (all of them).

יֵדְעוּ אוֹתִי The preformative and sufformative combination on the verb יֵדְעוּ identify it as Imperfect 3mp. The Tsere preformative vowel is diagnostic of the I-י (Type 1) weak verb class in the Qal stem. This verb is followed by the definite direct object marker with a 1cs pronominal suffix (they will know me).

לְמִקְטַנָּם וְעַד־גְּדוֹלָם This construction consists of two prepositional phrases with superlative adjectives and 3mp pronominal suffixes (from the *least* of them and unto the *greatest* of them). See Waltke-O'Connor, 14.5c.

אֶסְלַח לַעֲוֹנָם The form אֶסְלַח is the Qal Imperfect 1cs of סָלַח. Instead of the expected Holem stem vowel, II-Guttural and III-ע/ח verbs take a Pathach stem vowel (16.5.2). The object of the verb, עָוֹן with a 3mp pronominal suffix, is marked by the preposition לְ (I will forgive their iniquity).

וּלְחַטָּאתָם לֹא אֶזְכָּר־עוֹד This clause begins with its object, חַטָּאת with a 3mp pronominal suffix, marked by the preposition לְ. Because the Qal Imperfect 1cs verb אֶזְכָּר is joined by Maqqef to the adverb עוֹד, the Holem stem vowel changes to Qamets Hatuf (and their sins I will remember no longer).

Ezekiel 37:1-6

The Valley of Dry Bones

1 הָיְתָה עָלַי יַד־יְהוָה וַיּוֹצִאֵנִי בְרוּחַ יְהוָה וַיְנִיחֵנִי בְּתוֹךְ הַבִּקְעָה[1]
וְהִיא מְלֵאָה עֲצָמוֹת 2 וְהֶעֱבִירַנִי עֲלֵיהֶם סָבִיב סָבִיב וְהִנֵּה רַבּוֹת
מְאֹד עַל־פְּנֵי הַבִּקְעָה וְהִנֵּה יְבֵשׁוֹת[2] מְאֹד 3 וַיֹּאמֶר אֵלַי בֶּן־אָדָם
הֲתִחְיֶינָה הָעֲצָמוֹת הָאֵלֶּה וָאֹמַר אֲדֹנָי יְהוִה אַתָּה יָדָעְתָּ
4 וַיֹּאמֶר אֵלַי הִנָּבֵא עַל־הָעֲצָמוֹת הָאֵלֶּה וְאָמַרְתָּ אֲלֵיהֶם
הָעֲצָמוֹת הַיְבֵשׁוֹת שִׁמְעוּ דְּבַר־יְהוָה 5 כֹּה אָמַר אֲדֹנָי יְהוִה
לָעֲצָמוֹת הָאֵלֶּה הִנֵּה אֲנִי מֵבִיא בָכֶם רוּחַ וִחְיִיתֶם 6 וְנָתַתִּי
עֲלֵיכֶם גִּדִים[3] וְהַעֲלֵתִי עֲלֵיכֶם בָּשָׂר וְקָרַמְתִּי[4] עֲלֵיכֶם עוֹר וְנָתַתִּי
בָכֶם רוּחַ וִחְיִיתֶם וִידַעְתֶּם כִּי־אֲנִי יְהוָה

---

1. בִּקְעָה valley, plain (19).
2. יָבֵשׁ (adj) dry (9).
3. גִּיד tendon, sinew (7).
4. קָרַם (Q) to cover, spread over (2).

Parse the following verbs from Ezekiel 37:1-6.

Ezekiel 37:1

הָיְתָה ____________________

וַיּוֹצִאֵנִי ____________________

וַיְנִיחֵנִי ____________________

Ezekiel 37:2

וְהֶעֱבִירַנִי ____________________

Ezekiel 37:3

הֲתִחְיֶינָה ____________________

וָאֹמַר ____________________

יָדָעְתָּ ____________________

Ezekiel 37:4

הִנָּבֵא ____________________

וְאָמַרְתָּ ____________________

שִׁמְעוּ ____________________

Ezekiel 37:5

אָמַר ____________________

מֵבִיא ____________________

וִחְיִיתֶם ____________________

Ezekiel 37:6

וְנָתַתִּי ____________________

וְהַעֲלֵתִי ____________________

וְקָרַמְתִּי ____

וְנָתַתִּי ____

וִחְיִיתֶם ____

וִידַעְתֶּם ____

Grammatical Commentary: Ezekiel 37:1-6

Ezekiel 37:1

הָיְתָה עָלַי The form הָיְתָה is the Qal Perfect 3fs of הָיָה. Recall that with III-ה verbal roots, the Perfect 3fs form replaces the ה of the verbal root with ת before the Perfect sufformative (14.7.3). The verb is followed by the preposition עַל with a 1cs (Type 2) pronominal suffix.

יַד־יְהוָה This definite construct chain, translated, "the hand of Yahweh," is the subject of the verb הָיְתָה. The verb הָיְתָה is feminine singular because its subject יָד is an (endingless) feminine singular noun (the hand of Yahweh was upon me).

וַיּוֹצִאֵנִי With the identification of the 1cs pronominal suffix ֵנִי (19.2; 19.6), the Waw Consecutive and the Imperfect preformative identify this form as Imperfect 3ms. The Holem Waw following the Imperfect preformative is diagnostic of the I-י weak verb class (27.12-13), and the Hireq (Yod) stem vowel is diagnostic of the Hiphil stem (26.6.2).

בְרוּחַ יְהוָה In this context, the preposition בְּ marks the instrument of the verbal action expressed by the preceding verb (*by* the Spirit of Yahweh).

וַיְנִיחֵנִי This verb is similar in basic construction to וַיּוֹצִאֵנִי above. With the identification of the 1cs pronominal suffix (ֵנִי), the Waw Consecutive and Imperfect preformative identify this form as Imperfect 3ms. The Hireq Yod stem vowel is diagnostic of the Hiphil stem (27.14-15). The expected Qamets under the Imperfect preformative has reduced to Shewa (propretonic reduction) with the addition of the pronominal suffix. The verbal root may be identified by a process of elimination. With III-ה verbs, there is no Hireq Yod stem vowel (יַגְלֶה). With I-נ verbs, there is a Daghesh Forte in the remaining initial root letter (יַצִּיל). With I-י verbs, Holem Waw follows the Imperfect preformative (יוֹשִׁיב). In this case, the verbal root is the Biconsonantal נוּחַ (and he set me).

בְּתוֹךְ הַבִּקְעָה The construction בְּתוֹךְ is a combination of the preposition בְּ and the construct form of the ms noun תָּוֶךְ (middle, midst). This combination is common (319 times) in the Hebrew Bible. With the definite absolute noun הַבִּקְעָה, this expression is translated, "in the middle of the valley."

וְהִיא מְלֵאָה עֲצָמוֹת The conjunction וְ is prefixed to the 3fs personal pronoun הִיא. The pronoun's antecedent is the fs noun בִּקְעָה (valley) and the combination of the personal pronoun and the following fs adjective מְלֵאָה creates a verbless clause (and it *was* full). The fp noun עֲצָמוֹת is an adverbial modifier in the clause-final position (of bones). In Hebrew, modifiers of this type may be placed at the end of their clause without any explicit markers such as a preposition.

Ezekiel 37:2

וְהֶעֱבִירַנִי עֲלֵיהֶם The ה prefix and the Hireq Yod stem vowel identify וְהֶעֱבִירַנִי as the Hiphil Perfect 3ms of עָבַר with a 1cs pronominal suffix. The Seghol-Hateph Seghol vowel pattern is characteristic of the I-Guttural weak verb class (27.3.2). With the preposition עַל and the 3mp (Type 2) pronominal suffix, translate this expression, "and he caused me to pass over them."

סָבִיב סָבִיב This is an adverbial construction meaning "all around."

וְהִנֵּה רַבּוֹת מְאֹד עַל־פְּנֵי הַבִּקְעָה This verse ends with two verbless clauses, each of which is introduced by וְהִנֵּה (the conjunction וְ prefixed to the interjection הִנֵּה). The first verbless clause describes the number (רַבּוֹת מְאֹד) and location (עַל־פְּנֵי הַבִּקְעָה) of the bones. Translate this statement, "and behold, *there were* very many [bones] on the floor of the valley."

וְהִנֵּה יְבֵשׁוֹת מְאֹד The second verbless clause introduced by וְהִנֵּה describes the condition of the bones, "and behold, [the bones] *were* very dry." Both of the adjectives modifying the bones (עֲצָמוֹת in verse 1) are feminine plural. The form רַבּוֹת is the fp of the Geminate (7.4.4) adjective רַב (many) and the form יְבֵשׁוֹת is the fp of יָבֵשׁ (dry).

Ezekiel 37:3

בֶּן־אָדָם This construct chain is vocative, a construction used in direct address. In English translation, the vocative is often set off by commas (and he said to me, "*Son of man,...*").

הֲתִחְיֶינָה הָעֲצָמוֹת הָאֵלֶּה Once it is recognized that the הֲ prefix is the interrogative particle, the preformative תִ and the sufformative נָה clearly identify this form as Qal Imperfect 3fp or 2fp. The presence of an explicit subject following the verb, the fp הָעֲצָמוֹת, makes the 3fp identification correct. The verbal root, identified as III-ה by the Seghol Yod stem vowel (16.11.3), is the doubly weak חָיָה (will these bones live?).

וָאֹמַר The verb וָאֹמַר may be difficult to identify. The conjunction וָ spelled with Qamets must be the Waw Consecutive that is prefixed to the Imperfect conjugation. The Daghesh Forte of the Waw Consecutive is rejected by the guttural א and so the Pathach of the Waw consecutive lengthens to Qamets as a result of compensatory lengthening (17.2.2). Having recognized the Waw Consecutive, the א of this form must be the Imperfect 1cs preformative. An unusual feature of the I-א Type 3 weak verb class is that the א of the verbal root does not appear in this form (16.3.3). Note that in the Type 1 and Type 2 paradigms, the א of the verbal root is retained (e.g., אֶאֱסֹר).

אֲדֹנָי יְהוִה אַתָּה יָדָעְתָּ The expression אֲדֹנָי יְהוִה is vocative, as is בֶּן־אָדָם earlier in this same verse. Note that the spelling of the divine name is written with Hireq under the ו and so it is read as אֱלֹהִים and not the more common reading אֲדֹנָי. This convention prevents the reading of אֲדֹנָי אֲדֹנָי by reading אֲדֹנָי אֱלֹהִים. This vocative construction is followed by the 2ms personal pronoun and the Qal Perfect 2ms of יָדַע. This clause may be translated, "O Lord God, [only] you know."

Ezekiel 37:4

הִנָּבֵא The הִ prefix, Qamets under the first root letter, and Daghesh Forte in that same root letter identify הִנָּבֵא as the Niphal Infinitive Construct or Imperative 2ms. The correct identification is determined by the context. Given that this verbal form lacks any prepositional prefix, begins a section of direct discourse, and is followed by the Perfect with Waw Consecutive וְאָמַרְתָּ, this form is properly identified as Niphal Imperative 2ms.

וְאָמַרְתָּ This Qal Perfect 2ms with Waw Consecutive carries the full volitional force of the preceding Imperative הִנָּבֵא (prophesy … and say…). The Imperative followed by the Perfect with Waw Consecutive is one of the important verbal sequences with which it is necessary to become familiar (23.6.3).

הָעֲצָמוֹת הַיְבֵשׁוֹת The definite fp noun עֲצָמוֹת (bones) is followed by the definite fp adjective יְבֵשׁוֹת (dry) used attributively (7.5.1). Like בֶּן־אָדָם and אֲדֹנָי יְהוִה above, this construction is also vocative.

Ezekiel 37:5

אֲדֹנָי יְהוִה In this instance, the expression אֲדֹנָי יְהוִה is not vocative but the subject of the verb אָמַר (Yahweh God says).

אֲנִי מֵבִיא בָכֶם The מֵ prefix and Hireq Yod stem vowel are diagnostic of the Hiphil Participle ms of the Biconsonantal weak verb class. The verbal root is בּוֹא and may be translated, "to bring" in the Hiphil stem. Preceded by the 1cs personal pronoun אֲנִי and followed by the preposition בְּ with a 2mp pronominal (object) suffix, this expression is translated, "I am bringing upon you."

וִחְיִיתֶם The sufformative תֶם identifies the Perfect 2mp. The Hireq Yod stem vowel is diagnostic of III-ה weak verbs and so the verbal root is חָיָה (to live). The spelling of the Waw Consecutive on this Qal Perfect form is the result of the First Rule of Shewa. According to this rule, the first of two contiguous Shewas at the beginning of a word becomes Hireq in a closed syllable. In other words, וְחְ becomes וִח (4.11.1).

Ezekiel 37:6

וְנָתַתִּי עֲלֵיכֶם גִּדִים Verse 6 consists of six clauses, each beginning with a Perfect with Waw Consecutive. The first four clauses are first person with אֲדֹנָי יְהוִה as their subject (in verse 5 above). The last two clauses are 2mp with עֲצָמוֹת as their subject (in verse 5 above). In this first clause, the Qal verb is followed by the prepositional phrase עֲלֵיכֶם and the mp object גִּדִים (I will put tendons on you).

וְהַעֲלֵתִי עֲלֵיכֶם בָּשָׂר The ה prefix and sufformative תִּי identify וְהַעֲלֵתִי as the Hiphil Perfect 1cs with Waw Consecutive. The Pathach preformative vowel and the Hateph Pathach under the first root letter are the result of the guttural in first root position (27.2-3). The verbal root is the doubly weak עָלָה. This verb is followed by the preposition עַל with a 2mp (Type 2) pronominal suffix and the ms noun בָּשָׂר functioning as the verbal object (and I will make flesh come up on [cover] you).

וְקָרַמְתִּי עֲלֵיכֶם עוֹר This third clause is identical in structure to the two preceding clauses (and I will put [cover] skin on you).

וְנָתַתִּי בָכֶם רוּחַ This fourth clause is identical in structure to the three preceding clauses. In this case, however, the prepositional phrase following the verb begins with בְּ instead of עַל (and I will put breath in you).

וִחְיִיתֶם וִידַעְתֶּם In the last two clauses of this verse, the verbs shift from 1cs to 2mp. The stem of both verbs is Qal. The verbal root of the first form (וִחְיִיתֶם) is identified by the Hireq Yod stem vowel. This feature is diagnostic of III-ה weak verbs and so the verbal root is חָיָה (to live). The verbal root of the second form (וִידַעְתֶּם) is יָדַע (to know). With both verbs, the spelling of the Waw Consecutive is governed by the Rules of Shewa: the first form is governed by the First Rule of Shewa (4.11.1) and the second form by the exception to the First Rule of Shewa (4.11.2).

Translation 24

Joel 3:1-5 (English 2:28-32)

I Will Pour Out My Spirit

1 וְהָיָה אַחֲרֵי־כֵן אֶשְׁפּוֹךְ אֶת־רוּחִי עַל־כָּל־בָּשָׂר

וְנִבְּאוּ בְּנֵיכֶם וּבְנוֹתֵיכֶם

זִקְנֵיכֶם חֲלֹמוֹת יַחֲלֹמוּן

בַּחוּרֵיכֶם[1] חֶזְיֹנוֹת[2] יִרְאוּ

2 וְגַם עַל־הָעֲבָדִים וְעַל־הַשְּׁפָחוֹת

בַּיָּמִים הָהֵמָּה אֶשְׁפּוֹךְ אֶת־רוּחִי

3 וְנָתַתִּי מוֹפְתִים[3] בַּשָּׁמַיִם וּבָאָרֶץ

דָּם וָאֵשׁ וְתִימֲרוֹת[4] עָשָׁן[5]

---

1. בָּחוּר young man; (mp) בַּחוּרִים (44).
2. חִזָּיוֹן vision, revelation; (mp) חֶזְיֹנוֹת (9).
3. מוֹפֵת wonder, sign, miracle (36).
4. תִּימָרָה column, pillar (2).
5. עָשָׁן smoke (25).

4 הַשֶּׁמֶשׁ יֵהָפֵךְ לְחֹשֶׁךְ וְהַיָּרֵחַ[6] לְדָם

לִפְנֵי בּוֹא יוֹם יְהוָה הַגָּדוֹל וְהַנּוֹרָא

5 וְהָיָה כֹּל אֲשֶׁר־יִקְרָא בְּשֵׁם יְהוָה יִמָּלֵט

כִּי בְּהַר־צִיּוֹן וּבִירוּשָׁלַםִ תִּהְיֶה פְלֵיטָה[7]

כַּאֲשֶׁר אָמַר יְהוָה

וּבַשְּׂרִידִים[8] אֲשֶׁר יְהוָה קֹרֵא

Parse the following verbs from Joel 3:1-5 (English 2:28-32).

Joel 3:1

וְהָיָה ______________________________

אֶשְׁפּוֹךְ ______________________________

וְנִבְּאוּ ______________________________

יַחֲלֹמוּן ______________________________

יִרְאוּ ______________________________

---

6. יָרֵחַ moon (27).
7. פְּלֵיטָה survivor, escape, deliverance (28).
8. שָׂרִיד survivor (29).

Joel 3:2

אֶשְׁפּוֹךְ ______________________________

Joel 3:3

וְנָתַתִּי ______________________________

Joel 3:4

יֵהָפֵךְ ______________________________

בּוֹא ______________________________

וְהַנּוֹרָא ______________________________

Joel 3:5

יִקְרָא ______________________________

יִמָּלֵט ______________________________

תִּהְיֶה ______________________________

אָמַר ______________________________

קֹרֵא ______________________________

Grammatical Commentary: Joel 3:1-5 (English 2:28-32)

Joel 3:1 [2:28]

וְהָיָה אַחֲרֵי־כֵן This well-known passage from the book of the prophet Joel is quoted by the apostle Peter in Acts 2 on the day of Pentecost. The text begins with the temporal modifier וְהָיָה (Qal Perfect 3ms with Waw Consecutive) followed by the adverbial expression אַחֲרֵי־כֵן. Literally, these words translates as "and it shall come to pass afterward" (ESV) or, more idiomatically, "and afterward" (NIV).

אֶשְׁפּוֹךְ אֶת־רוּחִי The preformative א and the Holem Waw stem vowel identify אֶשְׁפּוֹךְ as the Qal Imperfect 1cs of שָׁפַךְ. The expected Holem stem vowel is written with full or *plene* spelling. This verb is followed by the definite direct object marker joined by Maqqef to רוּחַ with a 1cs pronominal suffix. Translate this clause, "I will pour out my Spirit."

וְנִבְּאוּ This verb is prefixed with the Waw Consecutive. The stem of this Perfect 3cp form can be difficult to identify. The Hireq under the נ and the Daghesh Forte in the ב are diagnostic features of the Piel stem. However, the identical spelling appears in the Niphal Perfect of the I-נ weak verb. In the spelling of the I-נ Niphal Perfect, the נ of the verbal root is assimilated and represented by Daghesh Forte in the second root consonant (25.9.1). The נ that appears in this spelling is the נ of the Niphal stem. In ambiguous instances such as this, a standard lexicon will normally provide the correct identification. In this case, it is to be learned from the lexicon that the verbal root נָבָא does not appear in the Piel stem and so this form must be Niphal.

בְּנֵיכֶם וּבְנוֹתֵיכֶם The mp noun בָּנִים (lexical form בֵּן) and the fp noun בָּנוֹת (lexical form בַּת), both with 2mp pronominal suffixes, are functioning as the compound subject of the verb וְנִבְּאוּ (and your sons and your daughters will prophesy).

זִקְנֵיכֶם חֲלֹמוֹת יַחֲלֹמוּן The word order for this clause is subject, object, and then verb. The subject is the mp adjective (used substantively) זְקֵנִים (lexical form זָקֵן) with a 2mp pronominal suffix, and the object is the irregular mp noun חֲלֹמוֹת (lexical form חֲלוֹם). The preformative and sufformative on the verb identify it as Imperfect 3mp. The Pathach preformative vowel and Hateph Pathach under the first root consonant appear in both Qal (16.2-3) and Hiphil (27.2-3) I-Guttural verbs. In this case, the Holem stem vowel is the diagnostic feature that makes the Qal stem the correct identification (your old men will have [dream] dreams). The final נ appearing on the verb is the Paragogic נ (see commentary on Exod 3:12 for a discussion of the Paragogic נ).

בַּחוּרֵיכֶם חֶזְיֹנוֹת יִרְאוּ This final clause in verse 1 is identical in word order to the preceding clause: subject, object, and then verb. The subject is the mp noun בַּחוּרִים (lexical form בָּחוּר) with a 2mp pronominal suffix. The object is the fp noun חֶזְיֹנוֹת (lexical form חִזָּיוֹן). The verb יִרְאוּ is the Qal Imperfect 3mp of רָאָה. This clause is translated as "your young men will see visions."

Joel 3:2 [2:29]

עַל־הָעֲבָדִים The preposition עַל is joined by Maqqef to its definite mp object עֲבָדִים (lexical form עֶ֫בֶד). In this context, because of the prepositional phrase that follows, translate עֲבָדִים with an explicit reference to gender, "male servants."

וְעַל־הַשְּׁפָחוֹת This prepositional phrase is connected to the preceding prepositional phrase by the conjunction וְ. In this case, the object of the preposition is the fp noun שְׁפָחוֹת (lexical form שִׁפְחָה) and is translated, "female servants."

בַּיָּמִים הָהֵמָּה The preposition בְּ is followed by the definite mp noun יָמִים (lexical form יוֹם) and the definite demonstrative adjective הֵמָּה (in those days).

Joel 3:3 [2:30]

וְנָתַתִּי מוֹפְתִים The תִּי sufformative identifies וְנָתַתִּי as Perfect 1cs with Waw Consecutive. The vowel pattern with Qamets followed by Pathach is diagnostic of the Qal stem. The verbal root is נָתַן. The נ in third root position has assimilated into the ת of the Perfect sufformative and is represented as a Daghesh Forte (13.9). The verb is followed by its mp object, מוֹפְתִים (lexical form מוֹפֵת). Translate this expression, "and I will display [give] wonders."

דָּם וָאֵשׁ וְתִימֲרוֹת עָשָׁן This series of nouns stands in apposition to the verbal object מוֹפְתִים (blood and fire and columns of smoke).

Joel 3:4 [2:31]

הַשֶּׁמֶשׁ יֵהָפֵךְ לְחֹשֶׁךְ The verb יֵהָפֵךְ is preceded by its subject, הַשֶּׁמֶשׁ. The preformative identifies the verb as Imperfect 3ms. The vowel pattern with the Tsere preformative vowel and Qamets under the first root letter is diagnostic of the I-Guttural Niphal Imperfect. The guttural in first root position rejects the expected Daghesh Forte (assimilated נ of the Niphal stem), and the expected Hireq preformative vowel lengthens to Tsere (25.7.1). In other words, יִקָּטֵל (Hireq with Daghesh Forte) becomes יֵהָפֵךְ (Tsere). With the prepositional phrase לְחֹשֶׁךְ, this clause translates as "the sun will be turned to darkness."

וְהַיָּרֵחַ לְדָם The construction וְהַיָּרֵחַ consists of three parts: the conjunction וְ, the definite article, and the noun יָרֵחַ (moon). It is followed by the preposition לְ prefixed to the noun דָּם (blood). In this clause, there is a subject and prepositional phrase, but no verb. The verb from the preceding clause is implied (and the moon [will be changed] to blood). This phenomenon is known as verbal ellipsis. Waltke-O'Connor (11.4.3d) explain ellipsis as "the omission of part of a grammatical structure when that part can be recovered from the context."

לִפְנֵי בּוֹא יוֹם יְהוָה This phrase begins with the preposition לְ prefixed to the mp construct form of פָּנֶה. This combination occurs over two hundred times in the Hebrew Bible and functions as a preposition with both spatial (in front of) and temporal (before) significance. The Qal Infinitive Construct form of בּוֹא is easy to identify because it appears in a construct chain and follows לִפְנֵי used as a temporal preposition (before). The ms construct noun יוֹם does not undergo spelling changes in the construct state because of its "unchangeable" long vowel. Finally, because the absolute noun יְהוָה is a proper name, the entire construct chain is definite (before the coming of the day of Yahweh).

הַגָּדוֹל וְהַנּוֹרָא This expression consists of the definite ms adjective גָּדוֹל, the conjunction וְ, and the definite ms Participle נוֹרָא. Both גָּדוֹל and נוֹרָא are used attributively (22.5.1). The stem of the Participle נוֹרָא is identified as Niphal by the נ prefix. The verbal root is identified by the Holem Waw prefix vowel (יָרֵא). Because a construct chain cannot be broken, any adjectives (or Participles) that modify a word within that construction must appear outside of it (10.2.6). Thus, in order to determine what noun the adjectives modify, they must be matched in gender, number, and definiteness. In the phrase לִפְנֵי בּוֹא יוֹם יְהוָה, both יוֹם and יְהוָה are masculine, singular, and definite. In this context, יוֹם is to be preferred (before the coming of the *great and terrible* day of Yahweh).

Joel 3:5 [2:32]

וְהָיָה Like verse 1 above, this verse begins with the temporal modifier וְהָיָה (Qal Perfect 3ms with Waw Consecutive). Because of the frequency with which temporal modifiers occur in certain contexts, they are often left untranslated, though you can still translate the conjunction as "and" (17.7). The NIV, for example, simply translates this expression as "and" in this context. The ESV, on the other hand, prefers an extended rendering, "and it shall come to pass."

כֹּל אֲשֶׁר־יִקְרָא בְּשֵׁם יְהוָה This entire expression constitutes the subject of the verb יִמָּלֵט that follows. More specifically, the subject is כֹּל, and it is modified by the following relative clause which begins with אֲשֶׁר and continues through יְהוָה (all who call on the name of Yahweh).

יִמָּלֵט The preformative י without an additional sufformative identifies יִמָּלֵט as Imperfect 3ms. The Qamets under the first root consonant and the Daghesh Forte in that same consonant are diagnostic of the Niphal Imperfect ([he] will be delivered).

תִּהְיֶה פְלֵיטָה The verb תִּהְיֶה is Qal Imperfect 3fs or 2ms of הָיָה. Here, the fs noun פְלֵיטָה is the subject of תִּהְיֶה and thus 3fs is the correct identification (there will be [those who] escape).

כַּאֲשֶׁר אָמַר יְהוָה The combination of the preposition כְּ and the relative pronoun אֲשֶׁר occurs over five hundred times in the Hebrew Bible (see *HALOT* 1:98-99). With אָמַר יְהוָה, this clause translates as "just as Yahweh has said."

וּבַשְּׂרִידִים There are four parts to this construction: the conjunction וְ (spelled וּ before ב, מ, and פ), the preposition בְּ, the definite article, and the mp noun שְׂרִידִים (lexical form שָׂרִיד).

אֲשֶׁר יְהוָה קֹרֵא This relative clause modifies the object of the preceding prepositional phrase (שְׂרִידִים). The verb קֹרֵא is easily identified as a Qal active Participle (ms) by the Holem with the the first root letter. With the preceding prepositional phrase, this construction translates, "even among the survivors whom Yahweh calls."

Psalm 23:1-6

Yahweh is My Shepherd

1 מִזְמוֹר לְדָוִד

יְהוָה רֹעִי לֹא אֶחְסָר[1]

2 בִּנְאוֹת[2] דֶּשֶׁא[3] יַרְבִּיצֵנִי[4]

עַל־מֵי מְנֻחוֹת[5] יְנַהֲלֵנִי[6]

3 נַפְשִׁי יְשׁוֹבֵב

יַנְחֵנִי[7] בְמַעְגְּלֵי[8]־צֶדֶק לְמַעַן שְׁמוֹ

---

1. חָסֵר (Q) to diminish, decrease, lack, be lacking (22).
2. נָוֶה pasture, dwelling (15). The fp cstr form נְאוֹת is irregular.
3. דֶּשֶׁא grass, vegetation (14).
4. רָבַץ (Q) to lie down, crouch (of animals), rest, stretch out (30).
5. מְנוּחָה rest, resting place (21).
6. נָהַל (Pi) to lead, guide, escort, help along, provide (with food), transport (10).
7. נָחָה (Q) to lead; (Hi) lead, guide, conduct (39).
8. מַעְגָּל path, wagon track (13).

4 גַּם כִּי־אֵלֵךְ בְּגֵיא צַלְמָוֶת[9] לֹא־אִירָא רָע

כִּי־אַתָּה עִמָּדִי[10]

שִׁבְטְךָ וּמִשְׁעַנְתֶּךָ[11] הֵמָּה יְנַחֲמֻנִי

5 תַּעֲרֹךְ לְפָנַי שֻׁלְחָן נֶגֶד צֹרְרָי[12]

דִּשַּׁנְתָּ[13] בַשֶּׁמֶן רֹאשִׁי כּוֹסִי[14] רְוָיָה[15]

6 אַךְ טוֹב וָחֶסֶד יִרְדְּפוּנִי כָּל־יְמֵי חַיָּי

וְשַׁבְתִּי בְּבֵית־יְהוָה לְאֹרֶךְ יָמִים

---

9. צַלְמָוֶת (ms) shadow of death, deep darkness, gloom (18).
10. עִמָּד (prep) with; (with 1cs suff) עִמָּדִי (45).
11. מִשְׁעֶנֶת staff, stick, support (11).
12. צָרַר (Q) to be hostile (toward), treat with hostility, attack (26).
13. דָּשֵׁן (Pi) to refresh, make fat (i.e. anoint), revive, clean away fat ashes; (Pu) be made fat (11).
14. כּוֹס (fs) cup (31).
15. רְוָיָה overflow(ing), abundance, saturation (2).

Parse the following verbs from Psalm 23:1-6.

Psalm 1:1

רֹעִי ______________________________

אֶחְסָר ______________________________

Psalm 1:2

יַרְבִּיצֵנִי ______________________________

יְנַהֲלֵנִי ______________________________

Psalm 1:3

יְשׁוֹבֵב ______________________________

יַנְחֵנִי ______________________________

Psalm 1:4

אֵלֵךְ ______________________________

אִירָא ______________________________

יְנַחֲמֻנִי ______________________________

Psalm 1:5

תַּעֲרֹךְ ______________________________

צֹרְרָי ______________________________

דִּשַּׁנְתָּ ______________________________

Psalm 1:6

יִרְדְּפוּנִי ______________________________

וְשַׁבְתִּי ______________________________

Grammatical Commentary: Psalm 23:1-6

Psalm 23:1

מִזְמוֹר The ms noun מִזְמוֹר occurs 57 times in the Hebrew Bible, each occurrence appearing in the first verse of a different psalm in the book of Psalms. In the Hebrew Bible, a song title, or superscription, may appear as part of the first verse in the Hebrew text. In certain instances, the superscription will constitute the whole of the first verse in the Hebrew text (Ps 3:1, "A psalm by David, when he fled from Absalom his son"). In such cases, the versification of the Hebrew Bible will not correspond to that of the English Bible. For example, in the Hebrew Bible Psalm 3 has nine total verses, but in the English Bible, it has only eight verses. The difference in versification is accounted for by the placement of the superscription or psalm title. In Hebrew, the title may represent the first verse. In English, the title is not counted among the verses but appears prior to the first verse, often in smaller, italicized script. When commentators cite an English verse number that differs from the Hebrew verse number, the Hebrew reference number will usually follow in brackets (for example, Ps 3:8[9]).

לְדָוִד The preposition לְ is prefixed to the proper name דָּוִד. In this context, the preposition may indicate that the psalm was written either "*for* David" or "*by* David." For a discussion of the preposition לְ denoting authorship, see Waltke-O'Connor, 11.2.10d.

יְהוָה רֹעִי The divine name is followed by the Qal active Participle ms of רָעָה with a 1cs pronominal suffix. The identifying mark of the Participle is the Holem that appears with the first root consonant. Before the addition of a pronominal suffix, the expected ה ֶ vowel letter (רֹעֶה) drops off.

With a psalm that begins with the statement, "Yahweh is my shepherd," its attribution to David is of some significance. In the account of his anointing by Samuel (1 Sam 16:1-13), before David's name is revealed, we are told (in v. 11), "Behold, he is shepherding the flock" (וְהִנֵּה רֹעֶה בַּצֹּאן). The shepherd metaphor provides us with a hint for understanding the rest of the psalm. In the ancient world, the shepherd was to protect and to provide for his flock. In this psalm, Yahweh is described as the one who provides in verses 1-3 and the one who protects in verses 4-5. In verse 6, the conclusion of the psalmist is based upon these two realities.

לֹא אֶחְסָר The negative particle לֹא is followed by the Qal Imperfect 1cs of חָסֵר. The verb חָסֵר is Tsere-Stative, so the Imperfect stem vowel should be Pathach, as in אֶחְסַר (15.6). However, in pause, Pathach lengthens to Qamets (36.3.1). In *BHS*, this form appears with Silluq under the ס (אֶחְסָֽר). This construction may be translated, "I shall not be in [a state of] want."

Psalm 23:2

בִּנְאוֹת דֶּשֶׁא The preposition בְּ is prefixed to the fp construct noun נְאוֹת (lexical form נָוֶה) followed by the absolute Segholate noun דֶּ֫שֶׁא. Translate as "in pastures of grass" or "in green pastures."

יַרְבִּיצֵנִי The י preformative and the lack of any sufformative identify this form as Imperfect 3ms of רָבַץ. The Pathach preformative vowel and the Hireq Yod stem vowel are diagnostic of the Hiphil stem. The pronominal suffix ֵנִי is 1cs. With the Hiphil stem, this construction is translated as "he *makes* me lie down."

עַל־מֵי מְנֻחוֹת The preposition עַל is joined by Maqqef to the mp construct form of מַ֫יִם which is followed by the fp absolute form of מְנוּחָה. The construct chain מֵי מְנֻחוֹת is translated literally as "waters of resting." Idiomatically, however, this expression translates as "still" (KJV, RSV, ESV) or "quiet" (NIV, NASB) waters.

יְנַהֲלֵנִי Once again, the preformative י and the lack of any sufformative identify יְנַהֲלֵנִי as Imperfect 3ms of נָהַל. The Vocal Shewa under the Imperfect preformative and the Pathach under the first root letter are diagnostic of the Piel stem. The Daghesh Forte expected in the second root letter is rejected by the guttural ה but the Pathach does not lengthen to Qamets according to the pattern of virtual doubling (31.6-8). Translate this construction imperfectively in the present tense, "he leads me."

Psalm 23:3

נַפְשִׁי יְשׁוֹבֵב The Segholate noun נֶ֫פֶשׁ with a 1cs pronominal suffix is the object of the verb יְשׁוֹבֵב that follows. The form of this verb may be difficult to identify. Recall that Biconsonantal and Geminate verbs occur infrequently in the Piel stem. Instead, these weak verbs prefer an alternate stem formation called the Polel. The diagnostic features of the Polel conjugation are the Holem Waw following the first root letter and the doubling of the final Biconsonantal root letter in every form of every conjugation. In this case, the Imperfect preformative and the lack of any sufformative identify יְשׁוֹבֵב as

Polel Imperfect 3ms of the verbal root שׁוּב (he restores my soul). For additional information on the Polel and a listing of the paradigms, see 31.13.

יַנְחֵנִי Recognition of the suffix ֵ נִי (see יַרְבִּיצֵנִי and יְנַהֲלֵנִי above) and the Imperfect preformative leads to the identification of this verb as Imperfect 3ms with a 1cs pronominal suffix. The Pathach stem vowel is diagnostic of the Hiphil stem and the verbal root is נָחָה. Remember that forms ending in vowel letters spelled with ה (as in יַנְחֶה) drop that vowel letter before the addition of a pronominal suffix (he leads me).

בְמַעְגְּלֵי־צֶדֶק The preposition בְּ is prefixed to the mp construct form of מַעְגָּל followed by the ms absolute noun צֶדֶק (on paths of righteousness).

Psalm 23:4

גַּם כִּי The combination of the two conjunctions גַּם and כִּי in this context may be translated as "even when" or "even though." See *HALOT* 1:196 (use 9); 1:471 (use 12). In this psalm, גַּם כִּי marks the transition between Yahweh as the shepherd who provides and Yahweh as the shepherd who protects.

אֵלֵךְ The preformative א identifies this verb as Qal Imperfect 1cs. The Tsere preformative vowel is a diagnostic feature of the I-י (Type 1) weak verb class (16.6-7) in the Qal. In this case, you must recall that the verb הָלַךְ inflects just like the I-י (Type 1) weak verb (even when I walk).

בְּגֵיא צַלְמָוֶת The preposition בְּ is prefixed to the singular construct form of גַּיְא followed by a word that appears to be a combination of צֵל (shadow) and מָוֶת (death). See *HALOT* 2:1029.

לֹא־אִירָא רָע The negative particle לֹא is joined by Maqqef to the verb אִירָא, which is followed by its object, the adjective רָע used substantively. As with אֵלֵךְ above, the preformative א of אִירָא identifies it as Qal Imperfect 1cs verb. Both verbs belong to the I-י weak verb pattern of inflection. In this case, however, אִירָא is Type 2 while אֵלֵךְ is Type 1 (16.6-7).

כִּי־אַתָּה עִמָּדִי Here, the conjunction כִּי introduces a verbless clause in which the 2ms personal pronoun אַתָּה is the subject and the preposition עִמָּד with a 1cs pronominal suffix is the predicate (for you *are* with me). In this context, the כִּי clause provides the grounds for the preceding statement.

שִׁבְטְךָ וּמִשְׁעַנְתֶּךָ This phrase consists of the two nouns שֵׁבֶט and מִשְׁעֶנֶת (joined by the conjunction וְ), each of which appears with a 2ms pronominal suffix (your rod and your staff).

הֵמָּה יְנַחֲמֻנִי The 3mp personal pronoun הֵמָּה helps to identify the person, gender, and number of the verb that follows. This is confirmed by the verb's preformative י and the defectively written sufformative (Qibbuts for Shureq). The stem of the verb is identified by the Vocal Shewa preformative vowel and the Pathach under the first root letter. These features are diagnostic of the Piel stem. The Daghesh Forte of the Piel stem expected in the second root letter is rejected by the guttural in that position. The Pathach does not lengthen to Qamets, according to the pattern of virtual doubling. Finally, note the reoccurrence of the 1cs pronominal suffix נִי (they comfort me).

Psalm 23:5

תַּעֲרֹךְ לְפָנַי שֻׁלְחָן The preformative תּ, the Pathach preformative vowel, and the Hateph Pathach under the first root letter identify this verb as either Qal (16.3.2) or Hiphil (27.2) Imperfect 2ms of a I-Guttural verb. The Holem stem vowel makes the Qal identification correct. The Hiphil stem vowel is Hireq Yod. The construction לְפָנַי consists of the preposition לְ, the mp noun פָּנִים (lexical form פָּנֶה), and a 1cs (Type 2) pronominal suffix. The ms noun שֻׁלְחָן functions as the object of the verb. Translate this clause, "you prepare [set] a table before me."

צֹרְרָי The Holem appearing with the first root letter is diagnostic of the Qal active Participle. The 1cs Type 2 pronominal suffix identifies the gender and number as masculine and plural. The spelling of this Type 2 pronominal suffix with Qamets instead of Pathach (צֹרְרַי) is pausal (36.3.1) appearing with Athnach in *BHS* (צֹרְרָ֑י).

דִּשַּׁנְתָּ בַשֶּׁמֶן רֹאשִׁי The sufformative תָּ identifies דִּשַּׁנְתָּ as Perfect 2ms. The Hireq under the first root letter and the Daghesh Forte in the second root letter are diagnostic of the Piel stem. The prepositional phrase בַשֶּׁמֶן identifies the verbal instrument and the noun רֹאשׁ with a 1cs pronominal suffix functions as the verbal object. Literally, this clause translates as "you *make* my head *fat* with oil." Idiomatically, it may be translated as "you *anoint* my head with oil."

כּוֹסִי רְוָיָה The construction כּוֹסִי רְוָיָה is a verbless clause. The subject is the fs noun כּוֹס with a 1cs pronominal suffix. The predicate is the rare fs noun רְוָיָה (my cup *is* overflowing).

אַךְ The adverbial particle אַךְ (surely, indeed) begins the last verse in this psalm and highlights the significance of the psalmist's concluding statement.

יִרְדְּפוּנִי The preformative י and the sufformative וּ identify יִרְדְּפוּנִי as Qal Imperfect 3mp of רָדַף. For the fifth time in this psalm, the 1cs pronominal suffix נִי appears with an Imperfect verb. The verb's subjects טוֹב and חֶסֶד precede. Translate this clause, "surely goodness and mercy [steadfast love] pursue me."

כָּל־יְמֵי חַיָּי This construct chain consists of כָּל (lexical form כֹּל) joined by Maqqef to the mp construct noun יָמִים (lexical form יוֹם) and followed by the mp absolute noun חַיִּים with a 1cs (Type 2) pronominal suffix (all of the days of my life). As with צֹרְרָי above, the 1cs (Type 2) pronominal suffix is spelled with Qamets (חַיָּי) instead of Pathach (חַיַּי) because it appears in pause. In *BHS*, this form appears with Athnach under the first י (חַיָּ֑י).

וְשַׁבְתִּי The spelling of this form is Qal Perfect 1cs of the Biconsonantal root שׁוּב with Waw Consecutive. This construction translates, "and I will *return*." You will notice, however, that this is not the translation that appears in contemporary versions. For example, the NIV and NASB translations read, "and I will *dwell*." This difference in translation is occasioned by an alternative reading of the Hebrew text that arises from comparisons with the Septuagint (the Greek translations of the Hebrew Bible) and other, similar Hebrew texts such as Ps 27:4 (שִׁבְתִּי בְּבֵית־יְהוָה כָּל־יְמֵי חַיַּי). It is clear that there are a number of corresponding features between Ps 23:6 and Ps 27:4. Most important for us is a comparison of the two verbal forms וְשַׁבְתִּי in Ps 23:6 and שִׁבְתִּי in Ps 27:4. The first form (וְשַׁבְתִּי) is spelled with Pathach beneath the שׁ and the second form (שִׁבְתִּי) is spelled with Hireq beneath the שׁ. This minor change in spelling carries with it significant implications. It has already been observed that וְשַׁבְתִּי is Qal Perfect 1cs of שׁוּב with Waw Consecutive. However, the form שִׁבְתִּי from Ps 27:4 is Qal Infinitive Construct (שֶׁ֫בֶת) of יָשַׁב with a 1cs pronominal suffix. This one spelling variation carries with it both a change in conjugation (Perfect with Waw Consecutive to Infinitive Construct with the conjunction וְ) and a change in verbal root (שׁוּב to יָשַׁב). Most modern translations have preferred to read וְשַׁבְתִּי in Ps 23:6 as וְשִׁבְתִּי (agreeing with the Septuagint). Note that the two spelling options do not require any change in the Hebrew consonants, only the Masoretic vowel pointing. This vowel pointing was not added until the second half of the first millennium A.D. (2.1).

לְאֹרֶךְ יָמִים This expression is translated literally, "for length of days." It is one of several expressions common in the book of Psalms that communicate enduring periods of time. See, for example, לְעוֹלָם (forever) and וָעֶד־דֹּר וָדֹר (and from generation to generation) in Ps 100:5 or לְעוֹלָם וָעֶד (forever and ever) in Ps 119:44.

Translation 26

Psalm 100:1-5

Hymn of Praise

1 מִזְמוֹר לְתוֹדָה[1]

הָרִיעוּ[2] לַיהוָה כָּל־הָאָרֶץ

2 עִבְדוּ אֶת־יְהוָה בְּשִׂמְחָה

בֹּאוּ לְפָנָיו בִּרְנָנָה[3]

3 דְּעוּ כִּי־יְהוָה הוּא אֱלֹהִים

הוּא־עָשָׂנוּ וְלֹא [וְלוֹ] אֲנַחְנוּ עַמּוֹ וְצֹאן מַרְעִיתוֹ[4]

4 בֹּאוּ שְׁעָרָיו בְּתוֹדָה חֲצֵרֹתָיו בִּתְהִלָּה

הוֹדוּ־לוֹ בָּרֲכוּ שְׁמוֹ

---

1. תּוֹדָה thanksgiving, thank offering, song of thanksgiving (32).
2. רוּעַ (Hi) to shout, cry (out), sound a signal for war, cheer, shout in triumph (44).
3. רְנָנָה exultation, rejoicing, shout of joy (4).
4. מַרְעִית pasture, place of grazing (10).

5 כִּי־טוֹב יְהוָה לְעוֹלָם חַסְדּוֹ

וְעַד־דֹּר וָדֹר אֱמוּנָתוֹ[5]

Parse the following verbs from Psalm 100:1-5.

Psalm 100:1

הָרִיעוּ ________________________________

Psalm 100:2

עִבְדוּ ________________________________

בֹּאוּ ________________________________

Psalm 100:3

דְּעוּ ________________________________

עָשָׂנוּ ________________________________

Psalm 100:4

בֹּאוּ ________________________________

הוֹדוּ ________________________________

בָּרְכוּ ________________________________

5. אֱמוּנָה faithfulness, reliability (49).

Grammatical Commentary: Psalm 100:1-5

Psalm 100:1

מִזְמוֹר לְתוֹדָה For a discussion of the ms noun מִזְמוֹר, see commentary on Psalm 23:1. מִזְמוֹר is followed by the preposition לְ prefixed to the fs noun תּוֹדָה (a psalm for thanksgiving). The structure of this particular psalm consists of two summons to praise (vv. 1-2 and 4) each followed by a series of reasons or grounds for such praise (vv. 3 and 5). Each summons to praise contains three Imperative 2mp verbs.

הָרִיעוּ There are only eight verbs in Psalm 100, seven of which are Imperative 2mp (the exception is עָשָׂנוּ in verse 3). The stem of this Hiphil Imperative is identified by the ה prefix and Hireq Yod stem vowel. The verbal root is the Biconsonantal רוּעַ.

לַיהוָה In this context, the preposition לְ (prefixed to the divine name) is used to mark the indirect object of the preceding Imperative (shout to Yahweh). See Waltke-O'Connor, 11.2.10d.

כָּל־הָאָרֶץ This construct chain is vocative, the case of direct address. According to Waltke-O'Connor (4.7d), "Vocatives stand in apposition to the second-person pronoun, expressed or unexpressed, and may occur with either verbless or verbal clauses."

Psalm 100:2

עִבְדוּ אֶת־יְהוָה The Qal Imperative 2mp עִבְדוּ is followed by the definite direct object marker joined by Maqqef to the divine name (worship [serve] Yahweh).

בְּשִׂמְחָה This prepositional phrase is used adverbially, modifying the Imperative עִבְדוּ ("with joy" or "joyfully").

בֹּאוּ לְפָנָיו The Qal Imperative 2mp of בּוֹא is followed by the prepositional phrase לְפָנָיו (come before him). The Holem Waw of the verb is spelled defectively as Holem. In fact, of the 67 times that the Qal Imperative of בּוֹא (18.7) occurs in the Hebrew Bible, it is spelled defectively 61 times.

בִּרְנָנָה Like בְּשִׂמְחָה above, this prepositional phrase is also functioning adverbially, modifying the Imperative בֹּאוּ.

דְּעוּ This is the fourth Imperative 2mp in Psalm 100 and it introduces a series of statements providing the grounds for the Imperative calls to worship in the preceding verses. With only two root letters remaining and Vocal Shewa under the first root letter, the verbal root of this Qal Imperative is difficult to identify. Geminate Qal Imperative 2mp verbs are identified by a Holem following the first root letter and a Daghesh Forte in the remaining Geminate consonant (סֹ֫בּוּ; 18.5). Biconsonantal Qal Imperatives appear with medial vowel letters (בּ֫וֹאוּ or בֹּ֫אוּ). The pattern of spelling observed in דְּעוּ appears in III-ה, I-נ, and I-י weak verb classes. In cases such as this, context and a good knowledge of Hebrew vocabulary or a standard lexicon will provide the correct identification (יָדַע).

כִּי־יְהוָה הוּא אֱלֹהִים The particle כִּי introduces the object of the Imperative דְּעוּ. This כִּי clause consists of a verbless clause of identification (23.8.2; Waltke-O'Connor 8.4.1a) where the divine name יְהוָה is the subject and אֱלֹהִים is the predicate. Note the intervening 3ms personal pronoun. In verbless clauses of this type, an intervening pronoun may appear as what is called a pleonastic (i.e., redundant) or dummy (i.e., semantically empty) pronoun (Waltke-O'Connor, 8.4.1b). Pronouns of this type, appearing in this context, are usually left untranslated (know that Yahweh *is* God). See also 23.8.3; Waltke-O'Connor, 16.3.3.

הוּא־עָשָׂנוּ The 3ms personal pronoun is joined by Maqqef to the Qal Perfect 3ms of עָשָׂה with a 1cp pronominal suffix (he made us). The expected final vowel letter of the III-ה Perfect 3ms (ה ָ) is dropped before the addition of the pronominal suffix (נוּ ָ). This is the only verb in Psalm 100 that is not Imperative 2mp.

וְלֹא [וְלוֹ] אֲנַחְנוּ The form וְלֹא followed by the bracketed form [וְלוֹ] indicates a difference in reading according to the Kethiv and Qere of the Masoretic Text (36.5). In this case, what is written in the text (Kethiv) is וְלֹא (and not). However, what was read (Qere) by the Masoretes appears in the margin of the text as וְלוֹ (and to him). Both constructions are pronounced identically. With the Qere, the preposition לְ is prefixed to the 3ms pronominal suffix followed by the 1cp independent personal pronoun. Interpreting the preposition as the ל of possession (see Waltke-O'Connor, 11.2.10f), this expression translates as "we belong to him" or "we are his."

עַמּוֹ וְצֹאן מַרְעִיתוֹ The last few words of this verse stand in apposition to the 1cp personal pronoun אֲנַחְנוּ. In other words, these nouns stand together with the pronoun and specify, explain, or clarify the more ambiguous אֲנַחְנוּ. The form עַמּוֹ consists of the Geminate noun עַם with a 3ms pronominal suffix (his people). The definite construct chain beginning with the conjunction וְ consists of the singular construct noun צֹאן and fs absolute noun מַרְעִית with a 3ms pronominal suffix (his people and the sheep of his pasture).

Psalm 100:4

בֹּאוּ שְׁעָרָיו בְּתוֹדָה This verse constitutes the second summons to praise and contains the last three Imperative 2mp verbal forms in Psalm 100. The verb בֹּאוּ appeared above in verse 2. Here, it is followed by the mp object שְׁעָרִים (lexical form שַׁ֫עַר) with a 3ms pronominal suffix and the prepositional phrase בְּתוֹדָה (compare with לְתוֹדָה above) used adverbially (enter his gates with thanksgiving).

חֲצֵרֹתָיו בִּתְהִלָּה The plural noun חֲצֵרוֹת (lexical form חָצֵר) with a 3ms pronominal suffix is followed by the preposition בְּ prefixed to the fs noun תְּהִלָּה. This expression is parallel to the preceding שְׁעָרָיו בְּתוֹדָה and it is also controlled by the verb of that clause ([enter] his courts with praise).

הוֹדוּ־לוֹ The doubly weak Imperative 2mp הוֹדוּ is identified as Hiphil by the ה prefix of the Hiphil stem. The Holem Waw following the Hiphil prefix is diagnostic of the I-י weak verb class in the Hiphil stem (27.12-13). The third root letter is identified as ה (יָדָה) by a process of elimination (give thanks to him).

בָּרְכוּ שְׁמוֹ The stem of the Imperative 2mp of בָּרַךְ is identified as Piel by the Qamets under the first root letter. The expected Pathach is lengthened to Qamets when the guttural in second root position rejects the Daghesh Forte of the Piel stem (31.9-10). Note that the Piel Imperative 2mp of a II-Guttural verb with compensatory lengthening (בָּרְכוּ) may be confused with a Qal Perfect 3cp II-Guttural verb (בָּחֲרוּ). In this case, context (as well as the preference of בָּרַךְ for the Piel stem) makes the Piel Imperative identification correct (bless his name).

Psalm 100:5

כִּי־טוֹב יְהוָה Introduced by the conjunction כִּי, verse 5 constitutes the second set of reasons for praise. This verse consists of three verbless clauses, each beginning with a predicate followed by its subject (verbless clauses of classification). In this case, therefore, טוֹב is the predicate and the divine name is the subject. In English translation, the subject normally appears before the predicate (for Yahweh *is* good).

לְעוֹלָם חַסְדּוֹ The prepositional phrase לְעוֹלָם is the predicate of this verbless clause. The subject is the ms noun חֶסֶד with a 3ms pronominal suffix. As with טוֹב יְהוָה above, in English the subject is translated before the predicate (his steadfast love *is* eternal).

וְעַד־דֹּר וָדֹר אֱמוּנָתוֹ The prepositional phrase עַד־דֹּר וָדֹר (prefixed with the conjunction וְ) is the predicate of this verbless clause. With regard to the expression דֹּר וָדֹר (literally, "generation and generation"), in Hebrew, a singular noun may be repeated to indicate a distributive nuance and such a construction can be translated with "each," "every," or "all" (Waltke-O'Connor, 7.2.3b). The subject is the fs noun אֱמוּנָה with a 3ms pronominal suffix (and his faithfulness *is* to all generations).

Translation 27

Psalm 121:1-8

Yahweh Will Keep You

1 שִׁיר לַמַּעֲלוֹת[1]

אֶשָּׂא עֵינַי אֶל־הֶהָרִים מֵאַיִן[2] יָבֹא עֶזְרִי[3]

2 עֶזְרִי מֵעִם יְהוָה עֹשֵׂה שָׁמַיִם וָאָרֶץ

3 אַל־יִתֵּן לַמּוֹט[4] רַגְלֶךָ אַל־יָנוּם[5] שֹׁמְרֶךָ

4 הִנֵּה לֹא־יָנוּם וְלֹא יִישָׁן[6] שׁוֹמֵר יִשְׂרָאֵל

5 יְהוָה שֹׁמְרֶךָ יְהוָה צִלְּךָ עַל־יַד יְמִינֶךָ

6 יוֹמָם הַשֶּׁמֶשׁ לֹא־יַכֶּכָּה וְיָרֵחַ[7] בַּלָּיְלָה

---

1. מַעֲלָה ascent, step, stairs; (fp) מַעֲלוֹת (49).
2. אַיִן where (from)? whence? (17).
3. עֵזֶר help, assistance (17).
4. מוֹט (Q) to totter, shake, waver, sway, stagger; (Ni) be made to stagger, stumble or totter (39).
5. נוּם (Q) to fall asleep, slumber (6).
6. יָשֵׁן (Q) to sleep, go to sleep, be asleep (16).
7. יָרֵחַ moon (27).

7 יְהוָה יִשְׁמָרְךָ מִכָּל־רָע יִשְׁמֹר אֶת־נַפְשֶׁךָ

8 יְהוָה יִשְׁמָר־צֵאתְךָ וּבוֹאֶךָ מֵעַתָּה וְעַד־עוֹלָם

Parse the following verbs from Psalm 121:1-8.

Psalm 121:1

אֶשָּׂא ____

יָבֹא ____

Psalm 121:2

עֹשֵׂה ____

Psalm 121:3

יִתֵּן ____

יָנוּם ____

שֹׁמְרֶךָ ____

Psalm 121:4

יִישָׁן ____

שׁוֹמֵר ____

Psalm 121:6

יַכֶּכָּה ____

Psalm 121:7

יִשְׁמָרְךָ ____

יִשְׁמֹר ____

Psalm 121:8

צֵאתְךָ	________________________________
וּבוֹאֶךָ	________________________________

Grammatical Commentary: Psalm 121:1-8

Psalm 121:1

שִׁיר לַמַּעֲלוֹת The ms noun שִׁיר is followed by the preposition לְ prefixed to the definite article and the fp noun מַעֲלוֹת (lexical form מַעֲלָה). The expression is translated "a song for the ascents." This psalm belongs to a group of psalms known collectively as the Psalms of Ascent. There are fifteen psalms in this group, beginning in Psalm 120 and continuing through Psalm 134. Each psalm in this category, except for Psalm 121, appears with the title שִׁיר הַמַּעֲלוֹת (song of the ascents). Four of these songs are attributed to David (122, 124, 131, 133) and one to Solomon (127). These psalms may have been sung during those annual pilgrimages when worshipers would travel to Jerusalem to celebrate the feasts of Yahweh.

אֶשָּׂא עֵינַי The preformative א with Seghol identifies אֶשָּׂא as Qal Imperfect 1cs. The Daghesh Forte in the שׂ represents the assimilated נ of the first root letter (נָשָׂא). The object of the verb that follows is the dual עֵינַ֫יִם with a 1cs (Type 2) pronominal suffix (I lift up my [two] eyes).

אֶל־הֶהָרִים The preposition אֶל is joined by Maqqef to the mp noun הָרִים (lexical form הַר) prefixed with the definite article (to the mountains [hills]). For the spelling of the definite article with Seghol, see 5.4.3.

מֵאַיִן יָבֹא עֶזְרִי The preposition מִן is prefixed to the adverbial particle אַ֫יִן meaning "where" (not to be confused with the identically spelled particle of non-existence). The adverb אַ֫יִן appears only 17 times in the Hebrew Bible and, in each case, it is prefixed with the preposition מִן and may be translated, "from where?" With regard to the verb יָבֹא, the preformative י and the lack of a sufformative identify it as Imperfect 3ms. The Qamets preformative vowel and Holem (defectively written Holem Waw) following the first root letter identify it further as a Qal form of the Biconsonantal weak verb בּוֹא (where does my help come from?).

Psalm 121:2

עֶזְרִי מֵעִם יְהוָה This verbless clause of identification answers the question from the preceding verse. The subject is the ms Segholate noun עֵ֫זֶר with a 1cs pronominal suffix. The predicate is a prepositional phrase consisting of the preposition מִן prefixed to the preposition עִם followed by the divine name (my help *is* from Yahweh).

עֹשֵׂה שָׁמַיִם וָאָרֶץ The stem and conjugation of the verb עֹשֵׂה are identified by the Holem vowel in the first syllable, a spelling feature that is diagnostic of the Qal Participle (22.3.3). The ms ending Seghol He (עֹשֶׂה) has changed to Tsere He (עֹשֵׂה) in the construct state (10.3.2d). The construct chain עֹשֵׂה שָׁמַיִם וָאָרֶץ stands in apposition to the preceding divine name ([the] maker of heaven and earth).

Psalm 121:3

אַל־יִתֵּן Verse 3 consists of two clauses, each introduced by the negative particle אַל joined by Maqqef to the verb that follows (15.8.2). The verb יִתֵּן is the Qal Imperfect 3ms of נָתַן. The first root letter has assimilated into the second root letter as Daghesh Forte (16.16.2). The subject of this verb is יְהוָה from verse 2.

לַמּוֹט רַגְלֶךָ The construction לַמּוֹט is difficult to interpret. In form, it appears to be a combination of the preposition לְ prefixed to the definite article and the ms noun מוֹט. However, the noun מוֹט denotes a pole used for carrying objects (cf. Num 4:10, 12), and its appearance makes no sense in this context. In *HALOT* (1:555), this construction is identified as a possible Qal Infinitive Construct from the verbal root מוֹט prefixed with the preposition לְ, meaning "to totter, shake." According to *NIDOTTE*, the combination of the verb מוֹט and the noun רֶ֫גֶל "forms a figure of speech that denotes a falling into calamity" (*NIDOTTE* 2:865). This interpretation appears to make better sense in this context (cf. Ps 13:4[5]; 38:16[17]; 66:9). With the negative verbal construction that precedes, this expression is translated literally, "he does not give your foot to slipping" or, more idiomatically, "he will not let your foot slip" (NIV).

אַל־יָנוּם שֹׁמְרֶךָ In this second negative clause, אַל is followed by the Qal Imperfect 3ms of the Biconsonantal verb נוּם. The form following the Imperfect verb is identified as a Qal Participle (ms with a 2ms pronominal suffix) by the Holem following the first root letter. This Participle is functioning substantively as the subject of the verb (the one who protects you does not slumber). Note that the verbal root שָׁמַר appears six times in Psalm 121: three times as a Participle ms (in verses 3-5) and three times as an Imperfect 3ms (in verses 7-8). In each instance, "Yahweh" is the subject of the verbal action.

Psalm 121:4

לֹא־יָנוּם Similar in construction to verse 3, verse 4 also consists of two negative clauses with Imperfect verbs. In this verse, however, the negative particle is לֹא (15.8.1) instead of אַל. An additional point of similarity between verses 3 and 4 is the repetition of the verbal form יָנוּם (he never slumbers).

וְלֹא יִישָׁן Preceded by the conjunction וְ prefixed to the negative particle לֹא, the verbal form יִישָׁן is Qal Imperfect 3ms of יָשֵׁן (he never sleeps), a synonym of נוּם. The verbal root יָשֵׁן belongs to the I-י (Type 2) weak verb class where the initial root letter is seemingly preserved by the Hireq Yod vowel letter (16.6; 16.7.3). The expected Pathach stem vowel is lengthened to Qamets in pause (36.3.1), appearing in *BHS* with Athnach under the שׁ (יִישָׁ֑ן).

שׁוֹמֵר יִשְׂרָאֵל The Qal active Participle ms of שָׁמַר is in construct with the proper name יִשְׂרָאֵל. This construct chain functions as the subject of the preceding two verbs יָנוּם and יִישָׁן (the protector of Israel does not slumber nor does he sleep). Note that the Holem vowel characteristic of the Qal active Participle is spelled with Holem Waw (22.3.3).

Psalm 121:5

יְהוָה שֹׁמְרֶךָ A verbless clause (of identification) where the divine name is the subject and a Qal Participle (ms with a 2ms pronominal suffix) follows as the predicate ("Yahweh *is* your protector" or "Yahweh is the one who protects you").

יְהוָה צִלְּךָ A parallel verbless clause (which also includes the prepositional phrase עַל־יַד יְמִינֶךָ) with the divine name functioning as the subject and the Geminate ms noun צֵל with a 2ms pronominal suffix appearing as the predicate (Yahweh *is* your shadow [shade]). In this context, the noun צֵל is a metaphor for protection.

Psalm 121:6

יוֹמָם The ms noun יוֹם appears with an adverbial suffix ("daily" or "by day"). In Hebrew, some adverbs are formed by adding Qamets Mem (ָם) to a word. This is somewhat similar to the formation of adverbs in English with the -ly suffix. Other Hebrew examples include דּוּמָם (silently), רֵיקָם (vainly), and חִנָּם (gratuitously, for free). See GKC, 100g; Waltke-O'Connor, 5.7e; and Joüon-Muraoka, 102b.

הַשֶּׁמֶשׁ לֹא־יַכֶּכָּה The definite noun שֶׁמֶשׁ functions as the subject of the following negated verb. The identification of the verb is tricky. The preformative י identifies the Imperfect (3ms) conjugation. The Pathach preformative vowel is diagnostic of the Hiphil stem. The Daghesh Forte in the first כ represents the assimilated נ of the verbal root (נָכָה). The 2ms pronominal suffix ֶ כָּה is spelled with a final vowel letter instead of the more common form without it (ֶ ךָ). The 2ms pronominal suffix appears almost 7,000 times in the Hebrew Bible. It is spelled with a final ה vowel letter fewer than 40 times.

וְיָרֵחַ בַּלָּיְלָה This final clause in verse 6 appears without an explicit verb but assumes the verb יַכֶּכָּה from the preceding clause. The noun יָרֵחַ is the subject of the implied verb. The prepositional phrase בַּלָּיְלָה is adverbial (by day the sun will not injure you nor [will] the moon [injure you] by night).

Psalm 121:7

יְהוָה יִשְׁמָרְךָ The divine name is the subject of the verb that follows. The Qal Imperfect 3ms of שָׁמַר appears with a 2ms pronominal suffix. With the addition of this pronominal suffix, the Holem stem vowel reduces to Qamets Hatuf (Yahweh protects you).

מִכָּל־רָע The preposition מִן is prefixed to כָּל, which is joined by Maqqef to the substantive adjective רָע in the absolute position of the construct chain. The ms adjective רַע is spelled with Qamets instead of Pathach in pause (36.3.1), appearing in *BHS* with Athnach under the ר (רָ֑ע).

Psalm 121:8

יִשְׁמָר The Qamets Hatuf stem vowel in יִשְׁמָר appears because it is joined to the following word by Maqqef and so surrenders its primary accent, with the result that its final syllable is closed and unaccented (3.7.1).

צֵאתְךָ וּבוֹאֶךָ These two Infinitive Construct verbs function as the objects of the verb יִשְׁמָר. Both forms are Qal and each has a 2ms pronominal suffix. The verbal root of the first form is the I-י verb יָצָא. Recall that most I-י verbs in the Infinitive Construct conjugation will drop their first root letter and add ת after the third root letter (20.6). The Biconsonantal verbal root of the second form should be easy to identify (בּוֹא). With the preceding Imperfect verb יִשְׁמָר, the first half of this verse is translated, "Yahweh protects your going out and your coming [in]."

מֵעַתָּה וְעַד־עוֹלָם The final expression in this psalm consists of two adverbial prepositional phrases with a temporal nuance. The first consists of the preposition מִן prefixed to the adverb עַתָּה, "from now" or "from this moment." The second prepositional phrase is joined to the first by the conjunction וְ. This conjunction is prefixed to the preposition עַד, which is joined by Maqqef to the ms noun עוֹלָם (and forevermore).

Ezra 7:6-10

A Model for Generations to Come

6 הוּא עֶזְרָא[1] עָלָה מִבָּבֶל וְהוּא־סֹפֵר מָהִיר[2] בְּתוֹרַת מֹשֶׁה
אֲשֶׁר־נָתַן יְהוָה אֱלֹהֵי יִשְׂרָאֵל וַיִּתֶּן־לוֹ הַמֶּלֶךְ כְּיַד־יְהוָה אֱלֹהָיו
עָלָיו כֹּל בַּקָּשָׁתוֹ[3] 7 וַיַּעֲלוּ מִבְּנֵי־יִשְׂרָאֵל וּמִן־הַכֹּהֲנִים וְהַלְוִיִּם
וְהַמְשֹׁרְרִים וְהַשֹּׁעֲרִים[4] וְהַנְּתִינִים[5] אֶל־יְרוּשָׁלִָם בִּשְׁנַת־שֶׁבַע
לְאַרְתַּחְשַׁסְתְּא[6] הַמֶּלֶךְ 8 וַיָּבֹא יְרוּשָׁלַ͏ִם בַּחֹדֶשׁ הַחֲמִישִׁי[7] הִיא
שְׁנַת הַשְּׁבִיעִית לַמֶּלֶךְ 9 כִּי בְּאֶחָד לַחֹדֶשׁ הָרִאשׁוֹן הוּא יְסֻד[8]
הַמַּעֲלָה[9] מִבָּבֶל וּבְאֶחָד לַחֹדֶשׁ הַחֲמִישִׁי בָּא אֶל־יְרוּשָׁלִָם

1. עֶזְרָא Ezra (22).
2. מָהִיר skilled, experienced (4).
3. בַּקָּשָׁה wish, request, desire (8).
4. שׁוֹעֵר gatekeeper; (mp) שֹׁעֲרִים (37).
5. נָתִין temple servant; (mp) נְתִינִים (17).
6. אַרְתַּחְשַׁסְתְּא Artaxerxes (10).
7. חֲמִישִׁי (adj) fifth; (fs) חֲמִישִׁית (45).
8. יְסֻד foundation, beginning (1).
9. מַעֲלָה ascent, step, stairs; (fp) מַעֲלוֹת (49).

כְּיַד־אֱלֹהָיו הַטּוֹבָה עָלָיו 10 כִּי עֶזְרָא הֵכִין לְבָבוֹ לִדְרוֹשׁ
אֶת־תּוֹרַת יְהוָה וְלַעֲשֹׂת וּלְלַמֵּד בְּיִשְׂרָאֵל חֹק וּמִשְׁפָּט

Parse the following verbs from Ezra 7:6-10.

Ezra 7:6

עָלָה ____________________

נָתַן ____________________

וַיִּתֶּן ____________________

Ezra 7:7

וַיַּעֲלוּ ____________________

וְהַמְשֹׁרְרִים ____________________

Ezra 7:8

וַיָּבֹא ____________________

Ezra 7:9

בָּא ____________________

Ezra 7:10

הֵכִין ____________________

לִדְרוֹשׁ ____________________

וְלַעֲשֹׂת ____________________

וּלְלַמֵּד ____________________

Grammatical Commentary: Ezra 7:6-10

Ezra 7:6

הוּא עֶזְרָא עָלָה The Qal Perfect 3ms verb עָלָה is preceded by the 3ms personal pronoun הוּא and the proper name עֶזְרָא. The use of the pronoun in this context is rare and occurs primarily in books written after Israel's exile. In cases such as this, it precedes a personal name and communicates the nuance of "the same" or "this very" (see Waltke-O'Connor, 16.3.5d; Joüon-Muraoka, 146e1). The significance of the pronoun is to connect this reference to Ezra in verse 6 with the mention of him at the beginning of his genealogical description in verses 1-5 of the same chapter (*this same* Ezra came up).

וְהוּא־סֹפֵר מָהִיר The 3ms personal pronoun הוּא and the Participle סֹפֵר constitute a verbless clause of identification in which the pronoun is the subject and the Participle is the predicate. The adjective מָהִיר modifies (attributively) סֹפֵר (he was an experienced scribe).

בְּתוֹרַת מֹשֶׁה The object of the preposition בְּ is the construct chain תּוֹרַת מֹשֶׁה. This construct chain is definite because the absolute noun מֹשֶׁה is a proper name.

וַיִּתֶּן־לוֹ הַמֶּלֶךְ In the absence of a sufformative, the preformative י identifies וַיִּתֶּן as Imperfect 3ms with Waw Consecutive. The root of this Qal verb is נָתַן. The נ in first root position has assimilated into the second root consonant and is represented by the Daghesh Forte in the ת. The word order for this clause is verb, indirect object (לוֹ), subject (הַמֶּלֶךְ), and then direct object (below).

כֹּל בַּקָּשָׁתוֹ The object of the verb וַיִּתֶּן consists of a definite construct chain with כֹּל in the construct position and בַּקָּשָׁתוֹ in the absolute position. The absolute form consists of the fs noun בַּקָּשָׁה with a 3ms pronominal suffix (and the king granted to him *all of his request*).

Ezra 7:7

וַיַּעֲלוּ The presence of the preformative י and the sufformative וּ identify this form as Imperfect 3mp with Waw Consecutive. The stem of this III-ה verb could be either Qal (they came up) or Hiphil (they brought up). In this context, the Qal stem is the best choice.

מִבְּנֵי־יִשְׂרָאֵל The subject of the verb וַיַּעֲלוּ consists of the two prepositional phrases that follow, each beginning with a different form of the preposition מִן. With this first prepositional phrase, מִן is prefixed

(6.5.2) to the mp construct noun בָּנִים and rendered with its partitive (6.6.3) nuance (*some of* the children of Israel).

וּמִן־הַכֹּהֲנִים The second part of the verbal subject begins with the preposition מִן joined by Maqqef (6.5.1) to the definite mp noun הַכֹּהֲנִים and includes the four additional mp nouns that follow. The partitive (6.6.3) nuance continues with this second construction (*some of* the priests, Levites, singers, gatekeepers, and temple servants).

בִּשְׁנַת־שֶׁבַע This prepositional phrase is adverbial, modifying the verb וַיַּעֲלוּ at the beginning of the verse. The object of the preposition בְּ is the construct form of the fs noun שָׁנָה followed by the absolute noun שֶׁבַע (in the seventh year).

לְאַרְתַּחְשַׁסְתְּא The preposition לְ is prefixed to the proper name אַרְתַּחְשַׁסְתְּא, a Hebrew transliteration of the Persian original for Artaxerxes. Even those of us with limited exposure to Biblical Hebrew will recognize that this is not a regular Hebrew word form.

Ezra 7:8

וַיָּבֹא יְרוּשָׁלִָם The Qal Imperfect 3ms of בּוֹא with Waw Consecutive is followed by the proper name Jerusalem. This proper name is neither the subject nor the object of the verb. It appears as an unmarked adverbial modifier (and he came *to* Jerusalem).

בַּחֹדֶשׁ הַחֲמִישִׁי The prepositional phrase בַּחֹדֶשׁ הַחֲמִישִׁי is also adverbial, modifying the verb וַיָּבֹא (in the fifth month). For a similar construction, see בִּשְׁנַת־שֶׁבַע above in verse 7.

הִיא שְׁנַת הַשְּׁבִיעִית לַמֶּלֶךְ The second half of this verse consists of a verbless clause of identification. The subject is the 3fs personal pronoun הִיא. The predicate follows and consists of the construct chain שְׁנַת הַשְּׁבִיעִית and the prepositional phrase לַמֶּלֶךְ (it *was* [in] the seventh year of the king).

Ezra 7:9

בְּאֶחָד לַחֹדֶשׁ הָרִאשׁוֹן The preposition בְּ is prefixed to the ms form אֶחָד which identifies the day of the month. The identification of the day of the month is followed by the identification of the month of the year. The construction identifying the month of the year begins with the preposition לְ prefixed to the definite article and the ms noun חֹדֶשׁ modified by the ordinal number רִאשׁוֹן (11.6). The use of the preposition לְ in this context marks what is called the "paraphrastic genitive," where the item counted (בְּאֶחָד) requires further qualification (לַחֹדֶשׁ הָרִאשׁוֹן). See Waltke-O'Connor, 9.7b; Joüon-Muraoka, 138b (on the first [day] of the first month).

הוּא יְסֻד הַמַּעֲלָה מִבָּבֶל The 3ms personal pronoun is followed by a word that is difficult to interpret. As it stands, the ms noun יְסֻד is a *hapax legomenon* (a word that appears only one time in the Hebrew Bible) with the possible meaning "beginning." With this interpretation, הוּא יְסֻד הַמַּעֲלָה מִבָּבֶל is a verbless clause translated, "it *was* the beginning of the ascent from Babylon."

וּבְאֶחָד לַחֹדֶשׁ הַחֲמִישִׁי Except for the change in the number of the month and the addition of the conjunction וְ, this expression is identical in construction to בְּאֶחָד לַחֹדֶשׁ הָרִאשׁוֹן above (and on the first [day] of the fifth month).

בָּא This Biconsonantal verb form may be identified as either a Qal Perfect 3ms or a Qal Participle ms of בּוֹא. In this context, the Qal Perfect identification, with Ezra as the implied subject, is better. Translate as "he came" or "he entered."

כְּיַד־אֱלֹהָיו הַטּוֹבָה The preposition כְּ is prefixed to the fs construct noun יַד (lexical form יָד), which is followed by the mp absolute noun אֱלֹהִים with a 3ms (Type 2) pronominal suffix (according to the hand of his God). The adjective הַטּוֹבָה that follows the construct chain must modify יַד because they agree in gender, number, and definiteness (according to the *good* hand of his God). There are two significant grammatical realities that merit review at this point. First, the nouns of a construct chain cannot be separated by other words and so modifying adjectives must appear after the construct chain (10.2.6). Second, remember that the definiteness or indefiniteness of nouns in a construct chain is determined by the absolute noun (10.2.3). In this case, the construct noun is definite because the absolute noun appears with a pronominal suffix and, as such, is considered to be definite.

עָלָיו This final prepositional phrase is adjectival, modifying the fs construct noun יַד (lexical form יָד).

Ezra 7:10

כִּי עֶזְרָא הֵכִין לְבָבוֹ Verse 10 begins with כִּי introducing the reason for Ezra's journey from Babylon to Jerusalem. The proper name עֶזְרָא is the explicit subject of the verb that follows. The ה prefix and the Hireq Yod stem vowel of the verb הֵכִין identify it as the Hiphil Perfect 3ms of the Biconsonantal root כּוּן (27.14; 27.15.1). The object of the verb is the ms noun לֵבָב with a 3ms pronominal suffix. To "prepare" or "establish" the heart is a metaphor or figure of speech for intent or resolve (*HALOT* 1:465). This Hebrew metaphor translates directly into English (for Ezra had determined in his heart).

לִדְרוֹשׁ The verb הֵכִין is followed by three Infinitive Construct verbal forms that identify the purpose or intent of Ezra's decision (20.12.1; 20.15). This first Infinitive Construct is prefixed with the preposition לְ and exhibits the diagnostic points of spelling of the Qal stem (20.2). Note that the expected Holem stem vowel is spelled with Holem Waw in this case (to study [the law of Yahweh]).

וְלַעֲשֹׂת This Qal Infinitive Construct form is prefixed with the conjunction וְ (which joins it to the preceding Infinitive) and the preposition לְ. The Hateph Pathach under the first root letter appears in the I-Guttural verb class (20.3.2). The ת ֹ(וֹת) ending is characteristic of III-ה Infinitive Construct forms (20.4). The object of this Infinitive Construct is implied (to do [it]).

וּלְלַמֵּד This last Infinitive Construct form is also prefixed with the conjunction וְ and the preposition לְ. In this case, however, there is a Pathach under the first root letter and a Daghesh Forte in the second root letter, which identifies the stem of this Infinitive Construct as Piel (30.9; 30.13.1-3). In the Piel stem, the verbal root לָמַד is translated, "to teach."

Translation 29

2 Chronicles 1:7-10

Solomon Asks for Wisdom

7 בַּלַּיְלָה הַהוּא נִרְאָה אֱלֹהִים לִשְׁלֹמֹה וַיֹּאמֶר לוֹ שְׁאַל מָה
אֶתֶּן־לָךְ 8 וַיֹּאמֶר שְׁלֹמֹה לֵאלֹהִים אַתָּה עָשִׂיתָ עִם־דָּוִיד אָבִי
חֶסֶד גָּדוֹל וְהִמְלַכְתַּנִי תַּחְתָּיו 9 עַתָּה יְהוָה אֱלֹהִים יֵאָמֵן דְּבָרְךָ
עִם דָּוִיד אָבִי כִּי אַתָּה הִמְלַכְתַּנִי עַל־עַם רַב כַּעֲפַר הָאָרֶץ 10
עַתָּה חָכְמָה וּמַדָּע[1] תֶּן־לִי וְאֵצְאָה לִפְנֵי הָעָם־הַזֶּה וְאָבוֹאָה
כִּי־מִי יִשְׁפֹּט אֶת־עַמְּךָ הַזֶּה הַגָּדוֹל

---

1. מַדָּע knowledge, understanding, thought (6).

Parse the following verbs from 2 Chronicles 1:7-10.

2 Chronicles 1:7

נִרְאָה ______________________

וַיֹּאמֶר ______________________

שְׁאַל ______________________

אֶתֶּן ______________________

2 Chronicles 1:8

עָשִׂיתָ ______________________

וְהִמְלַכְתַּנִי ______________________

2 Chronicles 1:9

יֵאָמֵן ______________________

הִמְלַכְתַּנִי ______________________

2 Chronicles 1:10

תֶּן ______________________

וְאֵצְאָה ______________________

וְאָבוֹאָה ______________________

יִשְׁפֹּט ______________________

Grammatical Commentary: 2 Chronicles 1:7-10

2 Chronicles 1:7

בַּלַּיְלָה הַהוּא The ms noun לַיְלָה is prefixed with the preposition בְּ and the definite article. It is followed by the 3ms demonstrative adjective (in that night). The ms noun לַיְלָה is one of only a few masculine nouns that have a lexical form ending in Qamets He.

נִרְאָה The נִ prefix is diagnostic of the Niphal stem and the Qamets He ending is diagnostic of the III-ה (Perfect 3ms) weak verb. In the

Niphal stem, the verb רָאָה is translated, "to appear" (God appeared to Solomon).

שְׁאַל The Vocal Shewa and the Pathach stem vowel identify שְׁאַל as Qal Imperative 2ms. The Pathach stem vowel is occasioned by the guttural in second root position.

מָה אֶתֶּן־לָךְ This expression constitutes the object of the preceding Imperative שְׁאַל. The interrogative pronoun מָה (what?) precedes the Qal Imperfect 1cs of נָתַן. With regard to the form אֶתֶּן, the נ in first root position has assimilated into the second root letter and is represented by Daghesh Forte (תּ). The expected Tsere stem vowel has reduced to Seghol because the verb is joined by Maqqef to the prepositional phrase that follows and so surrenders its primary accent. It is also important to recognize that the pronominal suffix attached to the preposition לְ is 2ms with pausal spelling (36.3), appearing in *BHS* with Silluq under the ל (לָֽךְ). The pronoun's antecedent is שְׁלֹמֹה (ask what I should give to you).

2 Chronicles 1:8

אַתָּה עָשִׂיתָ The 2ms personal (subject) pronoun precedes the Qal Perfect 2ms of עָשָׂה. The sufformative תָ identifies the Perfect 2ms and the Hireq Yod between the second root letter and the Perfect sufformative is diagnostic of the III-ה weak verb class.

עִם־דָּוִיד אָבִי The preposition עִם is joined by Maqqef to its object דָּוִיד. The noun אָב with a 1cs pronominal suffix stands in apposition to the object of the preposition (with David my father).

חֶסֶד גָּדוֹל The ms noun חֶסֶד is followed by the attributive ms adjective גָּדוֹל. Together they function as the object of the verb עָשִׂיתָ. This verb-object combination may be translated in a number of different ways. The NIV and ESV, for example, translate the Hebrew verb עָשָׂה with the English verb, "to show," as in, "*you have shown* great kindness [great and steadfast love]." The NASB, for another example, prefers to translate עָשָׂה with a form of the English verb "to deal" and treats the object חֶסֶד גָּדוֹל as an adverbial modifier, translating it with a preposition, "*you have dealt* with my father David *with* great lovingkindness."

וְהִמְלַכְתַּנִי This Hiphil Perfect 2ms of מָלַךְ is prefixed with the conjunction וְ (not the Waw Consecutive) and it also has a 1cs pronominal suffix (ֽנִי). Note that when a pronominal suffix is added to a Perfect 2ms form, the verb's sufformative is spelled תּ (without Qamets) before the pronominal suffix (19.4.3). The הִ prefix and the Pathach stem vowel are diagnostic features of the Hiphil Perfect (2ms). In the Hiphil stem, the verb מָלַךְ is translated, "to make [someone] king" (and you have made me king).

2 Chronicles 1:9

יְהוָה אֱלֹהִים The divine name, appearing together with the common noun אֱלֹהִים, is vocative, that is, used for direct address. In translation, the vocative is usually set off by commas and, in more traditional English versions, may be preceded by "O" as in "O Lord God."

יֵאָמֵן דְּבָרְךָ The preformative י without an additional sufformative identifies the Imperfect 3ms. The Tsere under the Imperfect preformative followed by the Qamets under the first root letter is diagnostic of the I-Guttural Niphal Imperfect. In the Niphal Imperfect strong verb, the נ of the Niphal stem assimilates as Daghesh Forte into the first root letter. When, as in this case, that first root letter is a guttural consonant, the Daghesh Forte is rejected and the Hireq preformative vowel lengthens to Tsere according to the rules for compensatory lengthening (25.7.1). The verbal subject דָּבָר with a 2ms pronominal suffix follows (let your word be confirmed). The position of the verb in its clause and other contextual considerations suggest the volitional translation value.

כַּעֲפַר הָאָרֶץ The preposition כְּ is prefixed to the construct noun of a construct chain. The lexical form of the ms construct noun is עָפָר. The change in vocalization (the spelling of the vowels) is occasioned by the construct noun's surrendering its primary accent to the absolute noun (10.3.1a-b). The entire construct chain is definite because the absolute noun is definite with the prefixing of the definite article (like the dust of the earth).

2 Chronicles 1:10

חָכְמָה וּמַדָּע The nouns חָכְמָה and מַדָּע function as the objects of the Imperative verb that follows. In this context, their position at the beginning of the clause is intended to highlight their significance.

תֶּן־לִי Identification of the Imperative verb תֶּן can be difficult. Without a sufformative, the person, gender, and number must be 2ms. The verbal root is נָתַן (give to me wisdom and knowledge). The first root letter has dropped off in the formation of the Imperative (18.6). The regular form of this Imperative is תֵּן, spelled with Tsere.

However, when joined by Maqqef to the following word, it surrenders its primary accent and the originally closed, accented syllable becomes a closed, unaccented syllable (see 3.13).

וְאֵצְאָה The preformative א identifies this verb as Imperfect 1cs. The Tsere preformative vowel is diagnostic of the I-י (Type 1) weak verb class (יָצָא). This verb also appears with the conjunction וְ and the Paragogic ה. The Paragogic ה appears with the Imperfect (אֶקְטְלָה), Imperfect with Waw Consecutive (וָאֶקְטְלָה), and Imperative (קָטְלָה) conjugations. To date, the significance of this suffix is undetermined. Grammarians have suggested that it may be emphatic, imply submission or politeness, or indicate that the action of the verb is directed back toward, or done for the benefit of, the verbal subject (ventive). The most important feature of this verb, however, is the verbal sequence within which it appears. When an Imperative verb is followed by the Imperfect with the conjunction וְ, it creates a verbal sequence in which the second clause indicates the purpose or result of the preceding Imperative (18.12.3; 23.7.4). In this case, therefore, we do not translate וְאֵצְאָה as "and I will go out" but as a purpose clause, "*so that* I may go out."

וְאָבוֹאָה Except for the spelling differences occasioned by the verbal root, this construction is identical to וְאֵצְאָה. It is the Qal Imperfect 1cs of בּוֹא with the conjunction וְ and Paragogic ה (discussed above). This verb continues the Imperative-Imperfect verbal sequence, indicating a purpose or result clause (and *so that* I may come in).

כִּי־מִי יִשְׁפֹּט This clause, introduced by the conjunction כִּי, provides the reason or motivation for Solomon's request. The conjunction כִּי is followed by the interrogative pronoun מִי (who?), which frames Solomon's reason or motivation in the form of a question. In this context, the Imperfect verb may be translated with the modal (auxiliary) verb, "can" (for who can judge?).

אֶת־עַמְּךָ הַזֶּה הַגָּדוֹל The final portion of this verse constitutes the object of the preceding verb יִשְׁפֹּט. It begins with the definite direct object marker אֶת־ because the object of the verb (עַם) is made definite with the addition of a (2ms) pronominal suffix. The verbal object is further modified by the ms demonstrative adjective זֶה and the ms adjective גָּדוֹל (this great people of yours).

Translation 30

2 Chronicles 7:1-4

The Glory of Yahweh Fills the Temple

1 וּכְכַלּוֹת שְׁלֹמֹה לְהִתְפַּלֵּל וְהָאֵשׁ יָרְדָה מֵהַשָּׁמַיִם וַתֹּאכַל
הָעֹלָה וְהַזְּבָחִים וּכְבוֹד יְהוָה מָלֵא אֶת־הַבָּיִת׃ 2 וְלֹא יָכְלוּ
הַכֹּהֲנִים לָבוֹא אֶל־בֵּית יְהוָה כִּי־מָלֵא כְבוֹד־יְהוָה אֶת־בֵּית
יְהוָה׃ 3 וְכֹל בְּנֵי יִשְׂרָאֵל רֹאִים בְּרֶדֶת הָאֵשׁ וּכְבוֹד יְהוָה
עַל־הַבָּיִת וַיִּכְרְעוּ[1] אַפַּיִם אַרְצָה עַל־הָרִצְפָּה[2] וַיִּשְׁתַּחֲווּ וְהוֹדוֹת
לַיהוָה כִּי טוֹב כִּי לְעוֹלָם חַסְדּוֹ׃ 4 וְהַמֶּלֶךְ וְכָל־הָעָם זֹבְחִים זֶבַח
לִפְנֵי יְהוָה׃

---

1. כָּרַע (Q) to bow (down), kneel (down), fall to one's knees (36).
2. רִצְפָּה (stone or mosaic) pavement (7).

Parse the following verbs from 2 Chronicles 7:1-4.

2 Chronicles 7:1

וּכְכַלּוֹת

לְהִתְפַּלֵּל

יָרְדָה

וַתֹּאכַל

מָלֵא

2 Chronicles 7:2

יָכְלוּ

לָבוֹא

2 Chronicles 7:3

רֹאִים

בְּרֶדֶת

וַיִּכְרְעוּ

וַיִּשְׁתַּחֲווּ

וְהוֹדוֹת

2 Chronicles 7:4

זֹבְחִים

Grammatical Commentary: 2 Chronicles 7:1-4

2 Chronicles 7:1

וּכְכַלּוֹת שְׁלֹמֹה לְהִתְפַּלֵּל This expression consists of two Infinitive Constructs and the proper name שְׁלֹמֹה (functioning as the subject of the first Infinitive). The conjunction וְ and the preposition כְּ are prefixed to the Infinitive Construct כַּלּוֹת. The conjunction is spelled with Shureq before Vocal Shewa (5.7.2b). The preposition כְּ signals the temporal use of the Infinitive Construct (20.12.5). The Pathach under the first root letter and the Daghesh Forte in the second root letter identify the Piel stem, and the וֹת ending is diagnostic of the III-ה weak verb class (כָּלָה). The second Infinitive Construct is prefixed with the preposition לְ and is easily identified as Hithpael with the prefix הִתְ, Pathach under the first root letter, and Daghesh Forte in the second root letter. This second Infinitive is complementary (20.12.4) and the entire expression is translated, "and when Solomon finished praying."

וְהָאֵשׁ יָרְדָה The conjunction וְ and the definite article are prefixed to the fs noun אֵשׁ. This noun functions as the subject of the Qal Perfect 3fs verb that follows (and the fire came down).

וַתֹּאכַל הָעֹלָה וְהַזְּבָחִים The verb וַתֹּאכַל is Qal Imperfect 3fs or 2ms of אָכַל with Waw Consecutive (16.3.3). Since the subject of the verb is the fs noun אֵשׁ from the previous clause, the correct identification is 3fs. The verb is followed by two definite direct objects, though they are not marked by the definite direct object marker (and it [the fire] consumed the burnt offering and the sacrifices).

וּכְבוֹד יְהוָה The elements of the last clause in this verse appear in the order: subject, verb, object. The subject of the verb מָלֵא is the construct chain כְּבוֹד יְהוָה, which is prefixed with the conjunction וְ. The key to recognizing that כְּבוֹד is in the construct state is the Vocal Shewa under the first consonant. The absolute or lexical form is כָּבוֹד with Qamets and, in the construct state, the changeable long vowel in the open syllable reduces to Vocal Shewa (10.3.1b).

מָלֵא This Qal Perfect 3ms form belongs to the Tsere-Stative verb category (13.10). In the Perfect conjugation, only the 3ms form is spelled with Tsere. All other forms of the Tsere-Stative Perfect exhibit the strong verb spelling.

אֶת־הַבָּיִת Here, the definite direct object is marked by the definite direct object marker (accusative particle) אֶת־. Because the ms absolute noun בַּיִת is pausal (36.3.1), appearing in *BHS* with Silluq under the ב (הַבָּ֑יִת), the expected Pathach has changed to Qamets.

2 Chronicles 7:2

וְלֹא יָכְלוּ הַכֹּהֲנִים Preceded by the conjunction וְ and the negative particle לֹא, the verb יָכְלוּ is Qal Perfect 3cp of יָכֹל. In this case, the consonant י is not an Imperfect preformative but rather the first consonant of the verbal root. The verbal subject follows (and the priests were not able).

לָבוֹא With the prefixing of the preposition לְ, this Biconsonantal Qal Infinitive Construct (20.7) is easy to identify. This Infinitive Construct form complements the preceding Perfect verb יָכְלוּ (and the priests were not able *to enter*).

2 Chronicles 7:3

רֹאִים The Holem following the first root letter identifies this as a Qal active Participle of רָאָה. The inflectional ending is mp. The construct chain that precedes this Participle (וְכֹל בְּנֵי יִשְׂרָאֵל) functions as the subject of the verbal action (and all of the children of Israel were *watching*).

בְּרֶדֶת הָאֵשׁ The verbal construction בְּרֶדֶת is difficult to identify. Prefixed with the preposition בְּ, this Segholate word formation is identified as a Qal Infinitive Construct. Recall that both I-י and I-נ weak verbs may drop the first root letter and add ת after the third root letter in the formation of the Infinitive Construct (20.5-6). In this case, the verbal root is I-י (יָרַד). The subject of the verbal action follows and the preposition בְּ indicates the temporal use of the Infinitive Construct (when the fire came down).

וּכְבוֹד יְהוָה עַל־הַבָּיִת The combination of the definite construct chain כְּבוֹד יְהוָה (subject) and the following prepositional phrase עַל־הַבָּיִת (predicate) creates a verbless clause (and the glory of Yahweh *was* upon the house). See 23.8.1.

וַיִּכְרְעוּ אַפַּיִם אַרְצָה The verb וַיִּכְרְעוּ is easily identified as Qal Imperfect 3mp of כָּרַע with Waw Consecutive. It is followed by an adverbial expression that is literally translated, "nose to the ground." Idiomatically, this clause may be translated, "they bowed down with their face to the ground." Note that the fs noun אֶ֫רֶץ appears with the directional ending (7.7).

וַיִּשְׁתַּחֲוּוּ The preformative י and the sufformative וּ identify this verbal form as Imperfect 3mp with Waw Consecutive. The distinctive prefix and preformative combination (יִשְׁתּ) is diagnostic of the Hishtaphel Stem (34.16). This stem appears only 173 times in the Hebrew Bible and only with the verbal root חָוָה (and they worshiped).

וְהוֹדוֹת לַיהוָה The verbal form הוֹדוֹת may be difficult to identify at first. The prefix ה is diagnostic of the Hiphil stem. The Holem Waw prefix vowel is diagnostic of the I-י weak verb class and the וֹת ending is diagnostic of the III-ה Infinitive Construct verb. After all of these diagnostic features have been correctly interpreted, this form can be identified as the Hiphil Infinitive Construct of יָדָה (giving thanks to Yahweh).

כִּי טוֹב This verse concludes with two clauses that begin with כִּי, both of which are verbless clauses. In this first verbless כִּי clause, the ms adjective טוֹב is the predicate and the subject (הוּא) is implied (for [he] *is* good). See 23.8.1.

כִּי לְעוֹלָם חַסְדּוֹ In this second verbless clause (of classification), the subject follows the predicate לְעוֹלָם (for his steadfast love is everlasting). Note that this same verbless clause appears 26 times in Psalm 136, at the end of each verse. See 23.8.1.

2 Chronicles 7:4

זֹבְחִים זֶבַח The Holem following the first root letter identifies זֹבְחִים as a Qal active Participle of זָבַח. The inflectional ending is mp. The object of the verbal action follows. Note how both the object (זֶבַח) and the verb זֹבְחִים share a common root (זבח). When a verb and its object share a common root, the object is called a "cognate accusative" (see Waltke-O'Connor, 10.2.1g). With its subject, this expression may be translated literally, "and the king and all of the people *sacrificed a sacrifice*." A more idiomatic translation of this expression would be "*offered* a sacrifice."

Appendix 1: Parsing Answer Key

This answer key contains the parsing information for the 622 verbs selected for parsing in the *Graded Reader*. With verbs that have more than one possible parsing identification, we have selected the one that makes the best sense given the context in which it occurs.

Genesis 1:1-5

1:1

בָּרָא Qal Pf 3ms בָּרָא

1:2

הָיְתָה Qal Pf 3fs הָיָה

מְרַחֶפֶת Piel Ptc fs רָחַף

1:3

וַיֹּאמֶר Qal Imp 3ms אָמַר WC

יְהִי Qal Imp 3ms הָיָה

וַיְהִי Qal Imp 3ms הָיָה WC

1:4

וַיַּרְא Qal Imp 3ms רָאָה WC

וַיַּבְדֵּל Hiphil Imp 3ms בָּדַל WC

1:5

וַיִּקְרָא Qal Imp 3ms קָרָא WC

קָרָא Qal Pf 3ms קָרָא

Genesis 2:1-3

2:1

וַיְכֻלּוּ Pual Imp 3mp כָּלָה WC

2:2

וַיְכַל Piel Imp 3ms כָּלָה WC

עָשָׂה Qal Pf 3ms עָשָׂה

וַיִּשְׁבֹּת Qal Imp 3ms שָׁבַת WC

2:3

וַיְבָרֶךְ Piel Imp 3ms בָּרַךְ WC

וַיְקַדֵּשׁ Piel Imp 3ms קָדַשׁ WC

שָׁבַת Qal Pf 3ms שָׁבַת

בָּרָא Qal Pf 3ms בָּרָא

לַעֲשׂוֹת Qal Inf Cst עָשָׂה prep לְ

Genesis 26:1-6

26:1

וַיְהִי Qal Imp 3ms הָיָה WC

הָיָה Qal Pf 3ms הָיָה

וַיֵּלֶךְ Qal Imp 3ms הָלַךְ WC

26:2

וַיֵּרָא Niphal Imp 3ms רָאָה WC

וַיֹּאמֶר Qal Imp 3ms אָמַר WC

תֵּרֵד Qal Imp 2ms יָרַד

שְׁכֹן Qal Impv 2ms שָׁכַן

אֹמַר Qal Imp 1cs אָמַר

26:3

גּוּר Qal Impv 2ms גּוּר

וְאֶהְיֶה Qal Imp 1cs הָיָה conj וְ

וַאֲבָרְכֶךָּ Piel Imp 1cs בָּרַךְ 2ms suff conj וְ

אֶתֵּן Qal Imp 1cs נָתַן

וַהֲקִמֹתִי Hiphil Pf 1cs קוּם WC

נִשְׁבַּעְתִּי Niphal Pf 1cs שָׁבַע

26:4

וְהִרְבֵּיתִי Hiphil Pf 1cs רָבָה WC

וְנָתַתִּי Qal Pf 1cs נָתַן WC

וְהִתְבָּרְכוּ Hithpael Pf 3cp בָּרַךְ WC

26:5

שָׁמַע Qal Pf 3ms שָׁמַע

וַיִּשְׁמֹר Qal Imp 3ms שָׁמַר WC

26:6

וַיֵּשֶׁב Qal Imp 3ms יָשַׁב WC

Genesis 35:9-15

35:9

וַיֵּרָא Niphal Imp 3ms רָאָה WC

בְּבֹאוֹ Qal Inf Cst בּוֹא prep בְּ 3ms suff

וַיְבָרֶךְ Piel Imp 3ms בָּרַךְ WC

35:10

וַיֹּאמֶר Qal Imp 3ms אָמַר WC

יִקָּרֵא Niphal Imp 3ms קָרָא

יִהְיֶה Qal Imp 3ms הָיָה

וַיִּקְרָא Qal Imp 3ms קָרָא WC

35:11

פְּרֵה Qal Impv 2ms פָּרָה

וּרְבֵה Qal Impv 2ms רָבָה conj וְ

יִהְיֶה Qal Imp 3ms הָיָה

יֵצֵאוּ Qal Imp 3mp יָצָא

35:12

נָתַתִּי Qal Pf 1cs נָתַן

אֶתְּנֶנָּה Qal Imp 1cs נָתַן 3fs suff
אֶתֵּן Qal Imp 1cs נָתַן

35:13

וַיַּעַל Qal Imp 3ms עָלָה WC
דִּבֶּר Piel Pf 3ms דָּבַר

35:14

וַיַּצֵּב Hiphil Imp 3ms נָצַב WC
וַיַּסֵּךְ Hiphil Imp 3ms נָסַךְ WC
וַיִּצֹק Qal Imp 3ms יָצַק WC

Genesis 43:1-8

43:2

וַיְהִי Qal Imp 3ms הָיָה WC
כִּלּוּ Piel Pf 3cp כָּלָה
לֶאֱכֹל Qal Inf Cst אָכַל prep לְ
הֵבִיאוּ Hiphil Pf 3cp בּוֹא
שֻׁבוּ Qal Impv 2mp שׁוּב
שִׁבְרוּ Qal Impv 2mp שָׁבַר

43:3

הָעֵד Hiphil Inf Abs עוּד
הֵעִד Hiphil Pf 3ms עוּד
תִרְאוּ Qal Imp 2mp רָאָה

43:4

מְשַׁלֵּחַ Piel Ptc ms שָׁלַח
נֵרְדָה Qal Imp 1cp יָרַד
וְנִשְׁבְּרָה Qal Imp 1cp שָׁבַר conj וְ

43:5

נֵרֵד Qal Imp 1cp יָרַד
אָמַר Qal Pf 3ms אָמַר

43:6

הֲרֵעֹתֶם Hiphil Pf 2mp רָעַע
לְהַגִּיד Hiphil Inf Cst נָגַד prep לְ

43:7

שָׁאוֹל Qal Inf Abs שָׁאַל
שָׁאַל Qal Pf 3ms שָׁאַל
וַנַּגֶּד Hiphil Imp 1cp נָגַד WC
הֲיָדוֹעַ Qal Inf Abs יָדַע interrog הֲ
נֵדַע Qal Imp 1cp יָדַע
יֹאמַר Qal Imp 3ms אָמַר
הוֹרִידוּ Hiphil Impv 2mp יָרַד

43:8

שִׁלְחָה Qal Impv 2ms שָׁלַח
Paragogic ה
וְנָקוּמָה Qal Imp 1cp קוּם conj וְ
וְנֵלֵכָה Qal Imp 1cp הָלַךְ conj וְ
וְנִחְיֶה Qal Imp 1cp חָיָה conj וְ
נָמוּת Qal Imp 1cp מוּת

Exodus 3:1-12

3:1

הָיָה Qal Pf 3ms הָיָה
רֹעֶה Qal Ptc ms רָעָה
וַיִּנְהַג Qal Imp 3ms נָהַג WC
וַיָּבֹא Qal Imp 3ms בּוֹא WC

3:2

וַיֵּרָא Niphal Imp 3ms רָאָה WC
וַיַּרְא Qal Imp 3ms רָאָה WC
בֹּעֵר Qal Ptc ms בָּעַר
אֻכָּל Qal Pass Ptc ms אָכַל or Pual
Ptc ms אָכַל

3:3

וַיֹּאמֶר Qal Imp 3ms אָמַר WC
אָסֻרָה Qal Imp 1cs סוּר
וְאֶרְאֶה Qal Imp 1cs רָאָה conj וְ
יִבְעַר Qal Imp 3ms בָּעַר

3:4

סָר Qal Pf 3ms סוּר
לִרְאוֹת Qal Inf Cst רָאָה prep לְ
וַיִּקְרָא Qal Imp 3ms קָרָא WC

3:5

תִּקְרַב Qal Imp 2ms קָרַב
שַׁל Qal Impv 2ms נָשַׁל
עוֹמֵד Qal Ptc ms עָמַד

3:6

וַיַּסְתֵּר Hiphil Imp 3ms סָתַר WC
יָרֵא Qal Pf 3ms יָרֵא
מֵהַבִּיט Hiphil Inf Cst נָבַט prep מִן

3:7

רָאֹה Qal Inf Abs רָאָה

רָאִיתִי Qal Pf 1cs רָאָה
שָׁמַעְתִּי Qal Pf 1cs שָׁמַע
נֹגְשָׂיו Qal Ptc mp נָגַשׂ 3ms suff
יָדַעְתִּי Qal Pf 1cs יָדַע

3:8

וָאֵרֵד Qal Imp 1cs יָרַד WC
לְהַצִּילוֹ Hiphil Inf Cst נָצַל prep לְ 3ms suff
וּלְהַעֲלֹתוֹ Hiphil Inf Cst עָלָה conj וְ prep לְ 3ms suff
זָבַת Qal Ptc fs (construct) זוּב

3:9

בָּאָה Qal Pf 3fs בּוֹא
לֹחֲצִים Qal Ptc mp לָחַץ

3:10

לְכָה Qal Impv 2ms הָלַךְ Paragogic ה
וְאֶשְׁלָחֲךָ Qal Imp 1cs שָׁלַח conj וְ 2ms suff
וְהוֹצֵא Hiphil Impv 2ms יָצָא conj וְ

3:11

אֵלֵךְ Qal Imp 1cs הָלַךְ
אוֹצִיא Hiphil Imp 1cs יָצָא

3:12

אֶהְיֶה Qal Imp 1cs הָיָה
שְׁלַחְתִּיךָ Qal Pf 1cs שָׁלַח 2ms suff
בְּהוֹצִיאֲךָ Hiphil Inf Cst יָצָא prep בְּ 2ms suff
תַּעַבְדוּן Qal Imp 2mp עָבַד Paragogic ן

Exodus 6:1-8

6:1

וַיֹּאמֶר Qal Imp 3ms אָמַר WC
תִרְאֶה Qal Imp 2ms רָאָה
אֶעֱשֶׂה Qal Imp 1cs עָשָׂה
יְשַׁלְּחֵם Piel Imp 3ms שָׁלַח 3mp suff
יְגָרְשֵׁם Piel Imp 3ms גָּרַשׁ 3mp suff

6:2

וַיְדַבֵּר Piel Imp 3ms דָּבַר WC

6:3

וָאֵרָא Niphal Imp 1cs רָאָה WC
נוֹדַעְתִּי Niphal Pf 1cs יָדַע

6:4

הֲקִמֹתִי Hiphil Pf 1cs קוּם
לָתֵת Qal Inf Cst נָתַן prep לְ
גָּרוּ Qal Pf 3cp גּוּר

6:5

שָׁמַעְתִּי Qal Pf 1cs שָׁמַע
מַעֲבִדִים Hiphil Ptc mp עָבַד
וָאֶזְכֹּר Qal Imp 1cs זָכַר WC

6:6

אֱמֹר Qal Impv 2ms אָמַר
וְהוֹצֵאתִי Hiphil Pf 1cs יָצָא WC
וְהִצַּלְתִּי Hiphil Pf 1cs נָצַל WC
וְגָאַלְתִּי Qal Pf 1cs גָּאַל WC
נְטוּיָה Qal Pass Ptc fs נָטָה

6:7

וְלָקַחְתִּי Qal Pf 1cs לָקַח WC
וְהָיִיתִי Qal Pf 1cs הָיָה WC
וִידַעְתֶּם Qal Pf 2mp יָדַע WC
הַמּוֹצִיא Hiphil Ptc ms יָצָא definite article

6:8

וְהֵבֵאתִי Hiphil Pf 1cs בּוֹא WC
נָשָׂאתִי Qal Pf 1cs נָשָׂא
לָתֵת Qal Inf Cst נָתַן prep לְ
וְנָתַתִּי Qal Pf 1cs נָתַן WC

Exodus 34:1-6

34:1

וַיֹּאמֶר Qal Imp 3ms אָמַר WC
פְּסָל Qal Impv 2ms פָּסַל
וְכָתַבְתִּי Qal Pf 1cs כָּתַב WC
הָיוּ Qal Pf 3cp הָיָה
שִׁבַּרְתָּ Piel Pf 2ms שָׁבַר

34:2

וֶהְיֵה Qal Impv 2ms הָיָה conj וְ
נָכוֹן Niphal Ptc ms כּוּן
וְעָלִיתָ Qal Pf 2ms עָלָה WC

וְנִצַּבְתָּ Niphal Pf 2ms נָצַב WC

34:3

יַעֲלֶה Qal Imp 3ms עָלָה

יֵרָא Niphal Imp 3ms רָאָה

יִרְעוּ Qal Imp 3mp רָעָה

34:4

וַיִּפְסֹל Qal Imp 3ms פָּסַל WC

וַיַּשְׁכֵּם Hiphil Imp 3ms שָׁכַם WC

וַיַּעַל Qal Imp 3ms עָלָה WC

צִוָּה Piel Pf 3ms צָוָה

וַיִּקַּח Qal Imp 3ms לָקַח WC

34:5

וַיֵּרֶד Qal Imp 3ms יָרַד WC

וַיִּתְיַצֵּב Hithpael Imp 3ms יָצַב WC

וַיִּקְרָא Qal Imp 3ms קָרָא WC

34:6

וַיַּעֲבֹר Qal Imp 3ms עָבַר WC

Leviticus 19:1-4

19:1

וַיְדַבֵּר Piel Imp 3ms דָּבַר WC

לֵּאמֹר Qal Inf Cst אָמַר prep לְ Conjunctive Daghesh

19:2

דַּבֵּר Piel Impv 2ms דָּבַר

וְאָמַרְתָּ Qal Pf 2ms אָמַר WC

תִּהְיוּ Qal Imp 2mp הָיָה

19:3

תִּירָאוּ Qal Imp 2mp יָרֵא

תִּשְׁמֹרוּ Qal Imp 2mp שָׁמַר

19:4

תִּפְנוּ Qal Imp 2mp פָּנָה

תַעֲשׂוּ Qal Imp 2mp עָשָׂה

Numbers 6:22-26

6:22

וַיְדַבֵּר Piel Imp 3ms דָּבַר WC

לֵּאמֹר Qal Inf Cst אָמַר prep לְ Conjunctive Daghesh

6:23

דַּבֵּר Piel Impv 2ms דָּבַר

תְבָרְכוּ Piel Imp 2mp בָּרַךְ

אָמוֹר Qal Inf Abs אָמַר

6:24

יְבָרֶכְךָ Piel Imp 3ms בָּרַךְ 2ms suff

וְיִשְׁמְרֶךָ Qal Imp 3ms בָּרַךְ conj וְ 2ms suff

6:25

יָאֵר Hiphil Imp 3ms אוֹר

וִיחֻנֶּךָּ Qal Imp 3ms חָנַן conj וְ 2ms suff

6:26

יִשָּׂא Qal Imp 3ms נָשָׂא

וְיָשֵׂם Qal Imp 3ms שִׂים conj וְ

Deuteronomy 6:1-15

6:1

צִוָּה Piel Pf 3ms צָוָה

לְלַמֵּד Piel Inf Cst לָמַד prep לְ

לַעֲשׂוֹת Qal Inf Cst עָשָׂה prep לְ

עֹבְרִים Qal Ptc mp עָבַר

לְרִשְׁתָּהּ Qal Inf Cst יָרַשׁ prep לְ 3fs suff

6:2

תִּירָא Qal Imp 2ms יָרֵא

לִשְׁמֹר Qal Inf Cst שָׁמַר prep לְ

מְצַוֶּךָּ Piel Ptc ms צָוָה 2ms suff

יַאֲרִכֻן Hiphil Imp 3mp אָרַךְ Paragogic נ

6:3

וְשָׁמַעְתָּ Qal Pf 2ms שָׁמַע WC

וְשָׁמַרְתָּ Qal Pf 2ms שָׁמַר WC

יִיטַב Qal Imp 3ms יָטַב

תִּרְבּוּן Qal Imp 2mp רָבָה Paragogic נ

דִּבֶּר Piel Pf 3ms דָּבַר

זָבַת Qal Ptc fs (cstr) זוּב

6:4

שְׁמַע Qal Impv 2ms שָׁמַע

6:5

וְאָהַבְתָּ Qal Pf 2ms אָהַב WC

6:6

וְהָיוּ Qal Pf 3cp הָיָה WC

6:7

וְשִׁנַּנְתָּם Piel Pf 2ms שָׁנַן WC 3mp suff

וְדִבַּרְתָּ Piel Pf 2ms דָּבַר WC

בְּשִׁבְתְּךָ Qal Inf Cst יָשַׁב prep בְּ 2ms suff

וּבְלֶכְתְּךָ Qal Inf Cst הָלַךְ conj וְ prep בְּ 2ms suff

וּבְשָׁכְבְּךָ Qal Inf Cst שָׁכַב conj וְ prep בְּ 2ms suff

וּבְקוּמֶךָ Qal Inf Cst קוּם conj וְ prep בְּ 2ms suff

6:8

וּקְשַׁרְתָּם Qal Pf 2ms קָשַׁר WC 3mp suff

6:9

וּכְתַבְתָּם Qal Pf 2ms כָּתַב WC 3mp suff

6:10

וְהָיָה Qal Pf 3ms הָיָה WC

יְבִיאֲךָ Hiphil Imp 3ms הָיָה 2ms suff

נִשְׁבַּע Niphal Pf 3ms שָׁבַע

לָתֶת Qal Inf Cst נָתַן prep לְ

בָנִיתָ Qal Pf 2ms בָּנָה

6:11

מִלֵּאתָ Piel Pf 2ms מָלֵא

חֲצוּבִים Qal Pass Ptc mp חָצַב

חָצַבְתָּ Qal Pf 2ms חָצַב

נָטָעְתָּ Qal Pf 2ms נָטַע

וְאָכַלְתָּ Qal Pf 2ms אָכַל WC

וְשָׂבָעְתָּ Qal Pf 2ms שָׂבַע WC

6:12

הִשָּׁמֶר Niphal Impv 2ms שָׁמַר

תִּשְׁכַּח Qal Imp 2ms שָׁכַח

הוֹצִיאֲךָ Hiphil Pf 3ms יָצָא 2ms suff

6:13

תִּירָא Qal Imp 2ms יָרֵא

תַעֲבֹד Qal Imp 2ms עָבַד

תִּשָּׁבֵעַ Niphal Imp 2ms שָׁבַע

6:14

תֵלְכוּן Qal Imp 2mp הָלַךְ Paragogic נ

6:15

יֶחֱרֶה Qal Imp 3ms חָרָה

וְהִשְׁמִידְךָ Hiphil Pf 3ms שָׁמַד WC 2ms suff

Deuteronomy 11:18-23

11:18

וְשַׂמְתֶּם Qal Pf 2mp שִׂים WC

וּקְשַׁרְתֶּם Qal Pf 2mp קָשַׁר WC

וְהָיוּ Qal Pf 3cp הָיָה WC

11:19

וְלִמַּדְתֶּם Piel Pf 2mp לָמַד WC

לְדַבֵּר Piel Inf Cst דָּבַר prep לְ

בְּשִׁבְתְּךָ Qal Inf Cst יָשַׁב prep בְּ 2ms suff

וּבְלֶכְתְּךָ Qal Inf Cst הָלַךְ conj וְ prep בְּ 2ms suff

וּבְשָׁכְבְּךָ Qal Inf Cst שָׁכַב conj וְ prep בְּ 2ms suff

וּבְקוּמֶךָ Qal Inf Cst קוּם conj וְ prep בְּ 2ms suff

11:20

וּכְתַבְתָּם Qal Pf 2ms כָּתַב WC 3mp suff

11:21

יִרְבּוּ Qal Imp 3mp רָבָה

נִשְׁבַּע Niphal Pf 3ms שָׁבַע

לָתֵת Qal Inf Cst נָתַן prep לְ

11:22

שָׁמֹר Qal Inf Abs שָׁמַר

תִּשְׁמְרוּן Qal Imp 2mp שָׁמַר Paragogic נ

מְצַוֶּה Piel Ptc ms צָוָה

לַעֲשֹׂתָהּ Qal Inf Cst עָשָׂה prep לְ 3fs suff

לְאַהֲבָה Qal Inf Cst אָהַב prep לְ Paragogic ה

לָלֶכֶת Qal Inf Cst הָלַךְ prep לְ

וּלְדָבְקָה Qal Inf Cst דָּבַק conj וְ prep לְ Paragogic ה

11:23

וְהוֹרִישׁ Hiphil Pf 3ms יָרַשׁ WC

וִירִשְׁתֶּם Qal Pf 2mp יָרַשׁ WC

Deuteronomy 31:1-8

31:1

וַיֵּלֶךְ Qal Imp 3ms הָלַךְ WC

וַיְדַבֵּר Piel Imp 3ms דָּבַר WC

31:2

וַיֹּאמֶר Qal Imp 3ms אָמַר WC

אוּכַל Qal Imp 1cs יָכֹל

לָצֵאת Qal Inf Cst יָצָא prep לְ

וְלָבוֹא Qal Inf Cst בּוֹא conj וְ prep לְ

אָמַר Qal Pf 3ms אָמַר

תַעֲבֹר Qal Imp 2ms עָבַר

31:3

עֹבֵר Qal Ptc ms עָבַר

יַשְׁמִיד Hiphil Imp 3ms שָׁמַד

וִירִשְׁתָּם Qal Pf 2ms יָרַשׁ WC 3mp suff

דִּבֶּר Piel Pf 3ms דָּבַר

31:4

וְעָשָׂה Qal Pf 3ms עָשָׂה WC

עָשָׂה Qal Pf 3ms עָשָׂה

הִשְׁמִיד Hiphil Pf 3ms שָׁמַד

31:5

וּנְתָנָם Qal Pf 3ms נָתַן WC 3mp suff

וַעֲשִׂיתֶם Qal Pf 2mp עָשָׂה WC

צִוִּיתִי Piel Pf 1cs צָוָה

31:6

חִזְקוּ Qal Impv 2mp חָזַק

וְאִמְצוּ Qal Impv 2mp אָמַץ conj וְ

תִּירְאוּ Qal Imp 2mp יָרֵא

תַּעַרְצוּ Qal Imp 2mp עָרַץ

הַהֹלֵךְ Qal Ptc ms הָלַךְ definite article

יַרְפְּךָ Hiphil Imp 3ms רָפָה 2ms suff

יַעַזְבֶךָּ Qal Imp 3ms עָזַב 2ms suff

31:7

וַיִּקְרָא Qal Imp 3ms קָרָא WC

וַיֹּאמֶר Qal Imp 3ms אָמַר WC

חֲזַק Qal Impv 2ms חָזַק

וֶאֱמָץ Qal Impv 2ms אָמַץ conj וְ

תָּבוֹא Qal Imp 2ms בּוֹא

נִשְׁבַּע Niphal Pf 3ms שָׁבַע

לָתֵת Qal Inf Cst נָתַן prep לְ

תַּנְחִילֶנָּה Hiphil Imp 2ms נָחַל 3fs suff

31:8

יִהְיֶה Qal Imp 3ms הָיָה

יַרְפְּךָ Hiphil Imp 3ms רָפָה 2ms suff

יַעַזְבֶךָּ Qal Imp 3ms עָזַב 2ms suff

תִירָא Qal Imp 2ms יָרֵא

תֵחָת Qal Imp 2ms חָתַת

Joshua 24:14-18

24:14

יְראוּ Qal Impv 2mp יָרֵא

וְעִבְדוּ Qal Impv 2mp עָבַד conj וְ

וְהָסִירוּ Hiphil Impv 2mp סוּר conj וְ

עָבְדוּ Qal Pf 3cp עָבַד

24:15

רַע Qal Pf 3ms רָעַע

לַעֲבֹד Qal Inf Cst עָבַד prep לְ

בַּחֲרוּ Qal Impv 2mp בָּחַר

תַעֲבֹדוּן Qal Imp 2mp עָבַד Paragogic נ

יֹשְׁבִים Qal Ptc mp יָשַׁב

נַעֲבֹד Qal Imp 1cp עָבַד

24:16

וַיַּעַן Qal Imp 3ms עָנָה WC

וַיֹּאמֶר Qal Imp 3ms אָמַר WC

מֵעֲזֹב Qal Inf Cst עָזַב prep מִן

לַעֲבֹד Qal Inf Cst עָבַד prep לְ

24:17

הַמַּעֲלֶה Hiphil Ptc ms עָלָה definite article

עָשָׂה Qal Pf 3ms עָשָׂה

וַיִּשְׁמְרֵנוּ Qal Imp 3ms שָׁמַר WC 1cp suff

הָלַכְנוּ Qal Pf 1cp הָלַךְ

עָבַרְנוּ Qal Pf 1cp עָבַר

24:18

וַיְגָרֶשׁ Piel Imp 3ms גָּרַשׁ WC
יֹשֵׁב Qal Ptc ms יָשַׁב
נַעֲבֹד Qal Imp 1cp עָבַד

Judges 3:7-11

3:7

וַיַּעֲשׂוּ Qal Imp 3mp עָשָׂה WC
וַיִּשְׁכְּחוּ Qal Imp 3mp שָׁכַח WC
וַיַּעַבְדוּ Qal Imp 3mp עָבַד WC

3:8

וַיִּחַר Qal Imp 3ms חָרָה WC
וַיִּמְכְּרֵם Qal Imp 3ms מָכַר WC 3mp suff
וַיַּעַבְדוּ Qal Imp 3mp עָבַד WC

3:9

וַיִּזְעֲקוּ Qal Imp 3mp זָעַק WC
וַיָּקֶם Hiphil Imp 3ms קוּם WC
מוֹשִׁיעַ Hiphil Ptc ms יָשַׁע
וַיּוֹשִׁיעֵם Hiphil Imp 3ms יָשַׁע WC 3mp suff

3:10

וַתְּהִי Qal Imp 3fs הָיָה WC
וַיִּשְׁפֹּט Qal Imp 3ms שָׁפַט WC
וַיֵּצֵא Qal Imp 3ms יָצָא WC
וַיִּתֵּן Qal Imp 3ms נָתַן WC
וַתָּעָז Qal Imp 3fs עָזַז WC

3:11

וַתִּשְׁקֹט Qal Imp 3fs שָׁקַט WC
וַיָּמָת Qal Imp 3ms מוּת WC

Judges 10:10-15

10:10

וַיִּזְעֲקוּ Qal Imp 3mp זָעַק WC
חָטָאנוּ Qal Pf 1cp חָטָא
עָזַבְנוּ Qal Pf 1cp עָזַב
וַנַּעֲבֹד Qal Imp 1cp עָבַד WC

10:11

וַיֹּאמֶר Qal Imp 3ms אָמַר WC

10:12

לָחֲצוּ Qal Pf 3cp לָחַץ
וַתִּצְעֲקוּ Qal Imp 2mp צָעַק WC
וָאוֹשִׁיעָה Hiphil Imp 1cs יָשַׁע WC Paragogic ה

10:13

עֲזַבְתֶּם Qal Pf 2mp עָזַב
וַתַּעַבְדוּ Qal Imp 2mp עָבַד WC
אוֹסִיף Hiphil Imp 1cs יָסַף
לְהוֹשִׁיעַ Hiphil Inf Cst יָשַׁע prep לְ

10:14

לְכוּ Qal Impv 2mp הָלַךְ
וְזַעֲקוּ Qal Impv 2mp זָעַק conj וְ
בְּחַרְתֶּם Qal Pf 2mp בָּחַר
יוֹשִׁיעוּ Hiphil Imp 3mp יָשַׁע

10:15

וַיֹּאמְרוּ Qal Imp 3mp אָמַר WC
חָטָאנוּ Qal Pf 1cp חָטָא
עֲשֵׂה Qal Impv 2ms עָשָׂה
הַצִּילֵנוּ Hiphil Impv 2ms נָצַל 1cp suff

1 Samuel 15:10-24

15:10

וַיְהִי Qal Imp 3ms הָיָה WC
לֵאמֹר Qal Inf Cst אָמַר prep לְ

15:11

נִחַמְתִּי Niphal Pf 1cs נָחַם
הִמְלַכְתִּי Hiphil Pf 1cs מָלַךְ
שָׁב Qal Pf 3ms שׁוּב
הֵקִים Hiphil Pf 3ms קוּם
וַיִּחַר Qal Imp 3ms חָרָה WC
וַיִּזְעַק Qal Imp 3ms זָעַק WC

15:12

וַיַּשְׁכֵּם Hiphil Imp 3ms שָׁכַם WC
לִקְרַאת Qal Inf Cst קָרָא prep לְ
וַיֻּגַּד Hophal Imp 3ms נָגַד WC
בָּא Qal Pf 3ms בּוֹא
מַצִּיב Hiphil Ptc ms נָצַב

וַיִּסֹּב Qal Imp 3ms סָבַב WC

וַיַּעֲבֹר Qal Imp 3ms עָבַר WC

וַיֵּרֶד Qal Imp 3ms יָרַד WC

15:13

וַיָּבֹא Qal Imp 3ms בּוֹא WC

בָּרוּךְ Qal Pass Ptc ms בָּרַךְ

הֲקִימֹתִי Hiphil Pf 1cs קוּם

15:14

שֹׁמֵעַ Qal Ptc ms שָׁמַע

15:15

הֱבִיאוּם Hiphil Pf 3cp בּוֹא 3mp suff

חָמַל Qal Pf 3ms חָמַל

זְבֹחַ Qal Inf Cst זָבַח

הֶחֱרַמְנוּ Hiphil Pf 1cp חָרַם

15:16

הֶרֶף Hiphil Impv 2ms רָפָה

וְאַגִּידָה Hiphil Imp 1cs נָגַד conj וְ Paragogic ה

דִּבֶּר Piel Pf 3ms דָּבַר

דַּבֵּר Piel Impv 2ms דָּבַר

15:17

וַיִּמְשָׁחֲךָ Qal Imp 3ms מָשַׁח WC 2ms suff

15:18

וַיִּשְׁלָחֲךָ Qal Imp 3ms שָׁלַח WC 2ms suff

לֵךְ Qal Impv 2ms הָלַךְ

וְהַחֲרַמְתָּה Hiphil Pf 2ms חָרַם WC

וְנִלְחַמְתָּ Niphal Pf 2ms לָחַם WC

כַּלּוֹתָם Piel Inf Cst כָּלָה 3mp suff

15:19

שָׁמַעְתָּ Qal Pf 2ms שָׁמַע

וַתַּעַט Qal Imp 2ms עִיט WC

וַתַּעַשׂ Qal Imp 2ms עָשָׂה WC

15:20

שָׁמַעְתִּי Qal Pf 1cs שָׁמַע

וָאֵלֵךְ Qal Imp 1cs הָלַךְ WC

שְׁלָחַנִי Qal Pf 3ms שָׁלַח 1cs suff

וָאָבִיא Hiphil Imp 1cs בּוֹא WC

הֶחֱרַמְתִּי Hiphil Pf 1cs חָרַם

15:21

וַיִּקַּח Qal Imp 3ms לָקַח WC

לִזְבֹּחַ Qal Inf Cst זָבַח prep לְ

15:22

כִּשְׁמֹעַ Qal Inf Cst שָׁמַע prep כְּ

שְׁמֹעַ Qal Inf Cst שָׁמַע

לְהַקְשִׁיב Hiphil Inf Cst קָשַׁב prep לְ

15:23

הַפְצַר Hiphil Inf Abs פָּצַר

מָאַסְתָּ Qal Pf 2ms מָאַס

וַיִּמְאָסְךָ Qal Imp 3ms מָאַס WC 2ms suff

15:24

חָטָאתִי Qal Pf 1cs חָטָא

עָבַרְתִּי Qal Pf 1cs עָבַד

יָרֵאתִי Qal Pf 1cs יָרֵא

וָאֶשְׁמַע Qal Imp 1cs שָׁמַע WC

2 Samuel 7:1-9

7:1

יָשַׁב Qal Pf 3ms יָשַׁב

הֵנִיחַ Hiphil Pf 3ms נוּחַ

אֹיְבָיו Qal Ptc mp אָיַב 3ms suff

7:2

רְאֵה Qal Impv 2ms רָאָה

יוֹשֵׁב Qal Ptc ms יָשַׁב

יֹשֵׁב Qal Ptc ms יָשַׁב

7:3

לֵךְ Qal Impv 2ms הָלַךְ

עֲשֵׂה Qal Impv 2ms עָשָׂה

7:5

לֵךְ Qal Impv 2ms הָלַךְ

וְאָמַרְתָּ Qal Pf 2ms אָמַר WC

אָמַר Qal Pf 3ms אָמַר

תִּבְנֶה Qal Imp 2ms בָּנָה

לְשִׁבְתִּי Qal Inf Cst יָשַׁב prep לְ 1cs suff

7:6

יָשַׁבְתִּי Qal Pf 1cs יָשַׁב

הַעֲלֹתִי Hiphil Inf Cst עָלָה 1cs suff

וָאֶהְיֶה Qal Imp 1cs הָיָה WC

מִתְהַלֵּךְ Hithpael Ptc ms הָלַךְ

7:7

הִתְהַלַּכְתִּי Hithpael Pf 1cs הָלַךְ

דִּבַּרְתִּי Piel Pf 1cs דָּבַר

צִוִּיתִי Piel Pf 1cs צָוָה

לִרְעוֹת Qal Inf Cst רָעָה prep לְ

בְנִיתֶם Qal Pf 2mp בָּנָה

7:8

תֹאמַר Qal Imp 2ms אָמַר

לְקַחְתִּיךָ Qal Pf 1cs לָקַח 2ms suff

לִהְיוֹת Qal Inf Cst הָיָה prep לְ

7:9

הָלַכְתָּ Qal Pf 2ms הָלַךְ

וָאַכְרִתָה Hiphil Imp 1cs כָּרַת WC Paragogic ה

אֹיְבֶיךָ Qal Ptc mp אָיַב 2ms suff

וְעָשִׂתִי Qal Pf 1cs עָשָׂה WC

1 Kings 8:22-26

8:22

וַיַּעֲמֹד Qal Imp 3ms עָמַד WC

וַיִּפְרֹשׂ Qal Imp 3ms פָּרַשׂ WC

8:23

שֹׁמֵר Qal Ptc ms שָׁמַר

הַהֹלְכִים Qal Ptc mp הָלַךְ definite article

8:24

שָׁמַרְתָּ Qal Pf 2ms שָׁמַר

דִּבַּרְתָּ Piel Pf 2ms דָּבַר

וַתְּדַבֵּר Piel Imp 2ms דָּבַר WC

מִלֵּאתָ Piel Pf 2ms מָלֵא

8:25

שְׁמֹר Qal Impv 2ms שָׁמַר

יִכָּרֵת Niphal Imp 3ms כָּרַת

יֹשֵׁב Qal Ptc ms יָשַׁב

יִשְׁמְרוּ Qal Imp 3mp שָׁמַר

לָלֶכֶת Qal Inf Cst הָלַךְ prep לְ

הָלַכְתָּ Qal Pf 2ms הָלַךְ

8:26

יֵאָמֶן Niphal Imp 3ms אָמַן

2 Kings 17:34-40

17:34

עֹשִׂים Qal Ptc mp עָשָׂה

צִוָּה Piel Pf 3ms צָוָה

שָׂם Qal Pf 3ms שִׂים

17:35

וַיִּכְרֹת Qal Imp 3ms כָּרַת WC

וַיְצַוֵּם Piel Imp 3ms צָוָה WC 3mp suff

תִירְאוּ Qal Imp 2mp יָרֵא

תִשְׁתַּחֲווּ Hishtaphel Imp 2mp חָוָה

תַעַבְדוּם Qal Imp 2mp עָבַד 3mp suff

תִזְבְּחוּ Qal Imp 2mp זָבַח

17:36

הֶעֱלָה Hiphil Pf 3ms עָלָה

נְטוּיָה Qal Pass Ptc fs נָטָה

תִּירָאוּ Qal Imp 2mp יָרֵא

17:37

כָּתַב Qal Pf 3ms כָּתַב

תִּשְׁמְרוּן Qal Imp 2mp שָׁמַר Paragogic נ

לַעֲשׂוֹת Qal Inf Cst עָשָׂה prep לְ

17:38

כָּרַתִּי Qal Pf 1cs כָּרַת

תִשְׁכָּחוּ Qal Imp 2mp שָׁכַח

17:39

יַצִּיל Hiphil Imp 3ms נָצַל

אֹיְבֵיכֶם Qal Ptc mp אָיַב 2mp suff

17:40

שָׁמֵעוּ Qal Pf 3cp שָׁמַע

Isaiah 43:1-6

43:1

אָמַר Qal Pf 3ms אָמַר

בֹּרַאֲךָ Qal Ptc ms בָּרָא 2ms suff

וְיֹצֶרְךָ Qal Ptc ms יָצַר conj וְ 2ms suff

תִּירָא Qal Imp 2ms יָרֵא

גְאַלְתִּיךָ Qal Pf 1cs גָּאַל 2ms suff

קָרָאתִי Qal Pf 1cs קָרָא

43:2

תַעֲבֹר Qal Imp 2ms עָבַר

יִשְׁטְפוּךָ Qal Imp 3mp שָׁטַף 2ms suff

תֵלֵךְ Qal Imp 2ms הָלַךְ

תִכָּוֶה Niphal Imp 2ms כָּוָה

תִבְעַר Qal Imp 3fs בָּעַר

43:3

מוֹשִׁיעֶךָ Hiphil Ptc ms יָשַׁע 2ms suff

נָתַתִּי Qal Pf 1cs נָתַן

43:4

יָקַרְתָּ Qal Pf 2ms יָקַר

נִכְבַּדְתָּ Niphal Pf 2ms כָּבֵד

אֲהַבְתִּיךָ Qal Pf 1cs אָהַב 2ms suff

וְאֶתֵּן Qal Imp 1cs נָתַן conj וְ

43:5

תִּירָא Qal Imp 2ms יָרֵא

אָבִיא Hiphil Imp 1cs בּוֹא

אֲקַבְּצֶךָּ Piel Imp 1cs קָבַץ 2ms suff

43:6

אֹמַר Qal Imp 1cs אָמַר

תֵּנִי Qal Impv 2fs נָתַן

תִּכְלָאִי Qal Imp 2fs כָּלָא

הָבִיאִי Hiphil Impv 2fs בּוֹא

Jeremiah 31:31-34

31:31

בָּאִים Qal Ptc mp בּוֹא

וְכָרַתִּי Qal Pf 1cs כָּרַת WC

31:32

כָּרַתִּי Qal Pf 1cs כָּרַת

הֶחֱזִיקִי Hiphil Inf Cst חָזַק 1cs suff

לְהוֹצִיאָם Hiphil Inf Cst יָצָא prep לְ 3mp suff

הֵפֵרוּ Hiphil Pf 3cp פָּרַר

בָּעַלְתִּי Qal Pf 1cs בָּעַל

31:33

אֶכְרֹת Qal Imp 1cs כָּרַת

נָתַתִּי Qal Pf 1cs נָתַן

אֶכְתֲּבֶנָּה Qal Imp 1cs כָּתַב 3fs suff

וְהָיִיתִי Qal Pf 1cs הָיָה WC

יִהְיוּ Qal Imp 3mp הָיָה

31:34

יְלַמְּדוּ Piel Imp 3mp לָמַד

לֵאמֹר Qal Inf Cst אָמַר prep לְ

דְּעוּ Qal Impv 2mp יָדַע

יֵדְעוּ Qal Imp 3mp יָדַע

אֶסְלַח Qal Imp 1cs סָלַח

אֶזְכָּר Qal Imp 1cs זָכַר

Ezekiel 37:1-6

37:1

הָיְתָה Qal Pf 3fs הָיָה

וַיּוֹצִאֵנִי Hiphil Imp 3ms יָצָא WC 1cs suff

וַיְנִיחֵנִי Hiphil Imp 3ms נוּחַ WC 1cs suff

37:2

וְהֶעֱבִירַנִי Hiphil Pf 3ms עָבַר conj וְ 1cs suff

37:3

הֲתִחְיֶינָה Qal Imp 3fp חָיָה interrog הֲ

וָאֹמַר Qal Imp 1cs אָמַר WC

יָדָעְתָּ Qal Pf 2ms יָדַע

37:4

הִנָּבֵא Niphal Impv 2ms נָבָא

וְאָמַרְתָּ Qal Pf 2ms אָמַר WC

שִׁמְעוּ Qal Impv 2mp שָׁמַע

37:5

אָמַר Qal Pf 3ms אָמַר

מֵבִיא Hiphil Ptc ms בּוֹא

וִחְיִיתֶם Qal Pf 2mp חָיָה WC

37:6

וְנָתַתִּי Qal Pf 1cs נָתַן WC

וְהַעֲלֵתִי Hiphil Pf 1cs עָלָה WC

וְקָרַמְתִּי Qal Pf 1cs קָרַם WC

וְנָתַתִּי Qal Pf 1cs נָתַן WC

וִחְיִיתֶם Qal Pf 2mp חָיָה WC

וִידַעְתֶּם Qal Pf 2mp יָדַע WC

Joel 3:1-5 (English 2:28-32)

3:1

וְהָיָה Qal Pf 3ms הָיָה WC

אֶשְׁפּוֹךְ Qal Imp 1cs שָׁפַךְ

וְנִבְּאוּ Niphal Pf 3cp נָבָא WC

יַחֲלֹמוּן Qal Imp 3mp חָלַם Paragogic נ

יִרְאוּ Qal Imp 3mp רָאָה

3:2

אֶשְׁפּוֹךְ Qal Imp 1cs שָׁפַךְ

3:3

וְנָתַתִּי Qal Pf 1cs נָתַן WC

3:4

יֵהָפֵךְ Niphal Imp 3ms הָפַךְ

בּוֹא Qal Inf Cst בּוֹא

וְהַנּוֹרָא Niphal Ptc ms יָרֵא conj וְ definite article

3:5

יִקְרָא Qal Imp 3ms קָרָא

יִמָּלֵט Niphal Imp 3ms מָלַט

תִּהְיֶה Qal Imp 3fs הָיָה

אָמַר Qal Pf 3ms אָמַר

קֹרֵא Qal Ptc ms קָרָא

Psalm 23:1-6

23:1

רֹעִי Qal Ptc ms רָעָה 1cs suff

אֶחְסָר Qal Imp 1cs חָסֵר

23:2

יַרְבִּיצֵנִי Hiphil Imp 3ms רָבַץ 1cs suff

יְנַהֲלֵנִי Piel Imp 3ms נָהַל 1cs suff

23:3

יְשׁוֹבֵב Polel Imp 3ms שׁוּב

יַנְחֵנִי Hiphil Imp 3ms נָחָה 1cs suff

23:4

אֵלֵךְ Qal Imp 1cs הָלַךְ

אִירָא Qal Imp 1cs יָרֵא

יְנַחֲמֻנִי Piel Imp 3mp נָחַם 1cs suff

23:5

תַּעֲרֹךְ Qal Imp 2ms עָרַךְ

צֹרְרָי Qal Ptc mp צָרַר 1cs suff

דִּשַּׁנְתָּ Piel Pf 2ms דָּשֵׁן

23:6

יִרְדְּפוּנִי Qal Imp 3mp רָדַף 1cs suff

וְשַׁבְתִּי Qal Pf 1cs שׁוּב WC

Psalm 100:1-5

100:1

הָרִיעוּ Hiphil Impv 2mp רוּעַ

100:2

עִבְדוּ Qal Impv 2mp עָבַד

בֹּאוּ Qal Impv 2mp בּוֹא

100:3

דְּעוּ Qal Impv 2mp יָדַע

עָשָׂנוּ Qal Pf 3ms עָשָׂה 1cp suff

100:4

בֹּאוּ Qal Impv 2mp בּוֹא

הודוּ Hiphil Impv 2mp יָדָה

בָּרְכוּ Piel Impv 2mp בָּרַךְ

Psalm 121:1-8

121:1

אֶשָּׂא Qal Imp 1cs נָשָׂא

יָבֹא Qal Imp 3ms בּוֹא

121:2

עֹשֵׂה Qal Ptc ms עָשָׂה

121:3

יִתֵּן Qal Imp 3ms נָתַן

יָנוּם Qal Imp 3ms נוּם

שֹׁמְרֶךָ Qal Ptc ms שָׁמַר 2ms suff

121:4

יִישָׁן Qal Imp 3ms יָשֵׁן

שׁוֹמֵר Qal Ptc ms שָׁמַר

121:6

יַכֶּכָּה Hiphil Imp 3ms נָכָה 2ms suff

121:7

יִשְׁמָרְךָ	Qal Imp 3ms שָׁמַר 2ms suff
יִשְׁמֹר	Qal Imp 3ms שָׁמַר

121:8

צֵאתְךָ	Qal Inf Cst יָצָא 2ms suff
וּבוֹאֶךָ	Qal Inf Cst בּוֹא conj וְ 2ms suff

Ezra 7:6-10

7:6

עָלָה	Qal Pf 3ms עָלָה
נָתַן	Qal Pf 3ms נָתַן
וַיִּתֶּן	Qal Imp 3ms נָתַן WC

7:7

וַיַּעֲלוּ	Qal Imp 3mp עָלָה WC
הַמְשֹׁרְרִים	Polel Ptc mp שִׁיר definite article

7:8

וַיָּבֹא	Qal Imp 3ms בּוֹא WC

7:9

בָּא	Qal Pf 3ms בּוֹא

7:10

הֵכִין	Hiphil Pf 3ms כּוּן
לִדְרוֹשׁ	Qal Inf Cst דָּרַשׁ prep לְ
וְלַעֲשֹׂת	Qal Inf Cst עָשָׂה conj וְ prep לְ
וּלְלַמֵּד	Piel Inf Cst לָמַד conj וְ prep לְ

2 Chronicles 1:7-10

1:7

נִרְאָה	Niphal Pf 3ms רָאָה
וַיֹּאמֶר	Qal Imp 3ms אָמַר WC
שְׁאַל	Qal Impv 2ms שָׁאַל
אֶתֶּן	Qal Imp 1cs נָתַן

1:8

עָשִׂיתָ	Qal Pf 2ms עָשָׂה
וְהִמְלַכְתַּנִי	Hiphil Pf 2ms מָלַךְ conj וְ 1cs suff

1:9

יֵאָמֵן	Niphal Imp 3ms אָמַן
הִמְלַכְתַּנִי	Hiphil Pf 2ms מָלַךְ 1cs suff

1:10

תֶּן	Qal Impv 2ms נָתַן

וְאֵצְאָה	Qal Imp 1cs יָצָא conj וְ Paragogic ה
וְאָבוֹאָה	Qal Imp 1cs בּוֹא conj וְ Paragogic ה
יִשְׁפֹּט	Qal Imp 3ms שָׁפַט

2 Chronicles 7:1-4

7:1

וּכְכַלּוֹת	Piel Inf Cst כָּלָה conj וְ prep כְּ
לְהִתְפַּלֵּל	Hithpael Inf Cst פָּלַל prep לְ
יָרְדָה	Qal Pf 3fs יָרַד
וַתֹּאכַל	Qal Imp 3fs אָכַל WC
מָלֵא	Qal Pf 3ms מָלֵא

7:2

יָכְלוּ	Qal Pf 3cp יָכֹל
לָבוֹא	Qal Inf Cst בּוֹא prep לְ

7:3

רֹאִים	Qal Ptc mp רָאָה
בְּרֶדֶת	Qal Inf Cst יָרַד prep בְּ
וַיִּכְרְעוּ	Qal Imp 3mp כָּרַע WC
וַיִּשְׁתַּחֲווּ	Hishtaphel Imp 3mp חָוָה WC
וְהוֹדוֹת	Hiphil Inf Cst יָדָה conj וְ

7:4

זֹבְחִים	Qal Ptc mp זָבַח

Appendix 2: Hebrew-English Lexicon

This lexicon contains all 642 Hebrew words (excluding proper names) that occur 50 or more times in the Hebrew Bible. Its contents are derived from *The Vocabulary Guide to Biblical Hebrew and Aramaic*, 2nd edition (Zondervan, 2019). The numbers that appear in the left-hand column of this lexicon correspond to the numbers in the frequency list of the *Vocabulary Guide* and to those numbers that idenfity each of the vocabulary cards from *Old Testament Hebrew Vocabulary Cards*, 2nd edition (Zondervan, 2019). The numbers that appear in parenthesis at the end of each entry identify how many times that particular word appears in the Hebrew Bible.

א

34 אָב father, ancestor; (ms cstr) אֲבִי; (mp) אָבוֹת (1,210)

237 אָבַד (Q) to perish, vanish, be(come) lost, go astray; (Pi) cause to perish, destroy; (Hi) exterminate (185)

606 אָבָה (Q) to be willing, consent, yield to, want something (54)

549 אֶבְיוֹן (adj) poor, needy (61)

171 אֶבֶן (fs) stone; (fp) אֲבָנִים (276)

62 אָדוֹן lord, master; (of God 439x) אֲדֹנָי Lord (774)

91 אָדָם man, mankind, humankind (546)

202 אֲדָמָה ground, land, earth (222)

582 אֶדֶן base, pedestal (57)

206 אָהַב (Q) to love (of human and divine love); (Pi ptc) lover (217)

139 אֹהֶל tent (348)

147 אוֹ (conj) or (321)

552 אוּלָם porch; also spelled אֵילָם (61)

436 אָוֶן iniquity, wickedness, evildoer (81)

447 אוֹצָר treasure, treasury, storehouse (79)

332 אוֹר (cs) light, daylight, sunshine (120)

448 אוֹת (cs) sign, mark, pledge; (cp) אֹתוֹת (79)

288 אָז then, since, before (141)

233 אֹזֶן (fs) ear; (fd cstr) אָזְנֵי (188)

76 אָח brother; (ms cstr) אֲחִי; (mp) אַחִים (629)

45 אֶחָד one; (fs) אַחַת (976)

335 אָחוֹת sister, relative, loved one (119)

534 אָחַז (Q) to seize, grasp, take hold (of), hold fast (63)

518 אֲחֻזָּה property, possession (66)

256 אַחֵר (adj) other, another; (fs) אַחֶרֶת (166)

629 אַחֲרוֹן (adj) last, behind, west (51)

72 אַחֲרֵי (prep) after, behind; also spelled אַחַר (718)

550 אַחֲרִית end, extremity, last (61)

165 אֹיֵב enemy (285)

625 אַיֵּה where? (52)

551 אֵיךְ how? (61)

247 אַיִל ram, ruler; (adj) mighty (171)

60 אַיִן (particle of nonexistence) is not, are not, nothing; most often spelled אֵין (790)

23 אִישׁ man, husband; (mp) אֲנָשִׁים (2,188)

263 אַךְ only, surely, nevertheless (161)

58 אָכַל (Q) to eat, consume; (Ni) be eaten, consumed; (Hi) feed (820)

71 אַל (neg particle) no, not (729)

8 אֶל־ (prep) to, toward, into; (with 3ms suff) אֵלָיו (5,518)

188 אֵל God, god (237)

68 אֵלֶּה (cp dmstr pron and adj) these (744)

18 אֱלֹהִים God, gods (2,602)

578 אֱלוֹהַּ God, god (58)

557 אַלּוּף tribal chief, leader (60)

593 אַלְמָנָה widow (55)

101 אֶלֶף thousand; (md) אַלְפַּיִם two thousand (496)

204 אֵם (fs) mother; (with 3ms suff) אִמּוֹ (220)

42 אִם if (1,070); כִּי־אִם but, except, only

587 אָמָה female slave or servant, maidservant (56)

183 אַמָּה cubit (distance between elbow and tip of middle finger), forearm (249)

387 אָמַן (Ni) to be reliable, faithful or trustworthy; (Hi) believe (in), trust, have trust in, put trust in (97)

11 אָמַר (Q) to say; (Ni) be said, called; (Hi) declare, proclaim (5,316)

318 אֱמֶת truth, fidelity; (with 2ms suff) אֲמִתְּךָ (127)

330 אֲנַחְנוּ (1cp pers pron) we (121)

52 אֲנִי (1cs pers pron) I (874)

136 אָנֹכִי (1cs pers pron) I (359)

223 אָסַף (Q) to gather (in), take in, take away, destroy; (Ni) be gathered, taken away, assemble (200)

479 אָסַר (Q) to tie, bind, fetter, imprison (73)

170 אַף nostril, nose; (metaphorically) anger; (md) אַפַּיִם (277)

309 אַף (conj) also, indeed, even (133)

543 אֵצֶל (prep) beside, near (62)

111 אַרְבַּע four; (fs) אַרְבָּעָה; (mp) אַרְבָּעִים forty (455)

222 אֲרוֹן (cs) ark, chest, coffin (202); אֲרוֹן הַבְּרִית "the ark of the covenant"

480 אֶרֶז cedar (73)

568 אֹרַח (cs) road, path, way (59)

394 אֹרֶךְ length (95)

21 אֶרֶץ (fs) land, earth, ground (2,505)

535 אָרַר (Q) to curse (63)

131 אֵשׁ (cs) fire (376)

61 אִשָּׁה woman, wife; (fs cstr) אֵשֶׁת; (fp) נָשִׁים (781)

522 אִשֶּׁה (ms) offering by fire (65)

9 אֲשֶׁר (rel pron) who, that, which (5,503)

5 אֵת (definite direct object marker) not translated; also spelled אֶת־ with loss of accent or (with 3ms suff) אֹתוֹ (10,978)

50 אֵת (prep) with, beside; also spelled אֶת־ with loss of accent or (with 3ms suff) אִתּוֹ (890)

512 אַתְּ (2fs pers pron) you (67)

67 אַתָּה (2ms pers pron) you (749)

166 אַתֶּם (2mp pers pron) you (283)

ב

4 בְּ (prep) in, at, with, by, against (15,559)

208 בֶּגֶד clothes, garment, covering (216)

231 בְּהֵמָה animal(s), beast(s), cattle (190)

19 בּוֹא (Q) to go in, enter, come to, come upon; (Hi) bring (in), come (in); (Hoph) be brought (2,592)

513 בּוֹר pit, cistern, well (67)

322 בּוֹשׁ (Q) to be ashamed; (Hi) put to shame (125)

246 בָּחַר (Q) to choose, test, examine (172)

339 בָּטַח (Q) to trust, rely upon (118)

487 בֶּטֶן (fs) belly, stomach, womb (72)

248 בִּין (Q) to understand, perceive, consider, give heed to; (Ni) be discerning, have understanding; (Hi) understand, teach; (Hith) show oneself perceptive (171)

121 בֵּין (prep) between (409)

25 בַּ֫יִת (ms) house, household, (metaphorically) dynasty; (1497x ms cstr) בֵּית; (mp) בָּתִּים (2,047)

352 בָּכָה (Q) to weep (in grief or joy), weep (for) (114)

333 בְּכוֹר firstborn, oldest offspring (120)

481 בַּל (poetic) no, never (73); 69x in Isa, Pss, Prov

569 בְּלִי without, nothing (59)

356 בִּלְתִּי (negates Inf Cstr) not, except; also spelled לְבִלְתִּי (86x) with prep לְ (112)

369 בָּמָה (cultic) high place, sacred hill; (fp) בָּמוֹת (106)

13 בֵּן son; (ms cstr) בֶּן־; (mp) בָּנִים; (mp cstr) בְּנֵי (4,941)

130 בָּנָה (Q) to build (up), rebuild, build (establish) a family; (Ni) be built, have a child (by or from) (377)

371 בַּ֫עַד (prep) behind, through (104)

264 בַּ֫עַל owner, master, husband, (divine title) Baal (161)

558 בָּעַר (Q) to burn (up), consume; (Pi) kindle, burn (60)

630 בָּקַע (Q) to cleave, split, breach, break open; (Ni) be cleft, split (open); (Pi) split, rip open (51)

239 בָּקָר cattle, herd (183)

212 בֹּ֫קֶר morning (213)

198 בָּקַשׁ (Pi) to seek, search for, look for, discover, demand, require; (Pu) be sought (225)

460 בַּרְזֶל iron (76)

536 בָּרַח (Q) to run away, flee, go or pass through (63)

163 בְּרִית covenant (287)

145 בָּרַךְ (Q Pass ptc) blessed, praised, adored; (Pi) bless, praise (327)

494 בְּרָכָה blessing, gift (71)

175 בָּשָׂר flesh, meat, skin (270)

82 בַּת daughter; (fp) בָּנוֹת (587)

148 בְּתוֹךְ (prep) in the midst (middle) of, inside (319); combination of (prep) בְּ and (n) תָּ֫וֶךְ (middle, center); also מִתּוֹךְ (68x) and אֶל־תּוֹךְ (22x)

637 בְּתוּלָה virgin (50)

ג

372 גָּאַל (Q) to redeem, act as kinsman (perform the responsibilities of the next-of-kin), avenge (104)

181 גְּבוּל border, boundary, territory (251)

266 גִּבּוֹר (adj) mighty, valiant, heroic; (n) hero (160)

544 גְּבוּרָה power, strength; (fp) גְּבוּרוֹת mighty deeds (62)

488 גִּבְעָה hill (72)

519 גֶּ֫בֶר strong man, young man, hero (66)

93 גָּדוֹל (adj) great, big, large (527)

342 גָּדַל (Q) to grow up, be(come) great, strong, wealthy, important; (Pi) bring up (children), make great, extol; (Hi) make great, magnify, do great things (117)

87 גּוֹי nation, people; (mp) גּוֹיִם (567)

430 גּוּר (Q) to sojourn, dwell (stay) as a foreigner or alien (82)

457 גּוֹרָל lot, portion, allotment (77)

531 גַּיְא (cs) valley; also spelled גֵּיא (64)

235 גָּלָה (Q) to uncover, reveal, disclose; (Ni) uncover, reveal oneself, be revealed, exposed; (Pi) uncover, reveal, disclose; (Hi) take (carry away) into exile (187)

63 גַּם also, even (769)

607 גָּמָל camel; (mp) גְּמַלִּים (54)

594 גֶּפֶן (cs) vine, grapevine (55)

403 גֵּר stranger, sojourner, alien (92)

ד

595 דָּבַק (Q) to cling, cleave to, stick to; (Hi) cause to cling, cleave or stick to, pursue closely (55)

37 דָּבַר (Q) to speak (rare in Q); (Pi) speak (1,136)

30 דָּבָר word, matter, thing (1,454)

608 דְּבַשׁ honey (54)

553 דּוֹד beloved, uncle (61); 39x in Song

252 דּוֹר generation; also spelled דֹּר; (mp) דֹּרוֹת and דֹּרֹת (167)

415 דֶּלֶת door (88)

135 דָּם blood; bloodshed (361)

416 דַּעַת knowledge, understanding, ability (88)

537 דָּרַךְ (Q) to tread (often in the sense of pressing for wine or oil), march, draw a bow; (Hi) cause to tread, march or walk (63)

73 דֶּרֶךְ (cs) way, road, journey (712)

257 דָּרַשׁ (Q) to seek, inquire (of or about), investigate, require, demand (165)

ה

2 הַ· (definite article) the (24,058)

74 הֲ (interrog particle) prefixed to the first word of a question (664)

482 הֶבֶל vanity, futility, breath (73); 38x in Eccl

31 הוּא (3ms pers pron) he, it; (ms dmstr pron and adj) that (1,398)

631 הוֹי woe! oh! ha! (51)

104 הִיא (3fs pers pron) she, it; (fs dmstr pron and adj) that; also spelled הִוא in the Pentateuch (491)

15 הָיָה (Q) to be, become, happen, occur; (Ni) be done, brought about, come to pass, occur (3,576)

440 הֵיכָל temple, palace (80)

29 הָלַךְ (Q) to go, walk, (metaphorically) behave; (Pi) go, walk; (Hith) walk about, move to and fro (1,554)

282 הָלַל (Pi) to praise, sing hallelujah; (Pu) be praised, praiseworthy; (Hith) boast (146)

88 הֵם (3mp pers pron) they; (mp dmstr) those; also spelled הֵמָּה (565)

426 הָמוֹן multitude, crowd, sound, roar (85)

366 הֵן behold, if (107)

43 הִנֵּה behold, look; (with 1cs suff) הִנְנִי (1,061)

570 הֵנָּה here (59)

395 הָפַךְ (Q) to turn, overturn, overthrow, destroy; (Ni) be destroyed, turned into, changed (95)

89 הַר mountain, hill, hill country; (mp) הָרִים (558)

253 הָרַג (Q) to kill, slay (167)

ו

1 וְ (conj) and, but, also, even, then (50,524)

ז

79 זֹאת (fs dmstr pron and adj) this (605)

304 זָבַח (Q) to slaughter (for sacrifice), sacrifice; (Pi) offer sacrifice, sacrifice (134)

261 זֶבַח sacrifice (162)

35 זֶה (ms dmstr pron and adj) this (1,178)

127 זָהָב gold (392)

190 זָכַר (Q) to remember; (Ni) be remembered, thought of; (Hi) remind (235)

431 זָכָר male, man (82)

559 זָנָה (Q) to commit fornication, be a harlot (prostitute), be unfaithful (60)

483 זָעַק (Q) to cry (out), call for help, summon (73)

241 זָקֵן (adj) old; (n) elder, old man (180)

500 זָר (adj) foreign, strange (70)

408 זְרוֹעַ (fs) arm, forearm; (metaphorically) strength or power; (fp) זְרֹעוֹת (91)

588 זָרַע (Q) to sow, scatter seed (56)

195 זֶרַע seed, offspring, descendants (229)

ח

545 חַג feast, festival, procession; also spelled חָג; (mp) חַגִּים (62)

596 חָדַל (Q) to cease, end, stop, refrain (from) (55)

616 חָדָשׁ (adj) new, fresh (53)

167 חֹדֶשׁ month, new moon (283)

245 חָוָה (Hishtaphel) to bow down, worship (173)

310 חוֹמָה wall (133)

258 חוּץ outside, street; (mp) חוּצוֹת; (prefixed with prep מִן) מִחוּץ from outside, outside (164)

597 חָזָה (Q) to see, behold, perceive (55)

160 חָזַק (Q) to be(come) strong, have courage; (Pi) make strong, strengthen; (Hi) strengthen, seize, grasp, take hold of; (Hith) strengthen oneself, show oneself as strong or courageous (290)

583 חָזָק (adj) strong, mighty, hard (57)

186 חָטָא (Q) to miss (a goal or mark), sin, commit a sin; (Pi) make a sin offering; (Hi) cause to sin (240)

157 חַטָּאת sin, sin offering; (fs cstr) חַטַּאת; (fp cstr) חַטֹּאות and חַטֹּאת (298)

178 חַי (adj) living, alive; (mp) חַיִּים (254)

168 חָיָה (Q) to live, be alive, revive, restore to life; (Pi) preserve alive, let live, give life; (Hi) preserve, keep alive, revive, restore to life (283)

390 חַיָּה animal, beast, living thing (96)

291 חַיִּים life, lifetime (140)

185 חַיִל strength, wealth, army (246)

296 חָכָם (adj) wise, skillful, experienced (138)

71 חָכְמָה wisdom, skill (153)

404 חֵ֫לֶב fat; (metaphorically) best, choice part (92)

467 חָלָה (Q) to be(come) weak, tired, sick; (Ni) be exhausted; (Pi) appease, flatter (75)

523 חֲלוֹם dream (65)

396 חָלָל (adj) pierced, slain, defiled (94)

302 חָלַל (Ni) to be defiled, profaned, defile oneself; (Pi) profane, pollute, defile; (Hi) let something be profaned (135)

598 חָלַק (Q) to divide, share (with or in), apportion, distribute; (Pi) divide (in pieces), apportion, scatter (55)

520 חֵ֫לֶק portion, share (66)

323 חֵמָה wrath, heat, poison (125)

391 חֲמוֹר donkey (96)

560 חָמָס violence, wrong (60)

96 חָמֵשׁ five; (fs) חֲמִשָּׁה; (mp) חֲמִשִּׁים fifty (508)

507 חֵן favor, grace, charm (69)

286 חָנָה (Q) to decline, camp, encamp, pitch camp, lay siege to (143)

458 חָנַן (Q) to be gracious to, show favor to, favor; (Hith) plead for grace, favor or compassion (77)

184 חֶ֫סֶד loyalty, faithfulness, steadfast love, lovingkindness (249)

471 חָפֵץ (Q) to delight in, take pleasure in, desire, be willing (74)

599 חֵץ arrow; (mp) חִצִּים (55)

324 חֲצִי half, middle (125)

229 חָצֵר (cs) courtyard, village, settlement; (cp) חֲצֵרִים and חֲצֵרוֹת (192)

315 חֹק statute, appointed time, portion; (mp) חֻקִּים (131)

373 חֻקָּה statute, ordinance (104)

120 חֶ֫רֶב (fs) sword (413)

401 חָרָה (Q) to be(come) hot, burn with anger, become angry (93)

638 חָרַם (Hi) to devote to the ban, dedicate to destruction, exterminate (50)

484 חֶרְפָּה reproach, disgrace, shame (73)

327 חָשַׁב (Q) to think, consider, devise, plan, value, reckon; (Ni) be reckoned, accounted, considered (as); (Pi) think, consider, devise, plan (124)

441 חֹ֫שֶׁךְ darkness (80)

600 חָתַת (Q) to be shattered, dismayed, filled with terror (55)

ט

639 טַבַּ֫עַת ring, signet ring; (fp) טַבָּעֹת (50)

392 טָהוֹר (adj) clean, pure (96)

397 טָהֵר (Q) to be clean (ceremonially), pure (morally); (Pi) cleanse, purify, pronounce clean; (Hith) purify or cleanse oneself (94)

92 טוֹב (adj) good, pleasant (530)

262 טָמֵא (Q) to be(come) unclean; (Ni) defile oneself; (Pi) defile, pronounce or declare unclean; (Hith) defile oneself, become unclean (162)

417 טָמֵא (adj) unclean (88)

589 טֶ֫רֶם before, not yet; also spelled בְּטֶ֫רֶם with prep בְּ (56)

י

532 יְאֹר stream, river, Nile (64)

571 יָבֵשׁ (Q) to dry up, be(come) dry, wither; (Hi) make dry (up), make wither (59)

28 יָד (fs) hand; (metaphorically) power (1,627)

359 יָדָה (Hi) to thank, praise, confess; (Hith) confess (111)

47 יָדַע (Q) to know, know sexually (have intercourse with); (Ni) be(come) known, reveal oneself; (Hi) make known, inform (956)

22 יוֹם day; (mp) יָמִים (2,301)

617 יוֹמָם by day, daily, in the daytime (53)

393 יַחְדָּו together, at the same time (96)

343 יָטַב (Q) to be well with, go well with, be pleasing (to); (Hi) make things go well for, do good to, deal well with, treat kindly (117)

289 יַיִן wine; (ms cstr) יֵין (141)

572 יָכַח (Hi) to reprove, rebuke, reproach, chasten, punish, decide, mediate, arbitrate (59)

227 יָכֹל (Q) to be able, capable of, endure, prevail (193)

99 יָלַד (Q) to bear (children), give birth, bring forth, beget; (Ni) be born; (Pi) help at birth, serve as midwife; (Pu) be born; (Hi) become the father of, beget (499)

414 יֶלֶד child, boy, youth (89)

126 יָם sea; (mp) יַמִּים (396)

290 יָמִין (fs) right hand, south (141)

213 יָסַף (Q) to add, continue (to do something again); (Hi) add, increase, do again and again (213)

382 יַעַן on account of, because; 33x with אֲשֶׁר (9) as יַעַן אֲשֶׁר (100)

442 יָעַץ (Q) to advise, counsel, plan, decide; (Ni) consult or take counsel together (80)

584 יַעַר forest, woods, thicket (57)

40 יָצָא (Q) to go or come out; (Hi) cause to go or come out, lead out, bring out (1,076)

618 יָצַק (Q) to pour, pour out (liquid), cast (metal), flow (into); (Hoph) be cast, poured out, emptied out (53)

538 יָצַר (Q) to form, fashion, shape, create (63)

150 יָרֵא (Q) to fear, be afraid, in awe of, reverence; (Ni) be feared, held in honor (317)

539 יָרֵא (adj) fearful (63)

128 יָרַד (Q) to go down, descend; (Hi) bring down, lead down (382)

609 יְרִיעָה tent curtain (54)

194 יָרַשׁ (Q) to inherit, take possession of, dispossess, impoverish; (Hi) cause to possess or inherit, dispossess (232)

297 יֵשׁ (particle of existence) there is, there are (138)

38 יָשַׁב (Q) to sit (down), dwell, inhabit; (Hi) cause to sit or dwell, settle (a city) (1,088)

451 יְשׁוּעָה salvation, help, deliverance (78)

220 יָשַׁע (Ni) to be delivered, victorious, receive help; (Hi) help, save, deliver, rescue, come to the aid of (205)

336 יָשָׁר (adj) upright, just (119)

370 יָתַר (Ni) to be left over, remain; (Hi) have (something) left over or remaining (106)

388 יֶתֶר rest, remainder, excess (97)

כ

16 כְּ (prep) as, like, according to; (with 2ms suff) כָּמ֫וֹךָ (3,053)

353 כָּבֵד (Q) to be heavy, weighty, honored; (Ni) be honored; (Pi) honor; (Hi) make heavy, dull or insensitive, harden (heart) (114)

224 כָּבוֹד glory, splendor, honor, abundance (200); כְּבוֹד יְהוָה "the glory of Yahweh"

632 כָּבַס (Pi) to clean, cleanse, wash away guilt (51)

367 כֶּ֫בֶשׂ lamb, sheep (107)

85 כֹּה thus, here (577)

66 כֹּהֵן priest; (mp) כֹּהֲנִים (750)

205 כּוּן (Ni) to be established, steadfast, ready, arranged, stand firm; (Hi) establish, set up, prepare, make ready, make firm; (Polel) set up, establish (219)

320 כֹּחַ strength, power (126)

14 כִּי that, because; (adversative) but, except; (emphatic) indeed, truly (4,487); כִּי־אִם but, except

511 כִּכָּר (fs) something round, talent (weight), valley; (fp) כִּכָּרִים (68)

10 כֹּל all, each, every; (cstr) כָּל־ (5,415)

218 כָּלָה (Q) to be complete, finished, at an end, accomplished, spent, exhausted, come to an end; (Pi) complete, finish, bring to an end (207)

146 כְּלִי vessel, implement, weapon; (mp) כֵּלִים; (mp cstr) כְּלֵי (325)

69 כֵּן so, thus (741)

360 כָּנָף (fs) wing, edge (111)

303 כִּסֵּא seat, chair, throne (135)

272 כָּסָה (Q) to cover, conceal, hide; (Pi) cover (up), conceal, clothe (153)

501 כְּסִיל fool, shameless person (70)

123 כֶּ֫סֶף silver, money (403)

601 כָּעַס (Q) to be angry, vexed; (Hi) vex, provoke, provoke (God) to anger (55)

226 כַּף (fs) hand, palm, sole of the foot (195)

377 כָּפַר (Pi) to cover (over), atone (for), make atonement (102)

409 כְּרוּב cherub; (mp) כְּרוּבִים cherubim (91)

398 כֶּ֫רֶם vineyard (94)

161 כָּרַת (Q) to cut, cut off, cut down; (idiom) to make a covenant (with בְּרִית); (Ni) be cut off (down); (Hi) cut off, destroy, exterminate (289)

524 כָּשַׁל (Q) to stumble, totter, stagger; (Ni) be caused to stumble, stumble (65)

199 כָּתַב (Q) to write (upon), register, record; (Ni) be written (225)

514 כָּתֵף (fs) side, shoulder (67)

ל

3 לְ (prep) to, toward, for (20,321)

12 לֹא (neg particle) no, not; also spelled לוֹא (5,189)

54 לֵב heart, mind, will; (mp) לִבּוֹת; also spelled לֵבָב (854)

265 לְבַד alone, by oneself; (with 3ms suff) לְבַדּוֹ (161)

357 לָבַשׁ (Q) to put on a garment, clothe, be clothed; (Hi) clothe (112)

249 לָחַם (Q, Ni) to fight, do battle with (rare in Q) (171)

140 לֶ֫חֶם bread, food (340)

192 לַ֫יְלָה (ms) night; (mp) לֵילוֹת (234)

495 לִין (Q) to remain overnight, spend the night (71)

331 לָכַד (Q) to take, capture, catch, seize; (Ni) be caught, captured (121)

420 לָמַד (Q) to learn; (Pi) teach (87)

242 לָ֫מָּה why? also spelled לָמָה (178)

174 לְמַ֫עַן (prep) on account of, for the sake of (272)

46 לָקַח (Q) to take, grasp, capture, seize; (Ni) be captured, taken away (967)

344 לָשׁוֹן (cs) tongue, language (117)

מ

156 מְאֹד very, exceedingly (300)

84 מֵאָה hundred; (fp) מֵאוֹת; (fd) מָאתַ֫יִם two hundred (583)

472 מָאַס (Q) to refuse, reject, despise (74)

561 מָגֵן (cs) shield; (cp) מָגִנִּים (60)

354 מִגְרָשׁ open land, pasture (114)

176 מִדְבָּר wilderness, desert, pasture (269)

626 מָדַד (Q) to measure, measure off (distance or expanse), measure out (grain) (52)

602 מִדָּה measure, measurement (55)

489 מַדּוּעַ why? (72)

619 מְדִינָה province, district (53)

86 מָה (interrog pron) what? also spelled מַה and מֶה (571)

437 מָהַר (Pi) to hasten, hurry, go or come quickly (81)

640 מוּסָר discipline, correction, instruction (50)

200 מוֹעֵד appointed time (of feast), meeting place, assembly (223)

56 מוּת (Q) to die; (Hi) kill, put to death; (Hoph) be killed (845)

273 מָ֫וֶת death, dying; (ms cstr) מוֹת (153)

124 מִזְבֵּחַ altar; (mp) מִזְבְּחוֹת (403)

585 מִזְמוֹר psalm, song (57); all in Pss

473 מִזְרָח east, sunrise (74)

210 מַחֲנֶה (cs) camp, army; (cp) מַחֲנוֹת and מַחֲנִים (215)

627 מָחָר tomorrow (52)

590 מַחֲשָׁבָה thought, plan, scheme (56)

179 מַטֶּה (ms) staff, rod, tribe; (mp) מַטּוֹת (252)

116 מִי (interrog pron) who? (424)

83 מַ֫יִם water; (md cstr) מֵי (585)

443 מָכַר (Q) to sell, hand over; (Ni) be sold, sell oneself (into slavery) (80)

180 מָלֵא (Q) to be full, fill (up); (Ni) be filled (with); (Pi) fill, perform, carry out, consecrate as priest (252)

554 מָלֵא (adj) full, filled (61)

214 מַלְאָךְ messenger, angel (213)

254 מְלָאכָה work, occupation, service (167)

149 מִלְחָמָה war, battle, struggle (319)

399 מָלַט (Ni) to escape, flee to safety, slip away; (Pi) let someone escape, save someone, leave undisturbed (94)

138 מָלַךְ (Q) to be(come) king or queen, reign, rule; (Hi) make someone king or queen, install someone as king or queen (350)

20 מֶ֫לֶךְ king, ruler (2,530)

410 מַלְכוּת kingdom, dominion, royal power (91)

345 מַמְלָכָה kingdom, dominion, reign (117)

6 מִן (prep) from, out of; also spelled · מִ (Nun assimilates as Daghesh Forte) when prefixed to another word (7,592)

217 מִנְחָה gift, offering, tribute (211)

305 מִסְפָּר number (134)

379 מְעַט (adj) little, few (101)

292 מַ֫עַל above, upward, on top of (140)

191 מַעֲשֶׂה (ms) work, deed, act (235)

110 מָצָא (Q) to find (out), reach, obtain, achieve; (Ni) be found (457)

620 מַצָּה unleavened bread (53)

238 מִצְוָה commandment; (fp) מִצְוֹת (184); מִצְוֹת יְהוָה "the commandments of Yahweh"

468 מִקְדָּשׁ sanctuary (75); 31x in Ezek

125 מָקוֹם place, location; (mp) מְקֹמוֹת (401)

461 מִקְנֶה cattle, livestock, property (76)

376 מַרְאֶה vision, sight, appearance (103)

610 מָרוֹם height, elevation, pride (54)

502 מָשַׁח (Q) to smear (with a liquid, oil or dye), anoint (with oil) (70)

294 מִשְׁכָּן dwelling place, tabernacle; (mp) מִשְׁכָּנוֹת (139)

438 מָשַׁל (Q) to rule, reign, govern, have dominion (81)

452 מִשְׁמֶ֫רֶת watch, guard, responsibility (78)

154 מִשְׁפָּחָה family, clan (304)

115 מִשְׁפָּט judgment, decision, ordinance, law, custom (425)

נ

122 נָא (emphatic particle) please, now, surely (405)

132 נְאֻם utterance, announcement, revelation (376); נְאֻם־יְהוָה "says (declares) Yahweh"

350 נָבָא (Ni) to prophesy, be in a state of prophetic ecstasy; (Hith) speak or behave as a prophet (115)

503 נָבַט (Hi) to look (at or out), gaze, behold (70)

151 נָבִיא prophet (317)

134 נָגַד (Hi) to tell, announce, report, declare, inform; (Hoph) be told, announced, reported (371)

276 נֶ֫גֶד (prep) opposite, in front of (151)

277 נָגַע (Q) to touch, strike, reach; (Hi) touch, reach, throw, arrive (150)

453 נֶ֫גַע plague, affliction (78)

325 נָגַשׁ (Q) to draw near, approach; (Ni) draw near; (Hi) bring (near), offer (a sacrifice) (125)

633 נָדַח (Ni) to be scattered, banished, driven away, thrust out; (Hi) scatter, drive away, disperse, thrust out (51)

562 נֶ֫דֶר vow; also spelled נֵ֫דֶר (60)

337 נָהָר river, stream; (mp) נְהָרוֹת and נְהָרִים (119)

293 נוּחַ (Q) to rest, settle down, repose; (Hi) cause to rest, secure rest, set, leave (behind or untouched) (140)

267 נוּס (Q) to flee, escape (160)

573 נָחַל (Q) to take (as a) possession, obtain (receive) property, give as an inheritance; (Hi) give as an inheritance (59)

299 נַ֫חַל stream, brook, wadi (137)

203 נַחֲלָה inheritance, property, possession (222)

364 נָחַם (Ni) to be sorry, regret, have compassion (on or for); (Pi) comfort, console (108)

295 נְחֹ֫שֶׁת copper, bronze (139)

209 נָטָה (Q) to spread out, stretch out, extend, pitch (a tent), turn, bend; (Hi) turn, incline, stretch out, spread out (216)

574 נָטַע (Q) to plant (59)

98 נָכָה (Hi) to strike, smite, beat, strike dead, destroy; (Hoph) be struck down dead, beaten (501)

641 נָכַר (Hi) to recognize, know, investigate, be acquainted with, acknowledge (50)

563 נֶ֫סֶךְ drink offering; also spelled נֵ֫סֶךְ (60)

283 נָסַע (Q) to pull (out or up), set out, start out, depart, journey (146)

187 נַ֫עַר boy, youth, servant (240)

462 נַעֲרָה young girl, newly married woman, maidservant (76)

113 נָפַל (Q) to fall, fall upon; (Hi) cause to fall, bring to ruin (435)

65 נֶ֫פֶשׁ (fs) soul, life, person, neck, throat (757)

474 נָצַב (Ni) to stand (firm), take one's stand, station oneself, be positioned; (Hi) station, set (up), place, establish (74)

525 נָצַח (Pi) to supervise, oversee or inspect works and activities related to the temple; מְנַצֵּחַ (ptc) used as title (superscription) in 55 psalms (65)

215 נָצַל (Ni) to be rescued, delivered, saved; (Hi) tear from, take away, deliver from (213)

540 נָצַר (Q) to keep watch, watch over, guard, protect, preserve (63)

75 נָשָׂא (Q) to lift, carry, raise, bear (load or burden), take (away); (Ni) be carried, lifted up, exalted; (Pi) lift up, exalt; (Hith) lift oneself up, exalt oneself (659)

642 נָשַׂג (Hi) to reach, overtake (50)

316 נָשִׂיא chief, leader, prince (130)

26 נָתַן (Q) to give, put, place, set; (Ni) be given (2,014)

ס

260 סָבַב (Q) to turn (about), go around, surround; (Ni) turn; (Hi) cause to go around, lead around; (Polel) encompass with protection (163)

141 סָבִיב around, about; (substantive) surroundings (338)

411 סָגַר (Q) to shut (in), close; (Hi) deliver (up), hand over, surrender, give up (91)

298 סוּס horse (138)

158 סוּר (Q) to turn (aside), turn off, leave (off), desist; (Hi) remove, take away, get rid of (298)

475 סֶ֫לָה technical poetic notation of undetermined meaning; in Pss and 3x in Habakkuk (74)

575 סֶ֫לַע rock, stone, cliff (59)

621 סֹ֫לֶת flour (53)

368 סָפַר (Q) to count; (Pi) count, recount, make known, proclaim, report, tell (107)

230 סֵ֫פֶר book, scroll, document (191); סֵפֶר הַתּוֹרָה "the book of the law"

611 סֹפֵר scribe, secretary (54)

432 סָתַר (Ni) to be hidden, hide oneself; (Hi) hide (82)

ע

162 עָבַד (Q) to work, serve, toil (289)

59 עֶ֫בֶד slave, servant (803)

284 עֲבֹדָה work, labor, service, worship (145)

90 עָבַר (Q) to pass over, pass through, pass by, cross; (Hi) cause to pass over, bring over, cause or allow to pass (through), cause to pass through fire, sacrifice (553)

405 עֵ֫בֶר beyond, other side, edge, bank (92)

508 עֵד witness (69)

33 עַד (prep) until, as far as (1,263)

250 עֵדָה congregation, assembly (171)

555 עֵדוּת witness, testimony; (fp) עֵדוֹת (61)

105 עוֹד again, still, as long as (491)

112 עוֹלָם forever, everlasting, ancient; also spelled עֹלָם (439)

193 עָוֹן transgression, iniquity, guilt, punishment (of sin); (mp) עֲוֹנוֹת (233)

496 עוֹף (coll) flying creatures, birds, insects (71)

383 עוֹר skin, hide, leather (99)

444 עוּר (Q) to be awake, stir up; (Hi) arouse, rouse, wake up, stir up; (Polel) arouse, disturb, awaken (80)

476 עֵז (fs) goat, goat's hair; (fp) עִזִּים (74)

463 עֹז strength, power, might; (with 3ms suff) עֻזּוֹ (76)

211 עָזַב (Q) to leave, leave behind, forsake, abandon, set free (214)

433 עָזַר (Q) to help, assist, come to the aid of (82)

48 עַ֫יִן (cs) eye, spring (900)

39 עִיר (fs) city, town; (fp) עָרִים (1,088)

7 עַל (prep) on, upon, on account of, according to (5,777)

49 עָלָה (Q) to go up, ascend; (Ni) be taken up; (Hi) bring or lead up or out, offer up (sacrifice) (894)

164 עֹלָה whole burnt offering (sacrifice that is completely burned) (286)

622 עֶלְיוֹן (adj) upper; (divine title) Most High (53)

27 עַם people; (mp) עַמִּים (1,869)

44 עִם (prep) with, together with; (with 3ms suff) עִמּוֹ (1,048)

94 עָמַד (Q) to stand (up), take one's stand, stand still; (Hi) station, set up, appoint, designate (524)

358 עַמּוּד pillar, column, tent pole (112)

612 עָמָל trouble, labor, toil (54)

504 עֵ֫מֶק valley, plain (70)

152 עָנָה (Q) to answer, respond, reply, testify; (Ni) be answered (316)

449 עָנָה (Q) to be afflicted, humbled; (Pi) afflict, oppress, humiliate, violate (79)

445 עָנִי (adj) poor, humble, afflicted (80)

421 עָנָן (coll) clouds (87)

362 עָפָר dust, dry earth (110)

143 עֵץ tree, wood (330)

422 עֵצָה counsel, plan, advice (87)

321 עֶ֫צֶם (fs) bone, skeleton (126)

306 עֶ֫רֶב evening, sunset (134)

564 עֲרָבָה desert plain, Arabah (60)

613 עֶרְוָה nakedness (54)

469 עָרַךְ (Q) to set in order, lay out, set in rows, arrange, stack (wood), draw up a battle formation (75)

17 עָשָׂה (Q) to do, make; (Ni) be done, made (2,632)

142 עָשָׂר ten; (fs) עֶשְׂרֵה; used in constructions to express numerals eleven to nineteen (337)

103 עֶ֫שֶׂר ten; (fs) עֲשָׂרָה; (mp) עֶשְׂרִים twenty, twentieth (492)

159 עֵת (cs) time, point of time; (cp) עִתִּים and עִתּוֹת (296)

114 עַתָּה now, after all, at last, then (435)

פ

424 פֵּאָה corner, side, edge (86)

565 פָּדָה (Q) to ransom, redeem, buy out (60)

434 פֹּה here, at this place; also spelled פּוֹ (82)

100 פֶּה (ms) mouth, opening; (ms cstr) פִּי (498)

526 פּוּץ (Q) to be spread, dispersed, scattered, overflow; (Ni) be scattered, dispersed; (Hi) scatter, disperse (65)

497 פָּלָא (Ni) to be extraordinary, wonderful; (Hi) do something wonderful (71)

428 פָּלַל (Hith) to pray, make intercession (84)

311 פֶּן־ lest, otherwise (133)

307 פָּנָה (Q) to turn (toward, from, to the side, away) (134)

24 פָּנִים (cp) face, front; לִפְנֵי (prep לְ prefixed to cstr) before, in front of (2,126)

579 פָּעַל (Q) to do, make, perform (58)

340 פַּ֫עַם (fs) foot, pace, time; (fp) פְּעָמִים (118)

155 פָּקַד (Q) to attend (to), pay attention to, take care of, miss (someone), number, appoint; (Ni) be missed, visited, appointed; (Hi) appoint, entrust (304)

312 פַּר bull, ox, steer (133)

338 פְּרִי fruit, offspring (119)

515 פָּרַשׂ (Q) to spread out (as with hands in prayer), stretch (out or over) (67)

586 פָּרָשׁ horseman, horse (57)

402 פֶּ֫שַׁע transgression, rebellion (93)

259 פֶּ֫תַח opening, entrance, doorway (164)

300 פָּתַח (Q) to open (up); (Ni) be opened, loosened, set free; (Pi) let loose, loosen (136)

צ

172 צֹאן (cs) flock(s), flock of sheep and goats (274)

107 צָבָא (cs) host, army, war, service; (cp) צְבָאוֹת (487); יְהוָה צְבָאוֹת "Yahweh of Hosts"

219 צַדִּיק (adj) righteous, just, innocent (206)

328 צֶ֫דֶק righteousness, equity (123)

268 צְדָקָה righteousness, righteous act, justice (159)

102 צָוָה (Pi) to command, give an order, charge; (Pu) be ordered, be told, receive a command (496)

485 צוּר rock, boulder (73)

623 צֵל shadow, shade, protection (53)

527 צָלַח (Q) to succeed, prosper, be successful; (Hi) be successful, succeed, cause to succeed or prosper (65)

603 צָעַק (Q) to shout, cry (out), call for help; (Ni) be called together, summoned (55)

274 צָפוֹן (fs) north, northern (153)

490 צַר adversary, enemy (72)

505 צָרָה distress, anxiety, trouble (70)

ק

319 קָבַץ (Q) to collect, gather, assemble; (Ni) be gathered, assembled; (Pi) gather together, assemble (127)

313 קָבַר (Q) to bury; (Ni) be buried (133)

516 קֶבֶר grave, burial site; (mp) קְבָרִים and קְבָרוֹת (67)

346 קָדוֹשׁ (adj) holy, set apart (117)

509 קָדִים east, eastern, east wind (69)

556 קֶדֶם east, ancient times (61)

251 קָדַשׁ (Q) to be holy, set apart or consecrated; (Ni) be honored or treated as holy; (Pi) set apart, consecrate or dedicate as holy; (Hi) consecrate, dedicate or declare as holy; (Hith) show or keep oneself holy (171)

108 קֹדֶשׁ holiness, something that is holy (470)

329 קָהָל assembly, community, crowd (123)

97 קוֹל voice, sound, noise; also spelled קֹל (505)

77 קוּם (Q) to rise, arise, get up, stand (up); (Hi) set up, put up, cause to arise, establish (627)

477 קָטֹן (adj) small, young, insignificant; (fs) קְטַנָּה (74)

351 קָטַר (Pi) to make a sacrifice go up in smoke, offer (a sacrifice) by burning; (Hi) cause a sacrifice to go up in smoke (115)

566 קְטֹרֶת incense, smoke (60)

486 קִיר wall; (mp) קִירוֹת (73)

435 קָלַל (Q) to be small, insignificant, of little account, swift; (Ni, Pi) declare cursed; (Hi) treat with contempt (82)

427 קָנָה (Q) to get, acquire, buy (85)

546 קָנֶה (ms) reed (62)

517 קֵץ end, border, limit (67)

406 קָצֶה (ms) end, border, outskirts (92)

70 קָרָא (Q) to call, summon, proclaim, read aloud, give a name to; (Ni) be called, summoned, proclaimed (739)

301 קָרָא (Q) to meet, encounter, happen; Inf Cstr with prep לְ (לִקְרַאת) toward, against, opposite (136)

169 קָרַב (Q) to approach, draw near, come near; (Hi) bring (near), present, offer a sacrifice or offering (280)

197 קֶרֶב inner part(s), organ(s), body; (prep) בְּקֶרֶב (155x) in the middle of, among (227)

446 קָרְבָּן gift, offering (80)

470 קָרוֹב (adj) near, close (75)

464 קֶרֶן (fs) horn (76)

541 קָרַע (Q) to tear, rend, cut up, tear away (63)

634 קֶרֶשׁ board, plank (51); 48x in Exod

465 קֶשֶׁת bow, weapon (76)

ר

32 רָאָה (Q) to see, perceive, understand; (Ni) appear; (Pu) be seen; (Hi) let or cause someone to see (something) (1,311)

80 רֹאשׁ head, top, chief; (mp) רָאשִׁים (600)

240 רִאשׁוֹן (adj) first, former; (fs) רִאשֹׁנָה; (mp) רִאשֹׁנִים (182)

635 רֵאשִׁית beginning, first (51)

278 רֹב multitude, abundance, greatness (150)

119 רַב (adj) great, many; (mp) רַבִּים (419)

196 רָבָה (Q) to be(come) numerous, great, increase; (Hi) make many, make great, multiply, increase (229)

604 רְבִיעִי (adj) fourth; (fs) רְבִיעִית (55)

182 רֶגֶל (fs) foot (251)

285 רָדַף (Q) to pursue, follow after, chase, persecute (144)

129 רוּחַ (cs) spirit, wind, breath; (cp) רוּחוֹת (378)

225 רוּם (Q) to be high, exalted, rise, arise; (Hi) raise, lift up, exalt, take away; (Hoph) be exalted; (Polel) exalt, bring up, extol, raise (children) (197)

374 רוּץ (Q) to run (104)

380 רֹחַב width, breadth, expanse (101)

429 רָחוֹק (adj) distant, remote, far away (84)

491 רָחַץ (Q) to wash (with water), wash (off or away), bathe, bathe oneself (72)

576 רָחַק (Q) to be(come) far or distant, keep far from; (Hi) remove, put (keep) far away, keep at a distance (59)

492 רִיב (Q) to strive, contend, quarrel, dispute, conduct a legal case (72)

547 רִיב dispute, quarrel, lawsuit (62)

580 רֵיחַ smell, odor, scent (58)

454 רָכַב (Q) to ride, mount and ride; (Hi) cause or make to ride (78)

334 רֶכֶב chariot, (coll) chariots or chariot riders (120)

624 רָנַן (Q) to call or cry aloud, shout with joy; (Pi) cry out (with joy), exult (53)

153 רַע (adj) bad, evil, wicked, worthless; also spelled רָע (312)

234 רֵעַ friend, companion, neighbor (188)

381 רָעָב famine, hunger (101)

137 רָעָה evil, wickedness, calamity, disaster (354)

255 רָעָה (Q) to pasture, tend (flocks), graze, shepherd, feed (167)

384 רָעַע (Q) to be bad, evil or displeasing; (Hi) do evil, do wickedly, do injury, harm, treat badly (98)

510 רָפָא (Q) to heal; (Ni) be healed, become whole; (Pi) heal, make healthy (69)

591 רָצוֹן pleasure, acceptance, favor (56)

363 רַק only, still, but, however (109)

177 רָשָׁע (adj) wicked, guilty (264)

שׂ

389 שָׂבַע (Q) to be satisfied, have one's fill (of), eat or drink one's fill; (Hi) satisfy (97)

144 שָׂדֶה (ms) field, pastureland (329)

81 שִׂים (Q) to set (up), put, place, set in place, establish; also spelled שׂוּם (588)

567 שָׂכַל (Hi) to understand, comprehend, have insight, make wise, have success (60)

614 שְׂמֹאל left, left side, north; also spelled שְׂמֹאול (54)

269 שָׂמַח (Q) to rejoice, be joyful, glad; (Pi) cause to rejoice, gladden, make someone happy (156)

400 שִׂמְחָה joy, gladness (94)

279 שָׂנֵא (Q) to hate; (Pi Ptc) enemy (148)

628 שָׂעִיר male goat (52)

243 שָׂפָה lip, language, edge, shore (178)

117 שַׂר ruler, prince (421)

347 שָׂרַף (Q) to burn (completely), destroy; (Ni) be burned (117)

שׁ

287 שֶׁ (prefixed rel pron) who, which, that (143)

528 שְׁאוֹל (cs) underworld, Sheol (65)

244 שָׁאַל (Q) to ask (of), inquire (of), request, demand (176)

314 שָׁאַר (Ni) to remain, be left over, survive; (Hi) leave (someone or something) remaining (133)

521 שְׁאֵרִית remnant, remainder (66); 37x in Isa, Jer, Ezek

232 שֵׁבֶט rod, staff, scepter, tribe (190); שִׁבְטֵי יִשְׂרָאֵל "the tribes of Israel"

385 שְׁבִיעִי (adj) seventh; (fs) שְׁבִיעִית (98)

236 שָׁבַע (Ni) to swear (take) an oath; (Hi) cause to take an oath, plead with someone (186)

106 שֶׁבַע (ms) seven; (fs) שִׁבְעָה; (mp) שִׁבְעִים seventy (490)

280 שָׁבַר (Q) to break (up), break in pieces, smash, shatter; (Ni) be smashed, broken, shattered or destroyed; (Pi) shatter, smash, break (148)

498 שָׁבַת (Q) to stop, cease, rest; (Hi) put an end to, remove, put away (71)

361 שַׁבָּת (cs) Sabbath, day or period of rest; (cp) שַׁבָּתוֹת (111)

577 שָׁדַד (Q) to devastate, ruin, deal violently with, violently destroy; (Pu) be devastated (59)

615 שָׁוְא worthlessness, vanity, emptiness (54)

41 שׁוּב (Q) to turn back, turn, return; (Hi) cause to return, bring back, restore; (Polel) bring back, restore (1,075)

493 שׁוֹפָר trumpet, ram's horn; (mp) שׁוֹפָרוֹת (72)

450 שׁוֹר ox, bull, cow (79)

439 שָׁחַט (Q) to slaughter (animals for sacrifice) (81)

275 שָׁחַת (Pi, Hi) to ruin, destroy, spoil, annihilate (152)

418 שִׁיר (Q) to sing (of); (Q and Polel ptc) singer (88)

455 שִׁיר song (78)

425 שִׁית (Q) to set, put, place, set one's mind to (86)

216	שָׁכַב	(Q) to lie down, have sexual intercourse (with) (213)
378	שָׁכַח	(Q) to forget; (Ni) be forgotten (102)
529	שָׁכַם	(Hi) to get up early, rise early, do (something) early (65)
317	שָׁכַן	(Q) to settle (down), abide, reside, dwell, inhabit; (Pi) abide, dwell (130)
189	שָׁלוֹם	peace, welfare, wholeness (237)
55	שָׁלַח	(Q) to send, stretch out; (Pi) send, stretch out, send away, expel; (Pu) be sent away (off) (847)
499	שֻׁלְחָן	table; (mp) שֻׁלְחָנוֹת (71)
365	שְׁלִישִׁי	(adj) third; (fs) שְׁלִשִׁית and שְׁלִישִׁיָּה (108)
326	שָׁלַךְ	(Hi) to send, throw, cast; (Hoph) be thrown, cast (125)
478	שָׁלָל	plunder, spoil (74)
349	שָׁלֵם	(Q) to be complete, finished; (Pi) complete, finish, make whole, restore, reward; (Hi) bring to completion, consummate (116)
423	שֶׁלֶם	peace offering (87)
78	שָׁלֹשׁ	(ms) three; (fs) שְׁלֹשָׁה; (mp) שְׁלֹשִׁים thirty (606)
53	שֵׁם	name, reputation (864)
57	שָׁם	there, then, at that time (835)
413	שָׁמַד	(Ni) to be exterminated, destroyed or annihilated; (Hi) exterminate, annihilate, destroy (90)
118	שָׁמַיִם	heaven, sky (421)
407	שָׁמֵם	(Q) to be deserted, uninhabited; (Ni) be made uninhabited, desolate, deserted; (Hi) make deserted or desolated (92)
592	שְׁמָמָה	desolation, waste, ruin (56)
228	שֶׁמֶן	oil, fat (193)
281	שְׁמֹנֶה	eight; (fs) שְׁמֹנָה; (mp) שְׁמֹנִים eighty (147)
36	שָׁמַע	(Q) to hear, listen to, understand, obey; (Ni) be heard; (Hi) proclaim (1,165)
109	שָׁמַר	(Q) to watch (over), guard, keep, observe, preserve, protect, take care of; (Ni) to be kept, protected, on one's guard (469)
308	שֶׁמֶשׁ	(cs) sun (134)
605	שֵׁן	(cs) tooth, ivory (55)
51	שָׁנָה	year; (fp) שָׁנִים (878)
270	שֵׁנִי	(adj) second; (fs) שֵׁנִית (156)
64	שְׁנַיִם	(md) two; (fd) שְׁתַּיִם (769)
133	שַׁעַר	gate (373)
542	שִׁפְחָה	female slave or servant, maidservant (63)
221	שָׁפַט	(Q) to judge, make a judgment, decide (between), settle (a dispute or controversy); (Ni) go to court, plead, dispute (204)
348	שָׁפַךְ	(Q) to pour (out), spill, shed (blood) (117)
548	שָׁקָה	(Hi) to give drink (to), irrigate (62)
419	שֶׁקֶל	shekel, measurement of weight (88)
355	שֶׁקֶר	lie, deception, falsehood (113)
386	שָׁרַת	(Pi) to minister, serve (98)
173	שֵׁשׁ	six; (fs) שִׁשָּׁה; (fs cstr) שֵׁשֶׁת; (mp) שִׁשִּׁים sixty (274)
207	שָׁתָה	(Q) to drink (217)

ת

581	תְּהִלָּה	praise, song of praise (58)

341 תּוֹעֵבָה abomination, abhorrence, offensive thing (118)

201 תּוֹרָה law, instruction, teaching (223)

95 תַּ֫חַת (prep) under, below, instead of (510)

375 תָּמִיד continually (104)

412 תָּמִים (adj) blameless, perfect, honest, devout (91)

533 תָּמַם (Q) to be(come) complete or finished, come to an end, cease, be consumed, burned out (64)

636 תָּעָה (Q) to err, wander (about), stagger, go astray (animal); (Hi) lead astray, cause to err (51)

459 תְּפִלָּה prayer (77)

530 תָּפַשׂ (Q) to take hold of, seize, capture, grasp; (Ni) be seized, caught, captured, conquered (65)

506 תָּקַע (Q) to drive or thrust (weapon into a person), pitch (tent), blow (trumpet), clap one's hands (70)

466 תְּרוּמָה offering, contribution, tribute (76)

456 תֵּ֫שַׁע nine; (fs) תִּשְׁעָה; (mp) תִּשְׁעִים ninety (78)